Interdisciplining Digital Humanities

T0385665

DIGITAL HUMANITIES

The Digital Humanities series provides a forum for ground-breaking and benchmark work in digital humanities, lying at the intersections of computers and the disciplines of arts and humanities, library and information science, media and communications studies, and cultural studies.

Series Editors:
Julie Thompson Klein, Wayne State University
Tara McPherson, University of Southern California
Paul Conway, University of Michigan

Teaching History in the Digital Age
T. Mills Kelly

Hacking the Academy: New Approaches to Scholarship and Teaching from Digital Humanities
Daniel J. Cohen and Tom Scheinfeldt, Editors

Writing History in the Digital Age
Jack Dougherty and Kristen Nawrotzki, Editors

Pastplay: Teaching and Learning History with Technology
Kevin Kee, Editor

Interdisciplining Digital Humanities: Boundary Work in an Emerging Field
Julie Thompson Klein

DIGITALCULTUreBOOKS, an imprint of the University of Michigan Press, is dedicated to publishing work in new media studies and the emerging field of digital humanities.

Interdisciplining Digital Humanities

Boundary Work in an Emerging Field

Julie Thompson Klein

University of Michigan Press
Ann Arbor

Published in the United States of America by the
University of Michigan Press
Manufactured in the United States of America
⊗ Printed on acid-free paper

2018   2017   2016   2015   4   3   2   1

A CIP catalog record for this book is available from the British Library.

DOI: http://dx.doi.org/10.3998/dh.12869322.0001.001

ISBN 978-0-472-07254-5 (hardcover : alk. paper)
ISBN 978-0-472-05254-7 (pbk. : alk. paper)
ISBN 978-0-472-12093-2 (e-book)

Gail Ryder, who created the cover art, is a graduate of the Master's in
Interdisciplinary Studies program at Wayne State University and an Associate
Professor of Humanities at Siena Heights University where she teaches liberal
arts courses and composition—online. Bringing her classroom to the virtual
world has given her the opportunity to merge a strong interest in the visual arts
with her passion for curriculum development. Her newest creation is a course on
the Harlem Renaissance. In her spare time, she works on collages, multi-media
journals, and one-act plays about the locker room at the local YMCA.

We are by now well into a phase of civilization when the terrain to be mapped, explored, and annexed is information space, and what's mapped is not continents, regions, or acres but disciplines, ontologies, and concepts.

—John Unsworth, "What is Humanities Computing and What is Not?" 2002, http://computerphilologie.uni-muenchen.de/jg02/unsworth.html

Foreword

Cathy N. Davidson

Julie Thompson Klein has written a capaciously definitional book. By that I mean, at this crucial moment in the formation of the many fields that, together, intertwine to be called "digital humanities," Klein provides an invaluable guidebook that resists the temptation to restrict and, instead, invites exploration. *Interdisciplining Digital Humanities: Boundary Work in an Emerging Field* challenges the reader to not only visit the intellectual bounty across, around, and in and about digital humanities, but also helps us to explain its evolution. How did we get here? Where are we now? How far can we go? For an emerging field to become an established field, this work marks a necessary and vital contribution at the right moment.

This book will have many audiences at once and is the rare publication that actually keeps those multiple audiences in mind. Whereas most books that have this level of sophistication do not explain their founding principles, Klein patiently (and provocatively) explicates the basics—keywords, disciplinary inheritances, historical legacies, originating voices. We are never left to feel as if there is a conversation happening and we are not part of it. Rather, by analyzing the deepest assumptions and principles of the field, Klein also brings the reader up to speed, allowing us to run along when she makes her most demanding and expansive case for the way interdisciplinarity forms digital humanities and the way the digital humanities offer a new formation to classic accounts of interdisciplinarity.

This book should be required reading for anyone interested in the digital humanities, beginning student or founding figure. Its appreciations are wide and original. That means Klein makes the best case for the importance of the field and shows us how some of its most seminal debates, arguments, differences, and disjunctions have, over the last decades now, helped to form its vibrancy, relevance, scope, and impact in the academy and in the more public intellectual work of museums, libraries, and other civic spaces.

To my mind, one of the most important audiences for this book sits on academic committees that judge the quality of work produced within it. Especially for those who make hiring, tenure, and promotion decisions, *Interdisciplining Digital Humanities* is indispensable. In the academy, we are often called upon to judge the integrity of research outside our own field of expertise. We often rely upon peers we trust for judgment and those peers may or may not carry our own prejudices and predilections as part of their judgments. When a disciplinary boundary is traversed, it can sometimes look, to the more clearly defined disciplinary peer, as if it has been violated, ignored, or, in the case of junior colleagues, not yet been mastered. Klein helps those who do not understand the digital humanities to see how they, in fact, can both contribute vitally to central disciplines and also work through the assumptions at the heart of those disciplines, including methodologically. Digital humanities do so not out of naïveté but out of the interdiscipline's own generic needs. A literary professor doing a close reading of one novel, for example, may not need to know how to use or design algorithms for network analysis; a digital humanist understanding word clustering in 200 nineteenth-century British novels most certainly does. The outcome of this second kind of work may well also be a critical interpretation of texts, but that final analysis is by no means the only part of the process that is of intellectual significance. In the manner of many fields in the quantitative social sciences, the process on the way to the analysis is itself something that needs to be carefully, clearly documented and, in the end, is something also to be evaluated by those determining scholarly contribution.

Klein defines the contours of several fields—from computation to data-driven or "Big Data" analysis to visualization on the "digital" or technology side and to the full array of the humanities and interpretive social sciences. More importantly, she shows how, in the digital humanities, it is often the combination of and interplay between and across fields that results in the most exciting work—including work that requires a "meta analysis" of the fields themselves.

For example, in addressing the formidable contribution of the journal *Vectors*, including its summer programs where scholars and designers worked together to learn about one another's respective fields in order to learn how to collaborate, Klein shows the merging of different media, different vocabularies, different expertise, and even different ways of "seeing" the world that are key to the digital humanities. Klein notes that what emerged in the *Vectors* seminars were "bottom-up . . . conversations about how scholarship might be reimagined in a dynamic digital vernacular. The outcome is not a pre-determined tool for delivery." She notes that the result of the *Vectors* seminars is not just an exploratory, multimodal publication but a cadre of trained interdisciplinary collaborators plus an array of tools (the middleware package, the Dynamic Backend Generator) that allow those collaborators to work together in a digital environment.

In walking us through examples with such patience, Klein shows how interdisciplinary is this field of digital humanities in its practices, its tools, its methods, and its publications. She also shows how all of those things—practices, tools, methodology, publication—are the *object of study* of the digital humanities. *Vectors* is not just a major scholarly publication, in other words, but an entire process that helps us to think about what we mean by "major scholarly publication." The published article, in other words, is by no means the only finished product of the research. The development of the middleware itself is part of the research, an outcome, a tangible asset, and needs to be judged as part of the scholarly productivity of the digital humanists who created it. Appointment, promotion, and tenure committees are accustomed to understanding such outcomes in the portfolios of engineers but rarely of literary scholars, art historians, classics scholars, and other humanists.

Klein shows us why our evaluation of "what counts" within digital humanities as a performed interdiscipline must change from the standard idea of "what counts" in most humanities fields. By the precision of her analysis, and her strong citation of individual exemplars, Klein provides those evaluating digital humanities with a new way of looking not just at the outcomes of scholarship (such as a single-author monograph as the gold standard in many humanities fields) but at the process leading to scholarship. She makes us understand why that process itself is a scholarly outcome. The classic scholarly monograph can report on digital humanities but it does not duplicate its actual, full, interactive, iterative, collaborative outcome.

Thus, in order to judge a digital humanist, if one judges *solely* by the production of a scholarly monograph, one is setting the bar too low. You do not win the DARPA Grand Challenge from a *blueprint* of a self-driving car. You win it for building the car that actually navigates down an actual road. That is my analogy, not Klein's. But through her astonishing breadth of knowledge, her generous assessment of so many areas of the field, Klein walks us through all of the reasons for making such a distinction as we evaluate the worth and contribution of the digital humanities.

Beyond that, Klein is suggesting, I believe, that we have entered an important moment in higher education where many of the disciplinary boundaries are not just being crossed but are being interwoven in exciting new ways. In that interweaving, digital humanities has an absolutely central place—as model, pioneer, and predecessor to many different kinds of interdisciplinary "mash-ups" yet to come.

Read this book. Share it with those who are interested in what will come next in higher education. What Julie Thompson Klein has given us here is not only a comprehensive analysis of a field. She has given us a glimpse of higher education's future.

Acknowledgments

Every story has a beginning. This one started when Cathy Davidson called to ask if I would host a local event in a new monthly series being sponsored by the Humanities, Science, and Technology Alliance and Collaboratory (HASTAC). Dubbed the In/Formation Year, the series featured innovative uses of digital technologies on selected campuses. The planning team at Wayne State University decided to focus our February 2007 symposium on "Digital Partnerships in Humanities," highlighting the University Libraries' Digital Collections and the work of English Department faculty Steve Shaviro and Jeff Rice. As stories go, one thing led to another . . . Our event was the catalyst for a multi-year experiment in fostering Digital Humanities. I thank Walter Edwards, director of Wayne State's Humanities Center, for a small working group grant that expanded into a faculty learning community with generous support from Sandra Yee (Dean of University Libraries), Kristi Verbeke (former assistant director of the Office for Teaching and Learning/OTL), and Nardina Namath Mein (former director of New Media and Information Technology and co-organizer of our HASTAC event). Sandy, Kristi, and Dina provided full access to the OTL and Technology Resource Center, and subsequently Dina and I became Co-PIs on a project aimed at enhancing use of the digital collections in teaching and learning. Supported by a Digital Humanities II Start-Up grant from the National Endowment for the Humanities, the project team also included web librarians Joshua Neds-Fox and Jonathan McGlone, instructional designer Anne-Marie Armstrong, and metadata librarian Adrienne Aluzzo.

I have also gained enormously from participation in Digital Humanities initiatives at the University of Michigan. Daniel Herwitz, former director of the Institute for the Humanities at the University of Michigan, was a munificent host for two periods in residence at the institute, the first as a visiting fellow in Digital Humanities in 2008 and the second as Mellon Fellow and visiting professor of Digital Humanities in fall 2011. We were also co-chairs of the 2011 HASTAC conference hosted by the University of Michigan. Being involved in creating a new publication series has been a bountiful source of ideas as well. As co-editor of *Digital Humanities@ digitalculturebooks,* I spent countless hours with Tom Dwyer, acquisitions editor of the University of Michigan Press, designing the format and testing the suitability of book projects. My co-editors Tara McPherson (University of Southern California) and Paul Conway (University of Michigan) have been valued partners in this effort, and the timing was propitious. As the Press was being moved into the University of Michigan Library, I was fortunate to work closely with Shana Kimball, former head of publishing services and outreach at MPublishing and now business development manager for digital initiatives at the New York Public Library. And, I thank Aaron McCollough, Christopher Dreyer, and Andrea Olson for helping guide the final production process at the Press, as well as Kelly Witchen, Jason Colman, and Jonathan McGlone for their work on the online version and Hypothes.is platform.

This project benefited as well from the help of two research assistants. Sherry Tuffin, former student assistant in the OTL and HASTAC scholar at Wayne State, provided early database searching and copyediting. Andy Engel, a PhD candidate in English and HASTAC scholar, and now assistant professor of English at Wiley College, worked two summers as my graduate research assistant. Andy's help with searching and managing our digital research platform, feedback on chapters, and responsibility for the "Resourcing" section made him a vital colleague, not simply an assistant. Finally, I thank Wayne State University, for providing much-needed sabbatical time at an early stage of the book's development, as well as Anne Balsamo, Patrik Svensson, and Kate Hayles for generously sharing prepublication copies of their work. Willard McCarty also kindly granted permission to use his graphic of Methodological Interdisciplinarity. Their collegiality exemplifies the widespread spirit of cooperation in the sometimes perplexing, perpetually dynamic, and ever-evolving field of Digital Humanities.

Interdisciplining Digital Humanities is also freely available to read online (DOI: http://dx.doi.org/10.3998/dh.12869322.0001.001), and it is the first scholarly monograph published by the University of Michigan Press to use the annotating and commenting tool Hypothes.is (http://hypothes .is/). This tool supports sentence-level annotations and allows for discussion at the paragraph level to enrich the reading and learning experience of others and to facilitate community peer review. You can register to use Hypothes.is at http://hypothes.is/.

Detroit, July 2014

Contents

Introduction

Emerging

Recent coverage of the digital humanities (DH) in popular publications such as the *New York Times*, *Nature*, the *Boston Globe*, the *Chronicle of Higher Education*, and *Inside Higher Ed* has confirmed that the digital humanities is not just "the next big thing," as the *Chronicle* claimed in 2009, but simply "the Thing," as the same publication noted in 2011 (Panna-packer).

—Matthew Gold, "The Digital Humanities Moment," in *Debates in the Digital Humanities*, ed. Matthew Gold (Minneapolis: U of Minnesota P, 2012), ix

It would be naïve to think that this boundary-breaking trajectory will happen without contestation. Moreover, practitioners in the field recall similar optimistic projections from fifteen or twenty years ago; in this respect, prognostica-tions for rapid change have cried wolf all too often.

—N. Katherine Hayles, *How We Think: Digital Media and Contempo-rary Technogenesis* (Chicago: U of Chicago P, 2012), 44

Keywords: interdisciplinarity, boundary work

The opening epigraphs frame an ongoing conversation about Digital Hu-manities (DH) as buoyed by optimism as it is laden with skepticism. Digi-tal Humanities is a rapidly growing field at the intersections of computing and the disciplines of humanities and arts, interdisciplinary fields of cul-ture and communication, and the professions of education and library and information science. To begin with . . . The following examples are most often associated with the term, grouped roughly by kind:

- computational linguistics and language processing
- electronic text production and editing
- digital collections, archives, and libraries

- computing practices in disciplines of the humanities and arts
- computing practices in related interdisciplinary fields
- computing practices in related professions

- new objects and subjects
- new methods of analysis and interpretation
- cultural impacts of the Internet and new media

- design and production
- digital tools and methodologies
- project and program management

- the history and theory of Digital Humanities
- the field's professionalization and institutionalization
- new approaches to teaching and learning
- changing modes of scholarly communication and publication.

As this list suggests, interest in digital technologies and new media is widespread. Not a day goes by without traffic in the blogosphere and Twitterverse announcing new developments, ranging from the first Cultural Heritage & Digital Humanities hackathon in Lithuania to a digital archive of materials about the Boston Marathon bombings. The academic press now routinely heralds new activities as well, from the local launch of an Annotation Studio or a week-long focus on DH sponsored by the library to a crowdsourced digital project in a discipline and DH-inflected sessions at its annual professional meeting. Scholarly interest has also expanded to the point the field is now anchored by a burgeoning body of publications, organizations, networks, research centers, academic programs, and funded projects. Some even believe the field is at a threshold point. At a 2008 workshop of Project Bamboo, John Unsworth declared a point of "emergence" had been reached. Project Bamboo began in early 2008 with funding from the Mellon Foundation for a planning and community design program aimed at defining scholarly practices and technological challenges. At the fourth workshop in the series, Unsworth heralded the increased number of participants and developments since work began five years earlier on a report on cyberinfrastructure for humanities. Genuine change, he quoted one participant declaring, now seemed possible. That same year, editors of the inaugural issue of the journal *Digital Studies/Le Champ Numérique* took a step further, proclaiming Digital Humanities is now an established "inter-discipline."

Digital Humanities is a growing international movement as well. Melissa Terras's 2011 infographic revealed large clusters of activity in North America, Europe, and Southeast Asia, with added presence in Africa and the Middle East. New organizations continue to emerge, including Australasian and Japanese associations for Digital Humanities. In 2009 the inaugural Digital Humanities Luxembourg Symposium took place and in 2012 the Primer Encuentro de Humanistas Digitales in Mexico City. The 2014 conference of the Humanities, Arts, Science, and Technology Alliance and Collaboratory (HASTAC) took place in Lima, Peru, and in 2015 the flagship conference of the Alliance of Digital Humanities Organizations will be held in Sydney, Australia. The THATCamp movement of "unconferences" also continues to spread, with events in Brazil; the Caribbean; Wellington, New Zealand; Slovakia; and Panama. Global Perspectives on Digital History brings together material from multiple sites and forums in English, German, and French. The annual online forum "Day of Digital Humanities" has expanded from English to Spanish and Portuguese. And, the Bilateral Digital Humanities Program, co-funded by the National Endowment for the Humanities and the Deutsche Forschungsgemeinschaft, supports collaborative efforts between the two countries.

Given this momentum, two figures of speech inevitably appear in the discourse of Digital Humanities—*revolution* and *transformation*. Proclamations of Humanities 2.0, University 2.0, Learning 2.0, and Web 4.0 beckon a New Academy. Mauro Carassai and Elisabet Takehana even declare "an all-encompassing ontological shift" is under way. Yet, claims of "revolution" are overstated, and the rate of change is slower than the rhetoric of "transformation" suggests. In a special issue of *Daedalus* on the current state of humanities, James O'Donnell also questions whether DH is a "revolution" or "only automation" (100). Writing in his blog, Stanley Katz acknowledged the "revolution" propelled by computing and information technology has begun to transform humanities, but he is equally mindful of the impediments. Despite the proliferation of DH centers, Diane Zorich also cites challenges to their sustainability, infrastructure, and preservation of digital content (1–2, 37). Still other threats stem from the weakened funding climate in humanities, inflexible publication policies, lack of common standards and evaluation criteria, the limits of copyright law, uneven development across institutions, and the entire range of infrastructure needs identified in Project Bamboo and in the 2006 report of the American Council of Learning Societies Commission on Cyberinfrastructure for the Humanities and Social Sciences (*Our Cultural Commonwealth*).

Ernesto Priego also questions uneven infrastructure across the globe. The Mexican Digital Humanities network, the Red de Humanidades Digitales, holds promise. Yet, shortages of "big money" underscore the need for innovations that use available and inexpensive technologies. Isabel Galina Russell concludes, in turn, "the full internationalization of the field has not been fully achieved," despite notable projects in Mexico. Without a comprehensive register or documentation, they are not easy to identify. The field is also relatively unknown, and even with funding a solid infrastructure for projects is lacking, including academic recognition and sustainability and preservation. Three areas, she admonished, will be key to promoting DH in Mexico and the Latin American region: lobbying, promoting, and dissemination; training; and guidelines and aids for evaluating projects. Precedents in other countries are important, but so is understanding DH in Mexico's academic, cultural, political, and economic contexts, while also conducting research and documentation in Spanish (202–4). In an address at Mexico City in November 2013, she also concurred with Domenico Fiormonte, who questioned why the Italian Comunidad Informática Umanistica has been largely neglected in official writing of the history of Digital Humanities.

In short, to echo Patrick Juola, an "emerging" discipline of Digital Humanities has been emerging for decades (83). In the academic world, emergence is documented formally in two classification schemes: knowledge taxonomies and organizational charts. These indicators, however, are slow to change. The National Research Council's report on research doctorates recommended an increase in the number of interdisciplinary fields in its authoritative taxonomy. Digital Humanities, though, was not one of them (Ostriker and Kuh; Ostriker, Holland, Kuh, and Voytuk). Nor is it recognized in the 2010 U.S. Department of Education Classification of Instructional Programs, though "Digital Arts" was added to the category of Visual and Performing Arts. The field's status is also uneven. At some universities it enjoys a high profile in the form of a research center. On other campuses, it is a small program or dispersed interests that never gain traction. Debate also continues on the field's identity. One of the most frequent claims is that Digital Humanities is interdisciplinary, an inevitable assumption given the marriage of technology and humanities in the name. Yet, discussion is rarely informed by the voluminous literature on interdisciplinarity. This book tests the claim by examining the boundary work of the field.

Boundary work is a composite label for the claims, activities, and structures by which individuals and groups work directly and through institutions to create, maintain, break down, and reformulate between knowledge units. Boundary work studies initially focused on disciplines, especially the demarcation of science from non-science. Subsequently, though, they were extended to interdisciplinarity (Fisher, 13–17; Klein, *Crossing Boundaries*, 57–84). The extension was inevitable, given widespread spatial images of disciplinary borders, domains, turf, and territory. Yet, Willard McCarty cautions in mapping Humanities Computing, metaphors of boundaries, walls, and spaces depict a barrier and confinement that disguises expanding structures (*Humanities Computing*, 133–34). In contrast, Michael Winter highlights organic images of generation, cross-fertilization, mutation, and interrelation that compare intellectual movements to ecological processes and the evolution of new species. Spatial and organic models may even be combined, Winter suggests, to form a third type that highlights interactions between social groups and environments. The Greek word *ecology* (*oikeo*) means household or settlement. The root idea is to make and reinforce jurisdictional claims and exploit resources to produce new forms and settlements (343–46). This study is an example of the third type. It examines both spatial and organic contours of Digital Humanities in order to understand the boundary work of establishing, expanding, and sustaining a new interdisciplinary field.

The Book

Given the scope of Digital Humanities, this book is written for a wide audience. The first and largest segment is comprised of individuals and groups who work in the field, whether they identify explicitly as digital humanists or as "doing" Digital Humanities in some way. They are as diverse as a scholar in literary studies designing a digital collection centered on a single author, an anthropologist or a historian creating a computer visualization of an ancient site, a music instructor mapping sound patterns in the canon of a composer while creating an electronic music curriculum, an artist mounting a multimodal installation while involving students in its production, a professor of Italian producing a digital archive for an entire historical period while directing a humanities lab, a scholar in women's studies doing research on the relationship of the body and technology, and a librarian building an online Digital Humanities research guide for faculty and students. To name but a few examples . . . Understanding the field's contours will enable them to situate their activities within the larger expanse of theory and practice while sharpening their understanding of what interdisciplinarity entails. For that reason, this volume may also be used as a textbook in courses on related topics, and as a scholarly reference for funding agencies and professional organizations.

This book has an additional audience as well: scholars, teachers, and students of interdisciplinarity. Lessons from the literature on interdisciplinarity are often ignored in Digital Humanities, resulting in imprecise use of terminology and shallow understanding of theory and practice. At the same time, only by mapping situated practices can scholars of interdisciplinarity test their theories. The complex challenges of navigating interdisciplinarity in the 21st century, Jill Vickers admonishes, require ending the search for universal and timeless characteristics. We can better understand interdisciplinarity by studying how it is manifested in the contexts in which it emerges and evolves ("Diversity"). Tracing the history of another field with close ties to Digital Humanities—cultural studies—Stuart Hall also cautions that any field is situated within the political, theoretical, educational, and economic circumstances from which it arises. Projects and fields do not have simple origins. They are comprised of multiple discourses with different histories, trajectories, methodologies, and theoretical positions ("Emergence"). Digital Humanities is especially ripe for a study of its boundary work because members of the field have been quick to historicize, categorize, and institutionalize it.

In making this study of their arguments and actions, this book is itself interdisciplinary, in a triangulation of historiographical, sociological, and rhetorical methods. *Historiographical analysis* uncovers genealogies of origin, benchmark events, periodizations, and tensions between continuity and change. *Sociological analysis* examines how knowledge is codified in conditions of group membership and sanctioned practices. *Rhetorical analysis* dissects the claims by which people construct a field, patterns of consensus and difference, and the ways keywords and taxonomies structure hierarchies of value. These methods are not isolated. In the manner of Michel Foucault's genealogical studies of knowledge, historiography considers how discursive objects, concepts, and strategies produce regularities, rules, and unities that are challenged by ruptures, refigurations, and transformations. In the manner of Pierre Bourdieu's studies of the academic sphere, questions about power, conflict, and change arise in tracking the production, circulation, and institutionalization of knowledge. And, in the manner of Tony Becher's studies of disciplinarity, tracing historical and rhetorical patterns also entails an anthropological interest in how influential figures, artifacts, and literature establish cognitive authority, reputational systems, cultural identity, and symbolism.

The integration of historical, sociological, and rhetorical perspectives is especially needed when tracking the naming of a field. "No name," Cathy Davidson advises, "ever encompasses a field, either at its moment of inception or in its evolution over time." Names are historical reference points that mark converging energies at particular moments. They define lacunae while demarcating what is tangential, intersectional, or orthogonal to a field ("Humanities and Technology," 207). Given the immense variety of activities under "Big Tent Digital Humanities," David Silver's witty epithet is tempting: "Internet/cyberculture/digital culture/newmedia/fill-in-the-blank studies" (qtd. in Gurak and Antonijevic, 497). When tallying names of another field with close links to Digital Humanities—composition studies—Armstrong and Fontaine concluded that naming entails a process of sorting and gathering, comparing and contrasting, and marking territorial relationships in political-semantic webs (7–8). Understandably, then, the same name is used for different purposes. Matthew Kirschenbaum calls DH a "mobile and tactical signifier," deployed for particular goals such as "getting a faculty line or funding a staff position, establishing a curriculum, revamping a lab, or launching a center" ("Digital Humanities," 415, 421).

In order to understand the complex connotations of the name, keyword clusters frame each chapter. When clustered together, Raymond Williams taught us, a particular set of words and references constitutes a field of meaning defined by their particularities and relationalities (22–25). Because individuals will be unevenly familiar with all of the field's disciplinary, interdisciplinary, and professional parts, the chapters also include short synopses of representative developments, arguments, and practices. The focus, though, remains on *interdisciplinary* theory and practice. Some will wonder why another book is needed. Matthew Gold's anthology *Debates in Digital Humanities* and David Berry's *Understanding Digital Humanities* provide textbooks, along with the predecessor Blackwell *Companion to Digital Humanities*. Two more recent textbooks also present an overview. Terras, Nyhan, and Vanhoutte's 2013 *Defining Digital Humanities: A Reader* compiles core readings on the meaning, scope, and implementation of this field, with commentaries by the editors and authors, an annotated bibliography, and sample postings and analysis of the definitional exercise "Day of Digital Humanities." Aimed at non-specialists, Gold's forthcoming *DH: A Short Introduction to the Digital Humanities* will present a broad historical picture from antecedents to recent expansion and future directions. Warwick, Terras, and Nyhan's *Digital Humanities in Practice* is a practical guide to key topics for academic and cultural heritage audiences, with bibliographies. And, Burdick and colleagues' *Digital_Humanities* includes synthetic mappings, emerging methods and genres, case studies, along with a short guide. However, none of these and other publications interrogates the claim of being "interdisciplinary."

Chapter 1: Interdisciplining

Keywords: *Multidisciplinarity*, *Interdisciplinarity*, *Transdisciplinarity*, interprofessionalism, *Methodological* versus *Theoretical ID*, *Instrumental* versus *Critical ID*, interdisciplinary humanities, crosshatching, travel, identity, transversality

Any book that places interdisciplinarity at its heart begs an overriding question: what does this ubiquitous word mean? In order to foster more informed use of terminology, chapter 1 presents a baseline vocabulary of the three most common terms—*multidisciplinarity*, *interdisciplinarity*, and *transdisciplinarity*, supplemented by a fourth term, *interprofessionalism*. It situates Digital Humanities within the baseline while elaborating on differences between Methodological and Theoretical forms of interdisciplinarity as well as Instrumental and Critical forms. It then places DH within the larger history of interdisciplinarity in humanities while considering the roles of disciplinary change, increased crossing of boundaries between humanities and social sciences, the cross-hatching of new developments, and the mobility of concepts. The chapter closes by drawing insights from other interdisciplinary fields about their identity and transversal intersections.

Chapter 2: Defining

Keywords: Humanities Computing, Digital Humanities, discipline, interdiscipline, modes of engagement, 2.0 interactivity, visualization, spatialization, code

The English word *definition* derives from the Latin *dēfinītiō-em*, referring to both a statement of the meaning of a word and the act of setting bounds or limits of explanation. Rafael Alvarado contends "there is no definition of digital humanities," if that means "agreement on theory, methods, professional norms, and criteria of evaluation." Instead, he posits "a genealogy, a network of family resemblances among provisional schools of thought, methodological interests, and preferred tools" (50–51). Closer analysis of six statements opens a more nuanced picture of how the field has been defined across nearly sixty-five years of work, comparing both resemblances and differences. The chapter then contextualizes Digital Humanities within three major disciplines where digital technologies and new media are changing the nature of practice—English, history, and archaeology. It concludes by weighing the significance of three themes that have emerged in the field's recent history—visualization, spatialization, and a computational turn in culture.

Chapter 3: Institutionalizing

Keywords: institutionalization, critical mass, overt versus concealed interdisciplinarity, location, migration, leveraging, partnership, infrastructure

Institutionalization is a process of establishing something within an organization or a social sphere, whether it is an idea, such as democracy, or an occupation, such as teaching. Categories of knowledge are also institutions, Steven Shapin suggests, not in the conventional sense of buildings and structures but a set of marks constructed and maintained in cultural space (355). Chapter 3 initiates a three-part exploration of how the category of Digital Humanities is located within the cultural space of the academy, through institutionalizing, professionalizing, and educating. It begins by providing a conceptual framework for thinking about institutionalization of interdisciplinarity. It then identifies patterns of affiliation of scholars and educators in the field, followed by an examination of the most prestigious structure, research centers, and closing reflection on the challenge of sustainability.

Chapter 4: Professionalizing

Keywords: professionalization, platforming, communities of practice, network, partnership, scholarly communication, federation, remixing, modularity

Professionalization is a process by which a group establishes and maintains control of a social world. In the academic sphere, the primary mechanisms of professionalizing disciplines and fields are representative organizations and their annual meetings, publication venues, educational credentials, qualifications for career advancement, skill sets, norms of conduct and values, specialized discourse, criteria of evaluation, and standards of practice. Chapter 4 examines two major mechanisms of professionalizing in Digital Humanities: the formation of communities of practice and scholarly publication. Communities of practice range from small informal groups to global partnerships. Scholarly publication, in turn, is changing as new digital forums are appearing, from enhancements of traditional formats to new platforms and multimodal genres. In the process, the nature of knowledge production is also changing, along with underlying concepts of authorship and communication.

Chapter 5: Educating

Keywords: context, balance, tractability, relationality, interplay, participatory, relationality, interplay, remixing, intentionality

Although research centers have been more prominent in the institutional profile of Digital Humanities, the number of courses and programs is increasing. Pedagogy is also a topic of growing interest. Yet, the pattern of development and implementation is uneven, and claims of interdisciplinarity need to be weighed against generic indicators of strong programs in interdisciplinary studies. Chapter 5 begins by examining the general picture of DH syllabi and then turns to the particularities of introductory courses, the balance of humanities content and technological skills, and the roles of theory and critique. Next, it defines pedagogies that promote interdisciplinary learning in Digital Humanities curricula and attendant learning styles and skills. Taken together, the overview of trends and traits advances a definition of digital teaching and learning as *interdisciplinary* practice. The chapter closes by comparing strategies in different institutional settings and the ongoing professional development of faculty and staff.

Chapter 6: Collaborating and Rewarding

Keywords: collaboration, trading zones, interactional expertise, associative thought processes, negotiation, mutual learning, hybridity, culture of recognition, interdisciplinary paradigm shift, triple efficacy, aggregate activity

The closing chapter deepens understanding by exploring two final topics essential to interdisciplinarity in Digital Humanities: collaboration and a culture of recognition. It begins by defining characteristics of interdisciplinary collaboration, common problems, dynamics of integration in trading zones of expertise, the roles of conflict and mutual learning, interdisciplinary work practices, and ethics of collaboration. It then explores parallels between efforts to legitimate interdisciplinarity and digital work in the academic reward system, including impediments in peer review that are countered by new authoritative guidelines for candidates preparing credentials for tenure and promotion. The chapter closes by returning to the question that prompted this book in the first place: Is Digital Humanities an interdisciplinary field? A triple "efficacy" is unfolding across disciplines, interdisciplinary fields, and professions; within and across their institutional locations; and within and across all organizations and groups that are grappling with implications of digital technologies and new media. "Strategic tractions" are located in particular contexts, but at the same time they have multiplicative effects in the "circuit of work" and evolving "network aggregate university" of Digital Humanities.

Resourcing

Keywords: contours, scatter, scale, strategies, aggregators, taxonomy versus folksonomy, depth vs. breadth, timeliness, degree of specialization, purpose

The final section of the book, by Andy Engel, guides readers to resources. It highlights primary sites and aggregations of resources, bibliographies and library guides, networks and professional organizations, and ways of keeping up to date in the future. Being up to date is a significant challenge in the fast-paced world of Digital Humanities, with new tools, approaches, and meetings appearing every day. Yet, there are good places to begin and strategies for continuing identification of new resources.

http//:www.and . . .

A final note: much of the discourse about Digital Humanities takes place online. As a result, this book draws on more online sources than customary in traditional research. Policies also differ on whether to cite URLs. Some publishers discourage their use, since the life of a link may be short and dead ends clog the Internet. Some publishers, though, make inclusion optional, and some authors contend that even a dormant link can furnish clues to finding a resource. I am one of the latter but respect the objection that a clutter of URLs interferes with the flow of reading. To the extent possible I have clustered multiple URLs at the end of paragraphs and chapters while selecting the most likely routes of access.

NOTE: Print and online sources are equally important in this book. Print sources appear at the end in a traditional References section. All URLs for online sources cited at the ends of chapters were confirmed accurate as of July 17, 2014.

Clustered Links for Introduction in Order of Appearance

Lithuania Hackathon, Hack4LT: http://pro.europeana.eu/web/guest/pro-blog/-/blogs/1713396

Boston bombings: http://www.northeastern.edu/news/2013/05/our-marathon-project/

Project Bamboo: http://projectbamboo.org/

John Unsworth: https://wikihub.berkeley.edu/display/pbamboo/John+Unsworth's+Remarks+about+Cyberinfrastructure+and+Bamboo

Melissa Terras's blog with infograph: http://melissaterras.blogspot.com/2011/11/stats-and-digital-humanities.html

Digital Humanities Luxembourg: http://www.digitalhumanities.lu/

Primer Encuentro in Mexico City: http://www.insidehighered.com/blogs/university-venus/digital-humanities-cognitive-dissidence

Global Perspectives on Digital History: http://gpdh.org/

NEH/DFG Bilateral Digital Humanities Program: http://www.neh.gov/divisions/odh/grant-%09news/announcing-4-nehdfg-bilateral-digital-humanities-program-awards

Stanley Katz's blog: http://chronicle.com/blogPost/the-emergence-of-the-digital-humanities/5848

Ernesto Priego's blog: http://www.insidehighered.com/blogs/globalisation-digital-humanities-uneven-promise

Commission on Cyberinfrastructure for the Humanities and Social Sciences. American Council of Learned Societies. Our Cultural Commonwealth. Published 2006 and downloadable at http://www.acls.org/cyberinfrastructure/ourcultural commonwealth.pdf

Isabel Galina's comments and slides from a presentation in Mexico City in November 2013: http://humanidadesdigitales.net/blog/2013/07/19/is-there-anybody-out-there-building-a-global-digital-humanities-community/

Department of Education, Classification of Instructional Programs: http://nces.ed.gov/ipeds/cipcode/crosswalk.aspx?y=55

Angus Stevenson (Ed.). *Oxford Dictionary of English, Third Edition*. Oxford: Oxford UP, 2010. Entry "Definition." (searchable online resource).

Interdisciplining

> Concepts are never simply descriptive; they are also pro-
> grammatic and normative. Hence, their use has specific
> effects. Nor are they stable; they are related to a tradition.
> But their use never has simple continuity.
> —Mieke Bal, *Traveling Concepts in the Humanities: A Rough Guide*
> (Toronto: U of Toronto P, 2002), 29

> Digital humanists are unlikely to come to clarity about their
> naming or usage conventions, and about the concepts these
> express, until they engage in much fuller conversation with
> their affiliated or enveloping disciplinary fields (e.g., literary
> studies, history, writing programs, library studies, etc.),
> cousin fields (e.g., new media studies), and the wider public
> about where they fit in, which is to say, how they contribute
> to a larger, shared agenda expressed in the conjunction and
> collision of many fields.
> —Alan Liu, "Is Digital Humanities a Field?—An Answer From the Point
> of View of Language," http://liu.english.ucsb.edu/is-digital-humani-
> ties-a-Field-an-answer-from-the-point-of-view-of-language/

Keywords: *Multidisciplinarity, Interdisciplinarity, Transdisciplinarity, Interprofessionalism, Methodological* **versus** *Theoretical ID, Instrumental* **versus** *Critical ID,* **interdisciplinary humanities, cross-
hatching, travel, identity, transversality**

Any book that places interdisciplinarity at its heart begs an overriding
question. What does this ubiquitous word mean? Too often it is merely
a buzzword. In order to foster more informed use of terminology, this

first chapter begins with a baseline vocabulary of the three most common terms—*multidisciplinarity*, *interdisciplinarity*, and *transdisciplinarity*—supplemented by a fourth term, *interprofessionalism*. It situates Digital Humanities (DH) within the baseline while explaining differences among methodological, theoretical, instrumental, and critical forms. It then places DH within the larger history of interdisciplinarity in humanities while considering the roles of disciplinary change, increased interactions with social sciences, the cross-hatching of new developments, and the mobility of concepts. This chapter closes by drawing insights from other interdisciplinary fields about their identity. The popular slogan "Big Tent Digital Humanities" signifies broad scope, but it does little to sort out what is under the tent in what has been variously dubbed a "discipline," an "interdiscipline," an "interdisciplinary field," an "array of convergent practices," a set of "heterogeneous constituencies," and a "nexus of fields."

A Conceptual Vocabulary of Interdisciplinarity

(For a comprehensive account of terminology see Klein, "Taxonomy," adapted here for a core vocabulary in Digital Humanities.)

The first and most basic distinction is crucial, because many purportedly "interdisciplinary" activities are actually "multidisciplinary."

> *Multidisciplinarity* (*MD*) is characterized by juxtaposition of separate disciplinary inputs. Juxtaposition fosters breadth of knowledge and diversity of approaches. Yet, they are typically aligned or in encyclopedia order at best. Inputs are not integrated around core questions, topics, themes, or problems. Individuals also remain anchored in their respective expertise, and collaboration is lacking.

Interdisciplinarity differs:

> *Interdisciplinarity* (*ID*) is typically characterized by integration of information, data, methods, tools, concepts, and/or theories from two or more disciplines or bodies of specialized knowledge. Proactive focusing, blending, and linking of disciplinary inputs foster a more holistic understanding of a question, topic, theme, or problem by individuals or teams.

As these thumbnail definitions suggest, interdisciplinarity is more complex, for several reasons. The scope varies, from *Narrow ID* involving disciplines with relatively compatible methods and epistemologies—such as history and literature—to *Broad ID* bridging disparate approaches—such as linguistics and biology. Scale also varies. A local project curating a digital archive, for instance, differs from the MacArthur Foundation's international Digital Media and Learning initiative. The disciplinary mix varies as well. The Computers and Writing conference engages a different set of interests than the Text Encoding conference, though both are associated with Digital Humanities. And, activities range across a spectrum from borrowing methods or tools to the focus of this book, forming a new field. The earliest documented uses of the word *interdisciplinary* appeared in the early 20th century, in problem-oriented social science research and the general education and core curriculum movements. Its association with new fields dates to the 1930s and 1940s, most notably at the time American studies and area studies. During the 1950s and 1960s, the list expanded to include social psychology, molecular biology, cognitive science, and materials science. It grew further in the 1960s and 1970s with the emergence of black/ethnic/women's/environmental/urban/and science, technology, and society studies. And, in the closing decades of the 20th century, cultural studies and clinical and translational science became prominent.

New fields emerge, Richard McKeon explained when defining the role that rhetoric plays in their construction, because subject matters are not ready made to respond to all of the questions, problems, and issues we encounter (18). Raymond Miller's typology of four major catalysts offers a starting point for thinking about Digital Humanities as an interdisciplinary field. *Topics* are associated with problem areas that became a basis for new fields, such as criminal justice, labor studies, environmental studies, urban studies, and gerontology. The category of *Life Experience* became prominent in the late 1960s and 1970s with the emergence of black/women's/and ethnic studies. "The Digital" is neither a problem area nor a category of life experience. However, the proliferation of new technologies and media has stimulated studies of their implications and the thematics of subjectivity, and identity in the mode of cultural studies. *Professional Preparation*, in turn, led to new fields with a vocational focus such as social work and nursing. DH is not a discrete profession, but its emergence has had significant consequences for the traditional professions of library science, education, and engineering. *Hybrids* are interstitial specializations or "interdisciplines" (Miller, 11–15, 19; Smelser, 61). Social psychology and molecular biology are leading examples and in this book "Humanities Computing" and "Digital Humanities."

Three finer-grained distinctions also apply. The first distinction is apparent in two major strands of argument about Digital Humanities:

> *Methodological ID* typically improves the quality of results, by using a method, concept, or tool from another discipline in order to test a hypothesis, to answer a research question, or to help develop a theory. In contrast, *Theoretical ID* develops a more comprehensive general view, typically in the form of new conceptual frameworks or syntheses.

Digital Humanities is widely viewed as methodological in nature. In answer to the question "What is the Digital Humanities?," for example, the website of the University Library at the University of Illinois at Urbana-Champaign calls the field "an emerging discipline that applies computation to research in the humanities." In introducing an issue of the *Journal of Digital Humanities* on topic modeling, the Digital Humanities Specialist blogger at the Stanford University Libraries also calls DH "a Movement Expressed in a Method Enshrined in a Tool." Widespread focus on tools and methods has fostered the notion that DH is a handmaiden to humanities. Authors of the Digital Humanities *Manifesto 2.0* cite common dismissals: "it's *just* a tool; it's *just* a repository; it's *just* pedagogy." These judgments perpetuate a hierarchy of value that regards resource production as less worthy than interpretation, archival and library work as secondary to scholarship, and teaching of lesser value than research. The "knowledge jukebox" conception in particular, Willard McCarty laments, leaves technology makers "mere assistants or delivery boys to scholarship," rendering tools little more than "vending machines for knowledge" and reducing the machine to an efficient "servant" (*Humanities Computing*, 6).

The tension was evident in naming of the field. Stephen Ramsay claims that the term *digital humanities* was introduced at the University of Virginia's Institute for Advanced Technology in the Humanities to signify movement away from the equation of Humanities Computing with low-prestige computing support to an intellectual endeavor with its own professional practices, rigorous standards, and theoretical explorations (qtd. in Hayles, *How We Think*, 24). John Unsworth, for his part, traces the name to conversations with editorial and marketing staff about a title for Blackwell's *Companion to Digital Humanities*, recalling he suggested the name in order to move away from the connotation of "simple digitization" in the proposed title "Digitized Humanities." Patrik Svensson found roughly twice as many uses of "humanities computing" as "digital humanities" in the book, 139 versus 68 ("Humanities Computing," ¶36). Yet, the new name gained traction. The difference aligns with the distinction between *Methodological* and *Theoretical Interdisciplinarity*. Yet, it is not absolute. Schreibman, Siemens, and Unsworth describe technology as part of the process of knowledge representation ("Digital Humanities," xxv). "Thinking with" technology, Rockwell and Mactavish emphasize, is a craft with its own traditions of discourse, organizational forms, tools, and outcomes (117). Working with technology, Ramsay and Rockwell also note, has a hermeneutic power that generates an "epistemology of building" (78–79).

A second distinction marks the boundary between instrumentalism and critique:

> *Instrumental ID* typically aims at creating a product or meeting a designated pragmatic need. In contrast, *Critical ID* interrogates the dominant structure of knowledge and education with the aim of transforming them.

During the 1980s, interdisciplinarity gained heightened visibility in science-based areas of international economic competition, especially computers, engineering and manufacturing, and high technology. In this instance, interdisciplinarity serves instrumental needs in the marketplace and national defense, also dubbed "strategic" or "opportunistic" ID (Weingart, 39). In contrast, "critical" and "reflexive" forms raise questions of value and purpose that are silent in instrumental discourse. These questions are linked in humanities with new developments extending from importation of European philosophy and literary theories during the 1950s to social and political movements in the 1960s, and during the 1970s and 1980s widening interest in feminism and semiotics. Further into the 1980s, practices lumped under the umbrella term *poststructuralism* took root, including new historicism, Foucauldian studies of knowledge, and cultural and postcolonial critique. Together these developments fostered a "New Interdisciplinarity" that Ann Kaplan and George Levine deem nothing less than a transformation of humanities concerned with not only the canon and curriculum but also the organization of knowledge and all hierarchies that govern intellectual and political lives (3–4). In the process, older keywords of "plurality" and "heterogeneity" replaced "unity" and "universality." "Interrogation" and "intervention" supplanted "synthesis" and "holism," and a new rhetoric of "anti," " post-," "non-," and "de-" disciplinarity" emerged.

The advance of *Instrumental Interdisciplinarity* was met with growing critique within humanities, anchored by three warrants that place the current push for *Critical Interdisciplinarity* in Digital Humanities in historical context. In 1983, Jacques Derrida faulted programmed research on "applied" and "oriented" problems of technology, the economy, medicine, psycho-sociology, and military defense. Much of this research, he observed, is interdisciplinary (11–12). The following year the English translation of Jean-François Lyotard's 1979 book *La Condition Postmoderne: Rapport Sur Le Savoir* sharpened debate. The interdisciplinary approach, Lyotard argued, is specific to the age of delegitimation and its hurried empiricism. In the absence of a metalanguage or metanarrative in which to formulate the final goal and correct use of a complex conceptual and material machine, performative techniques of brainstorming and teamwork are marshaled for designated tasks. Even humanists are implicated in the production of "excellence" and training workers (52). In 1996, Bill Readings also linked interdisciplinarity with transformation of the Western university into a "transnational bureaucratic corporation" in service of the marketplace and an empty notion of excellence that is replacing the older appeal to "culture" (3).

Critique is a multi-layered concept. It connotes reflexivity in the design process. Echoing Derrida, Lyotard, and Readings, it questions mechanistic methods and the co-option of technology and information in a post-industrial global economy. And, it brings critical theory into the notion of "Critical Digital Humanities." Critical DH, Berry explains, builds on earlier work on race, ethnicity, gender, sexuality, and class. This form of critique has escalated with a number of initiatives: including *#transformDH* explorations of the intersections of DH and race, projects such as FemTechNet, a Google discussion document "Toward an Open Digital Humanities," a 2011 Southern California THATCamp SoCal session on diversity and DH, a session on "The Dark Side of Digital Humanities" at the 2013 conference of the Modern Language Association, and an open thread on Digital Humanities as a refuge from race, class, gender, sexuality, and disability on the website of Postcolonial Digital Humanities. It is further evident in studies of gender and race bias in digital collections and game design, as well as criticism of the "whiteness" of the field.

Dave Parry proposes a more general way of thinking about the relationship of technology and humanities: distinguishing *digital* as an adjective from *digital* as a transformative noun (434–35). The difference is apparent in Virginia Kuhn and Vicki Callahan's notions of *Horizontal* and *Vertical Interdisciplinarity*. *Horizontal Interdisciplinarity* is additive, linking fields such as history and literature without fundamental change to their disciplinary structures or logics. In contrast, *Vertical Interdisciplinarity* poses challenges to discursive categories and formal properties of a field. In the context of narrative, for example, verticality forces rethinking conceptions of the narrator, narrative forms, and the fundamental process of thinking, reflecting, critiquing, and expressing. At present, though, *Vertical Interdisciplinarity* is impeded by the way core materials are understood and implemented. Information from images and audio is still often aligned with creative/and critical thought/writing. In vertically integrated praxis, diverse materials and disciplinary strategies are engaged both within and across media, tools, formats, and philosophical categories. Each component is also in "ruthless interrogation of every possible formal boundary." Digital Humanities becomes more of a method than a field, with the potential to transform how teachers and scholars operate, the materials they engage, and the people they work with.

The third major term in the basic vocabulary moves beyond Interdisciplinarity:

> *Transdisciplinarity* transcends the narrow scope of disciplinary worldviews through an overarching synthesis associated with new conceptual frameworks or paradigms and, in a more recent connotation, problem-oriented research involving stakeholders in society.

The initial meaning of *Transdisciplinarity* (TD) was devised for the first international seminar on interdisciplinary teaching and research, held in France in 1970. It designated a common system of axioms such as anthropology conceived as a science of humans (*Interdisciplinarity*, 26). Other exemplars also emerged, including general systems theory, post/structuralism, feminist theory, sustainability, and in the United States a new meth-

odological and conceptual paradigm for health and wellness. The connotation of a new paradigm appears in Digital Humanities in arguments
that "the digital" is not simply one more new field but an overarching
framework that remakes all disciplinary research and education. In a posting to the 2011 online forum "Day of Digital Humanities," D. C. Spensley
called *Transdisciplinarity* the "new DH norm." The more recent European-
based connotation of trans-sector problem-oriented research involving
stakeholders in society is not cited explicitly in DH, but is implied in
two very different ways: instrumental alliances with stakeholders in commercial enterprises and engagement in the public sector. The former is
evident in financial partnerships for projects and proprietary ownership.
The latter is reinvigorating the older notion of "public humanities" on
new technological ground, engaging communities in the construction of
cultural heritage archives, participatory feedback, and use of digital tools
for self-representation.

Transdisciplinarity also heightens the difference between two metaphors of interdisciplinarity the Nuffield Foundation identified in 1970.
Bridge building occurs between complete and firm disciplines. *Restructuring*
detaches parts of disciplines to form a new whole (Nuffield). The distinction is apparent in differing views of the purpose of Digital Humanities.
For some, it serves traditional values encoded in legislation authorizing the
National Endowment for the Humanities: building bridges across humanities and technology in the interest of cultural heritage, history, and tradition. Editors of the Blackwell *Companion to Digital Humanities* emphasize
that even as the field broadened with the advent of World Wide Web it
remained in touch with founding goals of humanities—*illuminating* and
understanding the human record (Schreibman, Siemens, and Unsworth,
"Introduction," xxiii). For others, the purpose of DH is to refigure humanities. Authors of *Manifesto 2.0* acknowledge traditional values. Yet,
they bring design and development of new technologies, methodologies,
and information systems into the heart of humanities while expanding its
scope. *Transdisciplinarity* in DH is also aligned with "transgressive" critique
and critical imperatives in other interdisciplinary fields of cultural studies,
media and communication studies, women's and gender studies, and Canadian studies. And, in sketching a manifesto for "Artereality," Shanks and
Schnapp articulate a new vision for art education that bridges the divide of
art practice and historically grounded humanities while prioritizing teamwork, process, project- and performance-based learning, and a conception

of arts practice coterminous with research and pedagogy. Artereality moves beyond a conventional interdisciplinary agenda premised upon disciplinary borders in a transdisciplinary shift to broader human concerns anchored in themes such as representation and identity.

No discussion of Digital Humanities would be complete without mentioning a fourth term. To describe the field as "interdisciplinary" is an incomplete characterization, ignoring the triple boundary crossing that occurs across disciplines, interdisciplinary fields, and occupational professions.

> *Interprofessional* approaches involve collaboration of members of occupational professions, such as medicine, social work, education, law, and engineering.

The term *interprofessionalism* is associated most closely with health-care teams working with patients. The most prominent professions for Digital Humanities have been computer science, engineering, library and information science, and education. Law is also implicated, though not as often. Since occupational groups in DH projects often work with traditional academic areas, even when multiple professions are involved, *interdisciplinary* has tended to be a global term of convenience.

Echoing the reductive belief that DH is a handmaiden to humanities, tensions arise in the relationship between disciplines and professions when the former is regarded as doing the "real" work of scholarship and the latter playing only a support role. Collaborations are bridging this divide. However, Julia Flanders observes, in North American academic culture, diminution of technical roles to service is exacerbated by the distinction between "faculty" and "staff." Melissa Terras, likewise, cites hierarchical perceptions of the status of individuals depending on where they sit on the spectrum of ranks and roles ("Being the Other," 224). And, Flanders adds, tension persists between traditional values of scholarship and the business model of efficiency and productivity faced by library, IT, and other "para-academic" staff. The paradigm of the tenure-track professor also obscures a more complex reality as well: for every hour of faculty work, hundreds of hours are spent maintaining the infrastructure of physical and administrative space and the creation of scholarship and related resources ("Collaboration," 11).

Cross-hatching Interdisciplinary Humanities

No opening framework would be complete without also considering the nature of interdisciplinary humanities. Underlying ideas of synthesis, holism, and general knowledge were developed in ancient Greek philosophy and transmitted subsequently throughout the history of liberal education, perpetuating the ancient Greek ideal of *paideia*, Renaissance traditions of *studia humanitatis* and *litterae humaniore*, and a generalist model of culture and knowledge. When the unity found in the classical and humanistic tradition could no longer be assumed, Wilhelm Vosskamp recounted, interdisciplinarity emerged as a modern problem of *Wissenschaft*. From the 16th century forward, attempts at producing or bringing out unification appeared in the work of Comenius, Leibnitz, d'Alembert, Kant, Hegel, and von Humboldt ("From Scientific," 20; "Crossing," 45). In the 17th century, the idea of "ages of learning" also promoted cultural history as a master narrative of periodization for interart comparison. However, in the 18th century, the French Encyclopedists criticized the classical conception of humanities. Unity remained an ideal, but Diderot and Bacon regarded empirical science as the new basis of universality. Further into the 18th and 19th centuries, Vosskamp added, a pragmatic attitude developed toward reciprocal borrowing between neighboring disciplines, and interdisciplinary cooperation was increasingly institutionalized. The search for interdisciplinarity was framed increasingly as a limited endeavor as well ("From Scientific," 21).

There is no hard etymological proof of the first use of *interdisciplinarity* in humanities. Other terms were used more often, especially *integration, synthesis, unity,* and *holism*. During the opening decades of the 20th century, two differing conceptions of interdisicpinarity were apparent in humanities: one hearkening back to unity of knowledge and culture preserved in a canon of works and the other engaging the present in a historically situated problem focus. On the horizon, new developments would also foster *Critical Interdisciplinarity* and a transgressive connotation of *Transdisciplinarity*. In a 1993 report on humanities, Alberta Arthurs highlighted two wide-ranging developments. The first, "specializations of difference," was evident in black/ethnic/and women's studies. The second, Clifford Geertz's concept of "blurred genres," broke down established lines of intellectual inquiry, fostering intersections, overlays, juxtapositions, and new formulations. Moreover, Catherine Gallagher reported, by the late

20th century, faculty cultures began leaning toward synthetic projects such as Marxism, structuralism, feminism, semiotics, and cultural history (163–64). And, in a development that presaged Digital Humanities, scholars embarked on studies of media.

The identity of interdisciplinary humanists changed in kind. The earliest prototype, the synoptic philosopher of ancient Greece, was supplanted by the orator of Rome, the polymath of the Renaissance, the scholar gentleman of the 18th century, and upholders of a generalist model of culture and knowledge in the late 19th through early 20th centuries. As new interdisciplinary fields and cross-fertilization escalated over the course of the 20th century, a new model emerged, Richard Carp's notion of the "boundary rider" skilled at walking the borders of disciplinary expertise ("Relying on the Kindness of Strangers"). Stanley Katz also suggested the radicalism of the 1960s, redefinitions of culture and politics, and challenges to the structure of higher education encouraged methodological creativity and experiment. As a result, he found, many academics were by inclination or training "multi-", "inter-", or "non-" disciplinary ("Beyond the Disciplines"). Viewed as part of this history, Digital Humanities is both a hybrid specialization and a set of cross-fertilizing practices. Yet, conventional strategies of mapping interdisciplinarity are usually limited to tracing the most obvious sign—the relationship of one discipline to another.

In mapping interdisciplinarity in literary studies, Giles Gunn demonstrated the limits of this conjunctive strategy. "Literature and . . ." does not capture the emergence of new subjects and topics such as history of the book, materialism of the body, psychoanalysis of the reader, sociology of conventions, ideologies of gender, race, and class as well as intertextuality, power, and the status of "others." They, in turn, stimulated further lines of investigation that combined approaches from different disciplines and movements. This degree of complexity seems to defy mapping, let alone changes in correlate fields that are harder to track. Even at the level of new subjects and topics, Gunn concluded, "The threading of disciplinary principles and procedures is frequently doubled, tripled, and quadrupled in ways that are not only mixed but, from a conventional disciplinary perspective, somewhat off center." They are characterized by "overlapping, underlayered, interlaced, crosshatched affiliations, collations, and alliances" that are more like fractals than straight geometric lines (248–49).

The cross-hatching of influence will be strongly evident in chapter 2, when tracking Digital Humanities practices in the disciplines of English, history, and archaeology. More generally, Katherine Hayles observes, highly charged concepts appear in varied combinations throughout a culture. "Turbulence," for example, was viewed originally from the perspective of fluid flows, but it became associated more generally with "chaos." When concepts circulate within a cultural field they stimulate cross-fertilization, but they also bear the traces of local disciplinary economies (*Chaos Bound*, xiv, 4, 37, 116). Mieke Bal's notion of "traveling concepts" in humanities highlights the methodological potential of concepts as the backbone of interdisciplinary study of culture, including the exemplars of image, *mise en scène*, framing, performance, tradition, intention, and critical intimacy. The "digital," Carassai and Takehana suggest, should now be added to the list. Concepts, Bal advises, exhibit both specificity and inter-subjectivity. They do not mean the same thing for everyone, but they foster common discussion as they travel across disciplines, individuals, periods, and academic communities. In the process of travel, their meaning and use change. Their changeability, in fact, becomes part of their usefulness. Concepts also have analytical and theoretical force that stimulates productive propagation, prompting a new articulation and ordering of phenomena that does not impose transdisciplinary universalism.

Any discussion of the interdisciplinary nature of Digital Humanities must also acknowledge another development. The popular characterization of DH as the bridging of two cultures—humanities and technology—obscures the role of increased boundary crossing between humanities and a third culture—social sciences. Over the latter half of the 20th century a series of historical, sociological, and political turns in scholarship interrogated the notion of inherent meaning in an aesthetic work, reduction of context to a background gloss, and the placement of readers, viewers, and listeners outside of discipline proper. As humanities disciplines moved away from older paradigms of historical empiricism, positivist philology, and formalist criticism, the concept of culture also expanded from narrow elite forms to a broader anthropological notion, and discrete objects were reimagined as forces that circulate in a network of forms and actions. Subject matter further expanded with increased interest in marginalized groups and other cultures, and demands for social, political, and postmodern discourses reinvigorated scholarship and educational reform.

Increased interest in topics once regarded as the domain of social science signals yet another development. Over the latter half of the 20th century, disciplines in general have become more porous and multi- or interdisciplinary in character (Bender and Schorske, 12). In a posting to the 2009 "Day of Digital Humanities," Julia Flanders highlighted a new flux propelled by rapid technological, institutional, and cultural changes. Individuals still differ on the role of disciplines, however. McCarty admits the received notion of disciplinarity is an impediment in Humanities Computing. Yet, he accepts disciplines as "given." He is not concerned with reformulating them, rather focusing on relations and kinship in a more capacious sense of disciplinarity (*Humanities Computing*, 209). In contrast, Todd Presner's notion of Digital Humanities 2.0 problematizes where boundaries have been drawn in the past, accentuating new disciplinary paradigms, convergent fields, and hybrid methodologies ("Hypercities," 6). This stance also reflects the shared imperatives of *Critical Interdisciplinarity* and transgressive *Transdisciplinarity*, interrogating the existing structure of knowledge and education in order to change them.

Identity and Transversality

Tackling the question of what constitutes Digital Humanities from the perspective of language, Alan Liu asked whether DH is singular or plural, a "field" or "fields," or as the *Wikipedia* entry suggests, an "area." Liu drew parallels to the high-level generality of "media" for varied mediums, "data" for "datum," and singular verb "is" for the plurality of American studies. As he also suggested in the second epigraph to this chapter, the answer to the question of identity will depend on conversations not only with disciplines but also with "cousin" fields and the wider public. Exploring their fit within a shared agenda will not result in a false harmony. It will illuminate their "conjunction and collision." The final preliminary step for understanding interdisciplinarity in Digital Humanities lies in comparative lessons from "cousin" fields and their transversal operations.

Given its longevity, American studies furnishes deeper insight about shifts in identity over time. The institutional roots of the field lie in the 1920s and 1930s, when the first courses in American civilization were offered (Kerber, 417). The emergence of an identifiable field in English and history departments, though, is usually traced to the 1940s. When the American Studies Association (ASA) was founded in 1951, it adopted the explicit goal of studying American culture and history "as a whole," with the aim of unifying the plural and harmonizing differences (Wise, "Some

Elementary Axioms," 517; Brantlinger, 27). The actual practice of teaching and scholarship, though, was more multidisciplinary than interdisciplinary. Faculty also tended to retain their locations in departmental homes or hold dual appointments. Over time, increasing focus on themes and case-study problems fostered greater interaction. Even then, however, methods were not fused or a new holism, interdisciplinary synthesis, or metadiscipline created (Cowan, 107; Orvell, Butler, and Mechling, viii). If American studies were to achieve intellectual coherence, Mechling, Meredith, and Wilson implored, the concept of culture must occupy the center of a "discipline" of American studies. Achieving disciplinary status became the hallmark of legitimacy and social scientific methods the proposed means of achieving it ("American Culture Studies").

The period of the mid- to late 1960s and 1970s was a turning point in American studies, fueled by cultural revolutions, new subjects, and expanded methodology. Boundary crossing between humanities and social sciences accelerated, and over the latter half of the century the scope expanded to include ecological studies and environmental history; critiques of corporate capitalism and the global political economy; new area studies and African American, ethnic, women's, and urban studies; plus studies of popular, mass, and folk culture. Scholarship also opened to the full range of aesthetic expressions and social scientific analyses. In 1978, Gene Wise counted no less than seventy-four categories of specialization ("Paradigm Dramas," 519). During the 1980s, European cultural theory also became an important component of scholarship, and in the 1980s and 1990s increased attention was paid to gender, race, and ethnicity as well as region and class. New interests strained the unified synthesis of intellectual history and assumption that America is an integrated whole. In 1977 David Marcell called for a "critical interdisciplinarity" that would do justice to the pluralism of American culture, and by 1984 Giroux, Shumway, and Sosnoski were advocating a "counter-disciplinary praxis" of cultural studies that gave voice to oppositional and counterdisciplinary practices.

Several parallels stand out. In American studies, literature comprised a major body of content, along with American history. In Digital Humanities, linguistics and literature were early sites of computer-aided study of texts, and English and history are primary locations of DH work today. Over time, calls for *Critical Interdisciplinarity* also mounted in both fields, and the expanding plurality of approaches heightened boundary consciousness. Collective identity in American studies, George Lipsitz suggested, now derives from local incarnations across dispersed sites. The uneven variety of activities and plural practices coheres around common questions (106). Kathleen Fitzpatrick's description of Digital Humanities as a "nexus of fields" conveys a similar sense of plurality around shared interest in digital technologies: in this case "between those who've been in the field for a long time and those who are coming to it today, between disciplinarity and interdisciplinarity, between making and interpreting, and between the field's history and its future" ("The Humanities," 12, 14).

The question of disciplinary identity also arose in both fields. In framing historical and critical studies of disciplinarity, Messer-Davidow, Shumway, and Sylvan identified key traits. Disciplines constitute specialized subjects, objects, and methods. They produce economies of value. They manufacture discourse in the form of publication and discussion. They provide jobs. They secure funding in the form of awards, contracts, budgets, scholars, and salaries. They generate prestige in ranking, ratings, and reputation. And, they produce the idea of progress by proliferating objects for study, improving explanation, generating ideas that command assent, and telling stories of advancement (vii–viii). At the same time, disciplines are dynamic sites of change, including engagements with digital technologies. "Disciplinary traditions," Hayles observed, "are in active interplay with the technologies even as the technologies are transforming the traditions." Moreover, the shifts now under way are operating in recursive feedback loops that are expansive: "In broad view, the impact of these feedback loops is not confined to the humanities alone, reaching outward to redefine institutional categories, reform pedagogical practices, and re-envision the relation of higher education to local communities and global conversations" (*How We Think*, 53).

Louis Menand claims that interdisciplinarity is completely consistent with disciplinarity, because each field develops its own distinctive program of inquiry, thereby ratifying the logic of disciplinarity ("Undisciplined," 51; *Marketplace of Ideas*, 119). The relationship of disciplinarity and interdisciplinarity, however, is more complex. In a collection of "classic" articles published in *American Quarterly*, the American Studies Association held fast to the notion of disciplinary legitimacy (Maddox). Competing constructions of the field, though, envision a "framework," a "decentralized movement," and a "network." Patrik Svensson also drew parallels between Asian American studies and Digital Humanities. Both have accumulated mechanisms of disciplining in the form of faculty positions, book series, annual meetings, and core values. Both also originated in a sense of dissatisfaction with existing approaches and methods as well as the isolation of disciplinary specialization. Yet, their emergence did not result in complete separation. Both have played an "agentive role," mediating or "nourishing" disciplines to bring them into new alignment with the "real world." For area studies, the initial context was World War II. For Digital Humanities, it was new technologies and increasingly new media. Members of both fields also characterize themselves in an "in-between position," in a "dual citizenship" of dependency on disciplines ("Envisioning," 2–3).

A similar sense of being "in-between" appears in other fields as well. Diane Elam defines women's studies as both a "discipline of difference" and an "interdisciplinary discipline." Elam endorses departmental location, contending it does not deprive the field of radical politics. It harnesses funds and tenure lines. It also draws strength from disciplines without being reduced to them, at the same time interdisciplinarity is defined and advanced in the space of women's studies. Borders are crossed through continuous crossfertilization ("Ms. en Abyme," 294–98; "Taking Account"). In order to change the disciplines, one program coordinator remarked, women's studies had to be "of them, in them, and about them" (qtd. in Boxer, 671, 693). Consequently, Sandra Coyner found, practitioners typically identify with another community, as historian, literary critic, psychologist, or social worker (349–51). Likewise, practitioners of American studies call themselves Americanists, literary critics, historians, art historians, musicologists, and film and media critics, as well as feminists, African-Americanists, and members of other ethnic and national groups. Many see themselves as members of the field of cultural studies as well, or at least "doing cultural studies" in some way. In the case of Digital Humanities, John Walter posted to the "Day of Digital Humanities," identifying with a larger community does not mean surrendering identity as specialists. Anglo-Saxonists doing digital work, for example, do not relinquish their identity as Anglo-Saxonists or as linguists, literary scholars, historians, archeologists, or theologians. Mutual identification fosters dialogue with kindred spirits using different methods and perspectives.

Susan Stanford Friedman's description of working in two locations describes the movement that also occurs in Digital Humanities. Freidman's home base is literary studies. It provides an intellectual anchor and a substantive platform of knowledge and literature, narrative and figuration, representation, and a methodological base for strategies of reading texts in varied cultural contexts. Her political home base is feminism. It provides an approach to questions about gender, power relations, other systems of stratification, and an ethical commitment to social justice and change. From these two homes, she travels to other (inter)disciplinary homes, bringing back what she learned and is useful to her projects. Travel stimulates new ways of thinking, exposing the constructedness of what is taken for granted, dislodging unquestioned assumptions, and producing new insights, questions, and solutions to impasses at home ("Academic Feminism").

Travel, it must also be said, does not take place in a monolithic landscape of interdisciplinarity. Multiple kinds of fields, Jill Vickers explains, are now "in the mix." Some have "congealed" to the point they have a recognized canon or foundational theory. Effecting partial closure, they act like disciplines with a shared epistemological base, journals, learned societies, and, in some cases, separate departments. In contrast, "open or cross-roads interdisciplinary fields" do not have a paradigm, canon, foundation, or epistemology. Yet, two forces may be at work: an "integrative" tendency, evident in Canadian studies as area studies, and a self-asserting "disintegrating tendency" that draws attention away from the center of existing knowledge systems, evident in critical, oppositional, and self-studies. As new inter- and trans-disciplinary fields developed, the context also changed. Some fields, such as environmental studies, were problem driven. Others were part of a broad societal push for change, including the women's movement and Quebec and First Nations' movements for self-determination ("Unframed," 60).

Multiple interdisciplinarities are also "in the mix" of Digital Humanities. The field has "congealed" to the point it has a recognized canon, journals, organizations, and centers. An "integrative" tendency is evident in the formation of an identifiable field, though a "disintegrating tendency" is also evident in critical and oppositional stances that heighten debate on whether the purpose of DH is to serve traditional humanities or to transform them. Dean Rehberger and Andrew Prescott urge closer contact with cousin fields. Rehberger likens the challenge of authenticity digital humanists face to that of American studies. Rehberger remembered "the sting of being unreal," of not being a "real" historian or a "real" literary critic without regard to how traditional disciplines are always in flux and change. Rehberger urges making connections with others working in the margins: in black/women's/native/queer/and Latino[a] studies. Prescott advocates closer contact with cultural and media studies. When examining patterns in British DH centers, he found greater representation of early periods, geographical focus on the classical world and Western Europe, and standard cultural icons. Yet, culture, canon, and subject matter have widened, making games, popular media, and digital-born materials as legitimate a focus as ancient manuscripts.

Widening scope also increases cross-hatching, as the cousin field of media studies demonstrates. The Society for Cinema and Media Studies did not formally adopt "and Media" into its name until 2002. Yet, Jason Rhody of the National Endowment for Humanities Office of Digital Humanities recalls, the addition formalized a relationship that had been emerging in studies of electronic literature, video games, and the changing nature of cinema. Members were also interested in performance theory, Internet protocols, and critical race theory. They were not "digital humanists" per se. They were media scholars and literary historians, feminists and formalists, filmmakers and textual editors. The logic of adding "Media," Rhody suggests, underscores the recurring process of *refining* that produces new values emerging against the backdrop of traditions that have backstories threaded through multiple disciplinary backgrounds and institutional types. Moreover, they appear not only in universities but also in galleries, libraries, archives, museums, historic homes, and historical societies. From his vantage point reviewing grant applications, Rhody proposes DH operates as a kind of Boolean composition, in a process of invoking and refining combinations of disciplines, methods, subjects, and theories to investigate research questions of interest. Few people, he added, just "'do' DH.'"

David Scholle's options for mass communication studies raise further parallels, based on G. J. Shepherd's catalog of identities. The field was constructed as a practical enterprise in schools of mass communications and in speech departments. As a "boundary discipline," it is situated between the vocational interests of professional schools and the liberal arts. A "undisciplinary" response would continue to service disciplines. An "antidisciplinary" response would reject foundations, and a "disciplinary" response establish the field's own ontological grounding. Sholle rejects "undisciplinary" and "disciplinary" options, advocating a solution that lies between the "antidisciplinary" impetus of a democratic curriculum and a plurality of activities. Conceived as a "radically interdisciplinary" field, it would remain a locus of experiment and field of action ("Resisting Disciplines"). All of these identities are present in the discourse of Digital

Humanities. As a "boundary discipline," it is situated between professional schools and liberal arts, often in terms of "unidisciplinary" service. It leans overtly toward being a profession itself in specialized master's programs that prepare workers for jobs in the academy and the cultural heritage sector. Its alignment with traditional professions is strongly apparent in project-based work with experts in library and information science, engineering, and computer science. Resistance to disciplinary formation is strongest in arguments for embedding critique into all contexts, in pressing for "transdisciplinary" refiguration of humanities, and in "antidisciplinary" rejection of all foundations.

Comparison with cousin fields furnishes a final lesson foreshadowed by David Bathrick's prediction for culture studies. The diversity of practices, he concludes, means cultural studies will continue to be "elastic" and the name a "terminological mutant." Cultural studies is not *unified* in a totalizing sense but is *unifying* by virtue of gathering coalescing practices into a problematic and perhaps impossible synthesis (321). Echoing Bathrick, no single practice can metonymically represent Digital Humanities. Nor does it exist in a single space. It is located within disciplines, their subfields, and alternative practices. The field is multidisciplinary in scope. It is interdisciplinary in integrative work and collaborative practices. It is transdisciplinary in a broad-based reformulation of humanities that places technology and media at the heart of research and teaching, and in embedding critique in all practices and engaging the public sector.

What, then, is the proper object of study for Digital Humanities? Answering the question, Wendell Piez wonders if it will be media consciousness in a digital age? Or a critical attitude applied to cultural production in a nation or a period? Or a design and production art? (¶9). Pierre Bourdieu's definition of the intellectual field comes to mind. Like a magnetic field, the intellectual field is made up of a system of power lines. It cannot be reduced to a simple aggregate of isolated agents or the sum of juxtaposed elements. By their very existence, opposition, and combination, multiple forces determine its structure at a given moment (Bourdieu; Dhareshwar, 6–8). Moreover, the same field may serve different purposes simultaneously. Women's studies, Cornwall and Stoddard observe, may be viewed as an emergent discipline with its own canons, methods, and issues. At the same time, it is alternative and resistant to traditional discursive practices of disciplines (162). The same is true of Digital Humanities.

This level of complexity goes beyond plurality to transversality. Plurality is an additive concept, signified in descriptions of a "heterogeneous" and "polymorphous" field. "Transversality" signifies cross-hatching relationships at the intersections of disciplines and cousin fields, akin to a line in mathematics that intersects others in a system of lines. In an influential essay that still shapes thinking about interdisciplinarity in humanities, Roland Barthes linked the concept of transversality to reconfigurations that seek to produce or recover meaning that previous configurations tended to blur, camouflage, or efface. Interdisciplinarity, he wrote, is not "the calm of an easy security." The starting point is an "unease in classification," when the solidarity of an old discipline breaks down. From there a "certain mutation" may be detected. A sharp break may occur suddenly through disruptions of fashion, although change appears more often in the form of an epistemological slide. It is not enough, he added, to surround an object with multiple perspectives: "Interdisciplinarity consists in creating a new object that belongs to no one." The new object of "text," for example, displaced or overturned an older notion of a "work." Text was a wider methodological field invested with multiple meanings in an intersecting network of relations with other texts and influences (73–74).

To say that a new object belongs to no one, however, ignores the complexity of boundary work. Objects and concepts are not confined to bound domains. A prominent movement in humanities illustrates the complexity of transversality. *Theory* is an umbrella term for reflections on language and representation, historically oriented cultural criticism, and the role of gender and sexuality (Moran, 82). New syntheses of Marxism, psychoanalysis, semiotics, and feminism also emerged across literary studies, philosophy, and psychoanalysis, as well as law, anthropology, art history, music, classics, and history. The most notable approaches were deconstruction, poststructuralist Marxism, critiques of colonial discourse, theories of popular culture, and the discourses of identity fields. Vivek Dhareshwar's notion of Theory with a long view and a short view illustrates transversal operation. Theory with a "long view" was an expansive problem surveyed panoramically from a plurality of perspectives. Theory operated in horizontal fashion, moving above and between texts and disciplinary formations. Yet, it also took the form of a "close view," operating vertically through textual proddings in particular domains (6–8).

The "digital" and "media" operate in a similar manner. They are simultaneously expansive in their horizontal scope and located vertically within individual domains. Transecting between a long and a short view also moves past the dichotomy in Digital Humanities of "distant reading," based on a statistical picture of a large number of works, and "close reading," based on intensive analysis of a single work or artefact. Burdick et al. join a growing number of scholars who challenge the dichotomy. "Toggling" between distant and close, macro and micro, and surface and depth allows digital humanists to play with scale by "zooming in and out" in a search for large-scale patterns then focusing on finer-grained exegesis (30, 39). "Toggling" is also an apt metaphor for the study of complex topics across fields.

A 2011 Seminar in Experimental Critical Theory sponsored by the University of California Humanities Research Institute (UCHRI) focused on the theme "ReWired: Asian/TechnoScience/Area Studies." It provided a space for responding to rapidly transforming landscapes of technoscientific knowledge production and urban development across Asia. Comprehending the complex relationship of related movements, forces, and structures requires integrating deep understandings of history and politics represented by Asian and critical area studies with emergent work on transnational dynamics of science and technology, market economies, and their modes of governance. Computing practices are emerging via networks shaped by, in, and across the formerly "underdeveloped" world. Asia's hybrid modernities transect discourses of science and technology, digital revolution, political economy, community, nation, and identity. Critical knowledge of states, science, and social movements from histories and social sciences of Asia must also be integrated with studies of cultural production in Asia and studies of peer-to-peer creative and community-based practices generated by the transnational digital sphere. The core questions and themes also transect global studies and projects such as the UCHRI and HASTAC's Digital Media and Learning initiative.

Amidst the complexity of work across sites, Digital Humanities is also experiencing an identity crisis. This phenomenon is not new. Periodic identity crises have appeared in a number of interdisciplinary fields, usually centered on conceptual coherence (R. Miller, 13). It is not surprising, then, to see "(Digital) Humanities Revisited" as the title of a 2013 conference taking stock of "Challenges and Opportunities in the Digital Age." Melissa Terras also questioned in her blog whether "Big Tent Digital Humanities" has room for everyone practicing different kinds of interdisciplinarity. An ecumenical approach, she allows, gives individuals freedom to explore their interests while having a core of like-minded scholars. It also aids in networking and learning what new technologies are being appropriated. But, expansion is accompanied by "populist politics" that lack a clear remit, stance, or goal. A "Big Tent" provides strength in numbers. Yet, if everyone is a digital humanist then nobody is. The field does not really exist, Terras contends, if it is all-pervasive, too widely spread, ill-defined, and so loosely bound that deeper insights and understandings emanating from a community are lacking.

Clustered Links for Chapter 1 in Order of Appearance

Alan Liu. "Is Digital Humanities a Field?—An Answer From the Point of View of Language," http://liu.english.ucsb.edu/is-digital-humanities-a-Field-an-answer-from-the-point-of-view-of-language/

"What is Digital Humanities?" University of Illinois at Urbana-Champaign Library: http://www.library.illinois.edu/sc/services/Digital_Humanities/index.html

Digital Humanities Specialist, Stanford University: https://dhs.stanford.edu/the-digital-humanities-as/the-digital-humanities-as-a-movement-expressed-in-a-method-enshrined-in-a-tool/

Patrik Svensson. "Humanities Computing as Digital Humanities." *Digital Humanities Quarterly* 3, no. 3 (2009). http://www.digitalhumanities.org/dhq/vol/3/3/000065/000065.html

Michael Shanks and Jeffrey Schnapp's "Artreality: Rethinking Art as Craft in a Knowledge Economy. A Manifesto." http://documents.stanford.edu/Michael Shanks/Artereality

Carassai and Takehana's comment in "Introduction" to special issue on Futures of Digital Studies in *Digital Humanities Quarterly*, 5, no. 3 (2011): http://www.digitalhumanities.org/dhq/vol/5/3/000109/000109.html

Dave Berry's blog entry on Critical Digital Humanities: http://stunlaw.blogspot.com/2013/01/critical-digital-humanities.html

A Day in the Life of Digital Humanities postings: For 2009–11, http://tapor.ualberta.ca/taporwiki/index.php/How_do_you_define_Humanities_Computing_/_Digital_Humanities%3F#How_do_you_define_Digital_Humanities.3F; For 2012: http://dayofdh2012.artsrn.ualberta.ca/dh/; For 2013: http://dayofdh2013.matrix.msu.edu/

Alan Liu's blog: http://liu.english.ucsb.edu/is-digital-humanities-a-field-an-answer-from-the-point-of-view-of-language/

Patrik Svensson. "Envisioning the Digital Humanities." *Digital Humanities Quarterly* 6, no. 2 (2012). http://www.digitalhumanities.org/dhq/vol/6/1/000112/000112.html

Dean Rehberger's website: http://rehberger.us/archives/84

Andrew Prescott's blog: http://digitalriffs.blogspot.co.uk/2012/07/making-digital-human-anxieties.html

Jason Rhody's response to question of definition: http://mediacommons.future ofthebook.org/users/jasonrhody

Wendell Piez's comment: "Something Called 'Digital Humanities.'" *Digital Humanities Quarterly* 2.1 (2008).

UCHRI's "ReWired" Seminar in Experimental Critical Theory: http://rewired. uchri.org/?page_id=274?

German conferences on "Challenges and Opportunities in the Digital Age": http:// www.volkswagenstiftung.de/digitalhumanities

Melissa Terras's blog on "Peering Inside the Big Tent," July 26, 2011: http://melis saterras.blogspot.com/2011/07/peering-inside-big-tent-digital.html

< 2 >

Defining

When invited to post a definition of Humanities Computing/Digital Humanities in the online forum "Day of Digital Humanities":

"The digital humanities is whatever we make it to be." George H. Williams, 2011
"DH is best experienced as both theory and practice." Elli Mylonas, 2010
". . . just one method for doing humanistic inquiry." Brian Croxall, 2011
"A term of tactical convenience." Matthew Kirschenbaum, 2011
"I'm sick of trying to define it." Amanda French, 2011
"With extreme reluctance." Lou Bernard, 2011
"I try not to." Willard McCarty, 2011

Keywords: Humanities Computing, Digital Humanities, discipline, interdiscipline, modes of engagement, 2.0 interactivity, visualization, spatialization, code

In an age when many people turn to the Internet for information, keyword searching is a tempting strategy for defining a field. However, the most obvious search term—*digital humanities*—yields only a partial picture. It is not a recognized subject heading in the U.S. Library of Congress classification system and, Willard McCarty found, near equivalents of "Humanities Computing" appear in conjunction with other terms such as *humanities, arts, philosophy*, and variations of *computing, informatics, technology, data processing, digital,* and *multi-media* (*Humanities Computing*, 2–3, 215). Some subjects such as "arts" were also outside the scope of early print-dominated Humanities Computing. The words *digital* and *media*, Andy

37

Engel found in doing keyword searching for this book, appear often in titles of publications, educational programs, calls for conference papers, and job descriptions. Yet, as they have gained popularity their usefulness has diluted (e-mail, July 13, 2010). Database sleuthing, then, is only a blunt instrument. A closer analysis of six major statements furnishes a more nuanced picture of how the field is defined. This chapter then situates definition in the context of three major disciplines where new technologies and media are changing the nature of practice—English, history, and archaeology. It closes with a reflection on three trendlines that have emerged in those disciplines and Digital Humanities writ large—visualization, spatialization, and a computational turn in the field.

Declaring

Statement 1

This collection marks a turning point in the field of digital humanities: for the first time, a wide range of theorists and practitioners, those who have been active in the field for decades, and those recently involved, disciplinary experts, computer scientists, and library and information studies specialists, have been brought together to consider digital humanities as a discipline in its own right, as well as to reflect on how it relates to areas of traditional humanities scholarship.
—Susan Schreibman, Ray Siemens, and John Unsworth, "The Digital Humanities and Humanities Computing: An Introduction," in *A Companion to Digital Humanities* (Malden, MA; Oxford: Blackwell, 2004), xxiii

Publication of a Blackwell anthology in 2004 suggested that Digital Humanities had come of age in a history that is traced conventionally to the search for machines capable of automating linguistic analysis of written texts. The year 1949 is enshrined in most origin stories, benchmarked by Father Robert Busa's efforts to create an automated *index verborum* of all words in the works of Thomas Aquinas and related authors. In the opening chapter, Susan Hockey divides the history of the field into four stages: Beginnings (1949–early 1970s), Consolidation (1970s–mid-1980s), New Developments (mid-1980s–early 1990s), and the Era of the Internet (1990s forward). Hockey is mindful of the challenge of writing the history of an interdisciplinary area. Any attempt raises questions of scope, overlap, impact on other disciplines, and the difference between straightforward chronology and digressions from a linear timeline ("The History," 3). Willard McCarty also warns against the "Billiard Ball Theory of History," asserting impact for some developments while consigning others to lesser or no importance (*Humanities Computing*, 212–13). Jan Hajic, for instance, tracks emergence to 1948, citing broader scientific, economic, and political developments prior to and during World War II. Interest in natural language arose in fields distant from linguistics and other humanities disciplines, including computer science, signal processing, and information theory. The year 1948 also marks Claude Shannon's foundational work in information theory and the probabilistic and statistical description of information contents (80).

Nonetheless, the field has a strong historical identity with linguistics and computer-aided study of texts, signified by the early names *computational linguistics* and *humanities computing*. Typical activities included textual informatics, miniaturization, and stylometric analysis of encoded textual material that aided studies of authorship and dating. Vocabulary studies generated by concordance programs were prominent in publications and, during the period of Consolidation, literary and linguistic computing in conference presentations. Yet, papers also accounted for using computers in teaching writing and language instruction, music, art, and archaeology. Overall, emphasis tended to be on input, output, and programming, though early reproduction was more suited to journals and books than poetry and drama. Mathematics for vocabulary counts also exceeded humanists' traditional skills, and computer-based work was not widely respected in humanities (Hockey, "The History," 7–10).

The period of New Developments was marked by several advances. By the late 1980s, powerful workstations were affording greater memory, screen resolution, color capacity, and graphical user interface, facilitating display of not only musical notation software but also non-standard characters in Old English, Greek, Cyrillic, and other alphabets. Both textual and visual elements could be incorporated in digital surrogates of manuscripts and documents as well (Hockey, "The History"). Expectations for quality in graphics grew, Burdick et al. also recall, as bandwidth increased, and multimedia forms of humanistic research in digital environments emerged (9, 20). And, Melissa Terras adds, unprecedented investments and development in digitization were apparent in the heritage and cultural sector, along with changes in public policy that increased availability of funding ("Digitization," 51). The rhetoric of "revolution," the *Companion*'s editors caution, was more predictive in some disciplines than others (Schreibman, Siemens, and Unsworth, "The Digital Humanities," xxiv). Even so, an authoritative historical record could now be compiled for what they alternately called a "field" and a "discipline" with an "interdisciplinary core" located in "Humanities Computing." That label also marked a strong orientation to tools and methods reinforced in chapters on principles, applications, production, dissemination, and archiving.

The advent of personal computers and e-mail in the "Era of the Internet" ushered in a new relationship of humanities and technology. Burdick et al. characterize the change as acceleration of a transition in digital scholarship from processing to networking (8). The implications were evident in one of the early homes for Humanities Computing. Nancy Ide describes the period from the 1990s forward as a "golden era" in linguistic corpora. Prior to the Internet, the body of literature for stylistic analysis, authorship studies, and corpora for general language in lexicography was typically created and processed at single locations. Increased computer speed and capacity facilitated sharing more and larger texts while expanding possibilities for gathering statistics about patterns of language, and new language-processing software stimulated renewed interest in corpus composition in computational linguistics. Parallel corpora containing the same text in two or more languages also appeared, and automatic techniques were developed for annotating language data with information about linguistic properties. Yet, limits persisted. By 2004, few efforts had been made to compile language samples that were balanced in representing different genres and speech dialects (289–90).

Even with continuing limits, Hockey adds, by the early 1990s new projects in electronic scholarly editions were under way, libraries were putting the content of collections on the Internet, and the Text Encoding Initiative published the first full version of guidelines for representing texts in digital form. Services were being consolidated, and theoretical work in Humanities Computing and new academic programs signaled wider acceptance. And, early multimedia combinations of text with images, audio and video were appearing as well ("History," 10–16). The sea change prompted by the Internet also became the basis for new periodizations of the field. Cathy Davidson calls the time from 1991 to the dot-com bust in fall 2001 "Humanities 1.0." It was characterized by moving "from the few to the many." Websites and tools facilitated massive amounts of archiving, data collection, manipulation, and searching. For the most part, though, tools were created by experts or commercial interests. "Humanities 2.0" was characterized by new tools and relationships between producers and consumers of tools, fostering a "many-to-many" model marked by greater interactivity, user participation, and user-generated content. This shift was apparent in the corporate and social networking of Google and MySpace, collaborative knowledge building of *Wikipedia*, user-generated photo-sharing of Flickr, video-posting of YouTube, and blogs, wikis, and virtual environments. "If Web 1.0 was about democratizing access," Davidson sums up, "Web 2.0 was about democratizing participation" ("Humanities 2.0," 205).

Steven E. Jones highlights a more recent timetable over a ten-year period that gained momentum between 2004 and 2008. New digital products emerged along with social-network platforms and other developments such as Google Books and Google Maps. The change was not so much a "paradigm" shift as a "fork" in Humanities Computing that established a new "branch" of work and a "new, interdisciplinary kind of platform thinking." Borrowing from William Gibson, Jones styles the shift an "eversion" of cyberspace, a "turning itself inside out" marked by a diverse set of cultural, intellectual, and technological changes. Eversion parallels Katherine Hayles's conception of new phase in cybernetics that moved from "virtuality" to a "mixed reality." This phenomenon is not isolated to the academy: it is part of a larger cultural shift marked by emergence and convergence. The new DH associated with this shift is evident in digital forensics, critical code and platform studies, game studies, and a new phase of research using linguistic data, large corpora of texts, and visualizations documented in the latter half of this chapter in the disciplines of English, history, and archaeology. A more layered and hybrid experience of digital data and digital media, Jones adds, is occurring across contexts, from archived manuscripts to Arduino circuit boards. Conceptualized in terms of Hayles's notion of "intermediation" of humans and machines in "recursive feedback and feedforward loops," this experience is evident in new workflows and collaborative relationships examined more fully in chapter 6 (3–5, 11, 13, 31–32, 83, 91, 173).

Statement 2 signals another benchmark event that appeared three years after the *Companion* was published, the inaugural issue of *Digital Humanities Quarterly* (*DHQ*):

Statement 2

Digital humanities is by its nature a hybrid domain, crossing disciplinary boundaries and also traditional barriers between theory and practice, technological implementation and scholarly reflection. But over time this field has developed its own orthodoxies, its internal lines of affiliation and collaboration that have become intellectual paths of least resistance. In a world—perhaps scarcely imagined two decades ago—where digital issues and questions are connected with nearly every area of endeavor, we cannot take for granted a position of centrality.
—Julia Flanders, Wendell Piez, and Melissa Terras, "Welcome to *Digital Humanities Quarterly*," *Digital Humanities Quarterly* 1, no. 1 (2007): ¶3

In welcoming readers to the new journal, Flanders, Piez, and Terras resist defining the field as a discipline. They also defer the underlying question, "What is digital humanities?" Orthodoxies, codifications, and dominant practices had already formed, raising the danger of ossifying the history of a young field prematurely. They argue instead for letting definition emerge from practice, allowing submissions to represent contours of the field in Humanities Computing, other varieties of digital work, and initiatives and individuals not necessarily classified as "digital humanities." *DHQ* was conceived as an experimental model. Its innovative technical architecture afforded online, open-access publication under a Creative Commons license that allowed copying, distributing, and transmitting work for non-commercial purposes. Copyright remained with authors, enabling further publication or reuse. Giving all articles detailed XML encoding also facilitated marking genres, names, and citations, while other features fostered more nuanced searching, visualization tools, and other modes of exploration and tracking the evolving nature of the field. Moreover, the editors were looking forward to testing whether the nature of argument would change with the capacity for including interactive media, links to data sets, diagrams, and audiovisual materials.

Mindful of the multiple organizations serving related interests by 2007, the editors also hoped *DHQ* would become a meeting ground and space of mutual encounter. They hoped to bridge historic constituencies of Digital Humanities represented by the sponsoring Alliance of Digital Humanities Organizations (ADHO) and closely related domains that were emerging at that point. The journal's commitment to breadth has been borne out in the multidisciplinary scope of articles. Topics have spanned game studies and comic books, digital library resources, time-based digital media, digital editing, visual knowledge and graphics, sound, high-performance computing, copyright, endangered texts, and electronic literature, as well as teaching, learning, and curriculum and the reward system of tenure, promotion, and publication. Special clusters and numbers have also focused on project life cycles, data mining, classical studies, digital textual studies, the literary/studies, e-science for arts and humanities, theorizing connectivity, futures of digital studies, and oral histories of early Humanities Computing.

One year after the launch of *Digital Humanities Quarterly*, in May 2008, another benchmark of the field's evolution appeared when the National Endowment for the Humanities elevated a program-level initiative to a full-fledged Office of Digital Humanities (ODH). Brett Bobley, director of the office, addressed the question of definition in a presentation to the National Council on the Humanities:

Statement 3

We use "digital humanities" as an umbrella term for a number of different activities that surround technology and humanities scholarship. Under the digital humanities rubric, I would include topics like open access to materials, intellectual property rights, tool development, digital libraries, data mining, born-digital preservation, multimedia publication, visualization, GIS, digital reconstruction, study of the impact of technology on numerous fields, technology for teaching and learning, sustainability models, and many others.
—Brett Bobley, "Why the Digital Humanities?" Director, Office of Digital Humanities, National Endowment for the Humanities http://www.neh.gov/files/odh_why_the_digital_humanities.pdf

The mission of the ODH is to support innovative projects that use new technologies to advance the endowment's traditional goal of making cultural heritage materials accessible for research, teaching, and public programming. Elevation to a new office was widely considered a sign of maturity, signified as a "tipping" or "turning" point. In her report on DH for 2008, Lisa Spiro calls it a mark of credibility, and, in an article on

"The Rise of Digital NEH," Andy Guess remarks what began as a "grass-roots movement" was now anchored by funding agencies and a network of centers. The impact of technology on humanities, Bobley summed up, is characterized by four major game-changers:

(1) the changing relationship between a scholar and the materials studied;
(2) the introduction of technology-based tools and methodologies;
(3) the changing relationship among scholars, libraries, and publishers;
(4) the rise of collaborative, interdisciplinary work in the humanities.

The ODH expanded the endowment's support for digital work significantly. It provides funding for institutes on advanced topics and DH centers. Its Implementation Grants program supports a wide range of activities including the development of computationally based methods, techniques, or tools; completion and sustainability of existing resources often in alliance with libraries and archives; studies of philosophical or practical implications of emerging technologies in both disciplinary and interdisciplinary contexts; and digital modes of scholarly communication that facilitate peer review, collaboration, or dissemination scholarship. The ODH also partners with other funders, branches of government, organizations, and programs abroad. And, its Digital Humanities Start-Up Grants program supports smaller-scale prototyping and experimenting. Taking the April 2013 announcement of twenty-three new recipients of Start-Up Grants as a representative set of examples, projects span digital collections of visual, textual, and audio materials from early through modern periods, a mobile museum initiative, games development, and interests intersecting with fields of medieval studies, African American studies, and film studies. Older tools of computational linguistics are also being used in new contexts and novel ones developed for topic modeling, metadata visualization, open-source access, and preservation.

The Digging into Data Challenge, in particular, has accelerated boundary crossing between humanities and social sciences by providing funding for research using massive databases of materials, including digitized books and newspapers, music, transactional data such as web searches, sensor data, and cell-phone records. The "Big Data" initiative has also heightened the need for collaboration and inter-institutional cooperation in working with large data sets of complex topics over time, such as patterns of creativity, authorship, and culture. And, access to data on a large scale enhances prospects for interdisciplinary research and teaching by facilitating more comprehensive views. Describing the multidisciplinary scope of the project Civil War Washington, Kenneth Price lists history, literary studies, geography, urban studies, and computer-aided mapping. One of the reasons so little research had focused on the city during that period, Price speculates, was that the form of scholarship previously available could not represent adequately the complex interplay of literary, political, military, and social elements (293–94). Research on that scale, however, is expensive, rekindling debate about the relationship of humanities with commercial enterprises that set terms of access to and use of data. It has also stimulated a debate on marginalization of smaller projects in the force of "Big Humanities."

Taken together, statements 1–3 document significant developments in the institutionalization of new fields—a defining literature, a dedicated journal, and funding support. Statements 4 and 5 benchmark an added development, growing debate on definition of the field. Read comparatively, they reveal new positionings.

Statement 4:

Speculative computing arose from a productive tension with work in what has come to be known as digital humanities. That field, constituted by work at the intersection of traditional humanities and computation technology, uses digital tools to extend humanistic inquiry. Computational methods rooted in formal logic tend to be granted more authority in this dialogue than methods grounded in subjective judgment. But speculative computing inverts this power relation, stressing the need for humanities tools in digital environments.

—Johanna Drucker, *SpecLab: Digital Aesthetics and Projects in Speculative Computing* (Chicago: U of Chicago P, 2009), xi

Drucker distinguishes "digital humanities," characterized by a philosophy of Mathesis, from "speculative computing," characterized by a philosophy of Aesthesis. Her distinction is based on experiences during the 1990s and early 2000s at the Institute for Advanced Technology in the Humanities, in projects that became the core of the Speculative Computing Laboratory (SpecLab). By privileging principles of objectivity, formal logic, and instrumental applications in Mathesis, Drucker's formulation of "digital humanities" prioritizes the cultural authority of technical rationality manifested in quantitative method, automated processing, classification, a mechanistic view of analysis, and a dichotomy of subject and object. By privileging subjectivity, aesthetics, interpretation, and emergent phenomena, "speculative computing" prioritizes questions of textuality, rhetorical properties of graphicality in design, visual modes of knowing, and epistemological and ideological critique of how we represent knowledge. Mechanistic claims of truth, purity, and validity are further challenged by a probablitistic view of knowledge and heteroglossic processes, informed by theories of constructivism and post-structuralism, cognitive science, and the fields of culture/media/and visual studies (Drucker, *Spec Lab*, xi–xvi, 5, 19, 22–30; see also Drucker and Nowviskie).

Drucker's distinction elevates the aesthetics of computational work at the boundary of humanistic interpretation and computer science. In a comparable move, Burdick et al. bring a humanities conception of design—defined by information design, graphics, typography, formal and rhetorical patterning—to the center of the field framed by traditional humanities concerns—defined by subjectivity, ambiguity, contingency, and observer-dependent variables in knowledge production (vii, 92). Like Drucker, they also reconceptualize design from a linear and predictive process to generativity in an iterative and recursive process. Design, Drucker adds, becomes a "form of mediation," not just transmission and delivery of facts. Information visualization, she notes elsewhere, becomes genuinely humanistic, incorporating critical thought and the rhetorical force of the visual ("Humanistic Theory," 86). Not everyone, however, equates "digital humanities" narrowly with Mathesis. Drucker's positioning of speculative computing as the "other" to DH, Katherine Hayles responded, opens up the field. Yet, her stark contrast flattens its diversity. Many would also argue they are doing speculative computing (*How We Think*, 26). Moreover, Drucker bypasses the boundary work of Statement 5.

Statement 5 emanates from a group affiliated with UCLA's Digital Humanities and Media Studies program. The group focused directly on the task of definition in a Mellon-funded seminar in 2008–2009 at UCLA, a *Digital Humanities Manifesto 2.0*, and a March 2009 White Paper by Todd Presner and Chris Johanson on "The Promise of Digital Humanities."

Statement 5

Digital Humanities is not a unified field but **an array of convergent practices** that explore a universe in which: a) print is no longer the exclusive or the normative medium in which knowledge is produced and/ or disseminated; instead, print finds itself absorbed into new, multimedia configurations; and b) digital tools, techniques, and media have altered the production and dissemination of knowledge in the arts, human and social sciences.

—Jeffrey Schnapp and Todd Presner, "Digital Humanities Manifesto 2.0," http://www.humanitiesblast.com/manifesto/Manifesto_V2.pdf

The periodization of the *Manifesto* and the White Paper parallels Davidson's distinction between Humanities 1.0 and 2.0. A first wave of Digital Humanities in the late 1990s and early 2000s emphasized large-scale digitization projects and technological infrastructure. It replicated the world that print had codified over five centuries and was quantitative in nature, characterized by mobilizing search and retrieval powers of databases, automating corpus linguistics, and stacking HyperCards into critical arrays. In contrast, the second wave has been qualitative, interpretive, experiential, emotive, and generative in nature. It moved beyond the primacy of text to practices and qualities that can inhere in any medium, including time-based art forms such as film, music, and animation; visual traditions such as graphics and design; spatial practices such as architecture and geography; and curatorial practices associated with museums and galleries. The agenda of the field also expanded to include the cultural and social impact of new technologies and born-digital materials such as electronic literature and web-based artifacts. DH became an umbrella term for a multidisciplinary array of practices that extend beyond traditional humanities departments to include architecture, geography, information studies, film and media studies, anthropology, and other social sciences.

Interdisciplinary is a keyword in the second wave, along with *collaborative, socially engaged, global,* and *open access.* Their combination is not a simple sum of the parts. *Manifesto 2.0* invokes a "digital revolution," and the White Paper calls the effect of new media and digital technologies "profoundly transformative." The authors reject the premise of a unified field in favor of an interplay of tensions and frictions. Schnapp and Presner do not suggest that Digital Humanities replaces or rejects traditional humanities.

It is not a new general culture akin to Renaissance humanism either, or a new universal literacy. They see it as a natural outgrowth and expansion in an "emerging transdisciplinary domain" inclusive of both earlier Humanities Computing and new problems, genres, concepts, and capabilities. The vision of a transdisciplinary domain parallels trans-sector *Transdisciplinarity*. The *Manifesto* pushes into public spheres of the Web, blogosphere, social networking, and the private sector of game design. At the same time, it parallels the imperative of *Critical Interdisciplinarity*. If new technologies are dominated and controlled by corporate and entertainment interests, the authors ask, how will our cultural legacy be rendered in new media formats? By whom and for what? Elsewhere, Presner reported being told his HyperCities project using Google Maps and Google Earth puts him "in bed with the devil" (qtd. in Hayles, *How We Think*, 41).

The transdisciplinary momentum of statement 5 is further apparent in comparable declarations, notable among them the *Affiche du Manifeste des Digital Humanities*. Circulated at a THATCamp in Paris in May 2010, the French manifesto embraces the totality of social sciences and humanities. It acknowledges reliance on the disciplines but deems Digital Humanities a "transdiscipline" that embodies all methods, systems, and heuristic perspectives linked to the digital within those fields and communities with interdisciplinary goals. Like its U.S. counterpart, the *Manifeste* covers a wide scope of practices: including encoding textual sources, lexicometry, geographic information systems and web cartography, data-mining, 3-D representation, oral archives, digital arts and hypermedia literatures, as well as digitization of cultural, scientific, and technical heritage. The *Affiche* also calls for integrating digital culture into the definition of general culture in the 21st century.

Statement 6 sketches the broadest picture of the field in Svensson's typology of five paradigmatic modes of engagement between humanities and information technology or "the digital."

Engaging

Svensson's typology builds on Matthew Ratto's conception of "epistemic commitments." Differing commitments influence the identification of study objects, methodological procedures, representative practices, and interpretative frameworks.

Statement 6

Below, I will examine five major modes of engagement in some more detail: information technology as a tool, as a study object, as an expressive medium, as an experimental laboratory and as an activist venue. The first three modes will receive the most attention. Importantly, these should not be seen as mutually exclusive or overly distinct but rather as co-existing and co-dependent layers, and indeed, the boundaries in-between increasingly seem blurry. This does not mean, however, that it may not fruitful to analyze and discuss them individually as part of charting the digital humanities.
— Patrik Svensson, "The Landscape of Digital Humanities," *Digital Humanities Quarterly* 4, no. 1 (2010): ¶102 http://digitalhumanities.org/dhq/vol/4/1/000080/000080.html

In Svensson's first mode of engagement—as a tool—the field exhibits a strong epistemic investment in tools, methodology, and processes ranging from metadata schemes to project management. There is also a strong focus on text analysis, exemplified by use of text encoding and markup systems in corpus stylistics, digitization, preservation, and curation. This first mode aligns DH with the concept of Methodological Interdisciplinarity. In his book *Humanities Computing* McCarty identifies method, not subject, as the defining scholarly platform of the field (5–6). The *Wikipedia* entry on Digital Humanities retains a strong methodological orientation. Tom Scheinfeld argues that scholarship at this moment is more about methods than theory (125). And, posters to the "Day of Digital Humanities" online forum on the question "How do you define Humanities Computing/Digital Humanities?" associate the field strongly with "tools" and "application" of technology. McCarty and Harold Short have mapped relations in the "methodological commons" (see fig. 1).

The octagons above the commons in figure 1, McCarty explains in his book, demarcate disciplinary groups of application. The indefinite cloudy shapes below the commons suggest "permeable bodies of knowledge" that are constituted socially, even though lacking departmental or professional aspects. All disciplines, however, do not have the same kind of relation-

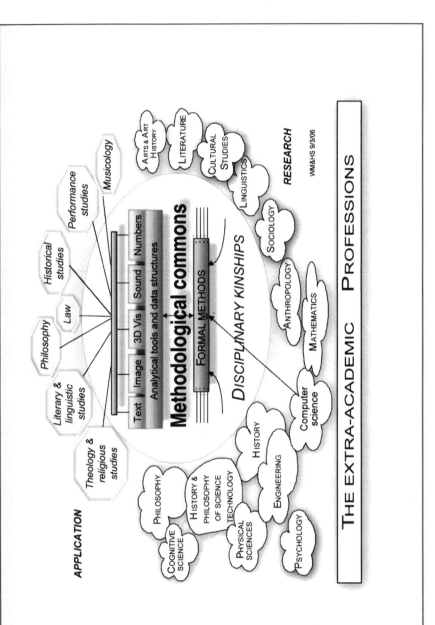

Fig. 1. An intellectual and disciplinary map of Humanities Computing. (From Willard McCarty, *Humanities Computing* [London and New York: Palgrave Macmillan, 2005].)

ship to the field. McCarty designates history as the primary discipline (especially history of science and technology), along with philosophy and sociology. All the rest are secondary (*Humanities Computing*, 4, 33, 119, 129). In a speech in March 2013, Raymond Siemens compared versions of the figure. The first version, he recalled, focused on content oriented toward digital modeling (emphasizing digitization). The second version, above, is more inclusive of media types and extra-academic partners while acknowledging process modeling (emphasizing analysis). Looking toward the future, Siemens proposed it is time to focus on problem-based modeling that moves past the rhetoric of revolution to a sustainable action-oriented agenda.

All of the shapes in figure 1, it should be said, are not strictly "disciplines," underscoring the need for the fourth major term in the baseline vocabulary for understanding interdisciplinarity—*interprofessionalism*. The figure also has a mix of traditional disciplines and interdisciplinary areas, in the latter case including cognitive science, performance studies, cultural studies, and the history and philosophy of science and technology. In addition, the profession of engineering appears. The commons in the middle of the figure is a hub for transcending the limits of specialized domains. In a separate though complementary reflection on the relationship of interdisciplinarity and *transdisciplinarity* in Digital Humanities, Yu-wei Lin calls models and tools for modeling "carriers of interdisciplinarity." Their carrying capacity fosters projects that may lead to more radical "transdisciplinary" movement beyond parent disciplines through a shared conceptual framework that integrates concepts, theories, and approaches from different areas of expertise in the creation of something new (296–97).

In Svensson's second mode of engagement—as a study object—the digital is an object of analysis with a strong focus on digital culture and transformative effects of new technologies of communication. Cyberculture studies and critical digital studies, for example, accentuate critical approaches to new media and their contexts. The scope of forms is wide: encompassing networked innovations such as blogging, podcasting, flashmobs, mashups, and RSS feeds as well as video-sharing websites such as MySpace and YouTube, *Wikipedia*, and massively multiplayer online role-playing games (MMORPGs). Creating and developing tools, Svensson adds, are not prominent activities in this mode, and use of information technology does not extend typically beyond standard tools and accessible data in online environments. The difference in the first two modes illustrates how definition varies depending on where the weight of priority falls: the algorithm or critical theory. Even the most fundamental terms, such as *access*, are used differently. From a technical standpoint, access connotes availability, speed, and ease of use. From the standpoint of cultural analysis, it connotes sharing materials and reinvigorating the notion of "public humanities" on digital ground.

In the third mode of engagement—as experimental laboratory—DH centers and laboratories are sites for exploring ideas, testing tools, and modifying data sets and complex objects. This kind of environment is familiar in science and technology but is relatively new to humanities. Svensson cites the Stanford Humanities Laboratory (SHL) and his own HUMlab at Umeå University. Digital platforms such as Second Life, he adds, may function as virtual spaces for experiments that are difficult to mount in physical spaces. Svensson likens such structures to Adam Turner's notion of "paradisciplinary" work born of exchanging ideas, sharing knowledge, and pooling resources. Turner compares modes of interaction and creativity in these spaces to the community collaboration at the heart of "hacker/ maker culture." Whether the site is a shed or a garage, "the space breathes life into the community" (qtd. in Svensson, "Landscape"). In their model of a new Artereality, Schnapp and Michael Shanks call the SHL both "a multimodal and fluid network" and "a diverse ecology of activity and interest." Established in 2001, the Stanford Lab was modeled on the platform of "Big Science." Activities within this collaborative environment comprise a form of "craftwork" where participants learn by making.

Comparably, Saklofske, Clements, and Cunningham liken the space of humanities labs to "experimental sandboxes" (325), and Ben Vershbow calls the New York Public Library Lab a kind of "in-house technology startup." The lab is occupied by "an unlikely crew of artists, hackers and liberal arts refugees" who focus on the library's public mission and collections. Envisioned as "inherently inter-disciplinary," their work has empowered curators "to think more like technologists and interaction designers, and vice versa." Vershbow credits their success to being able "to work agilely and outside the confines of usual institutional structures" (80). Bethany Nowviskie further likens such spaces to *skunkworks*, a term adopted by small teams of research and development engineers at the Lockheed Martin aeronautics corporation in the 1940s. Library-based DH skunkworks function as semi-independent "prototyping and makerspace labs" where librarians take on new roles as "scholar-practitioners." In the Scholars' Lab at the University of Virginia Library, collaborative research and development has led not only to works of innovative digital scholarship but also to technical and social frameworks needed for support and sustainability. The lab was a merger of three existing centers. It opened in 2006 in a renovated area of the humanities and social sciences research library that was conducive to open communication and flexible use of space (53, 56, 61).

In the fourth mode of engagement—as expressive medium—increased digitalization has afforded unparalleled access to heterogeneous types of content and media. Much of this content is born digital in multimodal forms that can be manipulated within a single environment, including moving images, text, music, 3-D designs, databases, graphical details, and virtual walk-throughs. Some areas—such as visual, media and digital studies—have been affected significantly and, Svensson found, work tends to focus on studying objects rather than producing them. Nevertheless, both the third and fourth modes heighten creativity. For builders of tools, Thomas Crombez posted to the 2010 "Day of Digital Humanities," DH is a "playground for experimentation." Innovation has led to technological advancements in the form of new software and more powerful platforms for digital archives. It has also fostered new digital-born objects and aesthetic forms of art and literature. Posting to the 2009 forum, Jolanda-Pieta van Arnhem called DH "about discovery and sharing as much as it is about archival and data visualization." It advances open communication, collaboration, and expression. At the same time it mirrors her own artistic process by incorporating art, research, and technology.

In Svensson's fifth mode of engagement—as activist venue—digital technology is mobilized in calls for change. He highlights several examples. *Public Secrets*, Sharon Daniel's work on women in prison and the prison system, is a hybrid form of scholarship that is simultaneously artistic installation, cultural critique, and activist intervention. Daniel moves from representation to participation, generating context in a database structure that allows self-representation. She describes her companion piece, *Blood Sugar*, as "transdisciplinary" in its movement beyond new ways of thinking about traditional rubrics to contesting those rubrics in open forms (cited in Balsamo, 87–88). Kimberly Christen's *Mukurtu: Wampurrarni-kari* website on aboriginal artifacts, histories, and images provides aboriginal users with an interface that offers more extensive access than the general public. And, another form of activist engagement occurs in conversations about *making* as a form of thinking about design and use. Preemptive Media is a space for discussing emerging policies and technologies through beta tests, trial runs, and impact assessments. Elizabeth Losh also cites the Electronic Disturbance Theater that adapted principles of the Critical Art Ensemble in virtual sit-ins, the b.a.n.g. lab at the California Institute for Telecommunications and Information Technology, the "Electronic Democracy" network's research on online practices of political participation, and acts of "political coding" and "performative hacking" by new-media dissidents (168–69, 171).

Svensson does not include *Critical Interdisciplinarity* and the "transgressive" and "trans-sector" connotations of *Transdisciplinarity* in the fifth mode. Yet, they can be viewed as activist modes of scholarship. Questions of social justice and democracy are prominent in cultural studies of digital technologies and new media. And, older topics of subjectivity, identity, community, and representation are being reinvigorated. Digital technologies are also sources of empowerment. Indigenous communities, for example, have used geospatial technologies to protect tribal resources, document sovereignty, manage natural resources, create databases, and build networking forums, and guidebooks. Yet, the same technologies are sources of surveillance, stereotyping, and subjugation. Amy Earhart has also interrogated the exclusion of non-canonical texts by women, people of color, and the GLBTQ community. Scrutinizing data from NEH Digital Humanities Start-Up Grants between 2007 and 2010, Earhart found that only 29 of the 141 awards focused on diverse communities and only 16 on preservation or recovery of the texts of diverse communities (314).

Distinct as they are, modes of engagement are not airtight categories. They may overlap, and even in the same mode differences arise. In an interview with Svensson, Charles Ess cites tension at a conference of the Association of Internet Researchers (AoIR) between German and philosophical senses of critical theory and radical critiques from the standpoint of race, gender, and sexuality in the Anglophone tradition. Moreover, although most researchers study the Internet as an artifact rather than engaging in experimentation, in Scandinavia there is a strong tradition of design. Internet research, Ess adds, could also be considered a subset of telecom research, digital studies, or other areas when it takes on their identities. Moreover, growing interest in research and instruction in multimedia art, design, and culture has aligned Humanities Computing with visual and performing arts. Svensson's statistical tracking of the twenty to fifty most frequent words in programs of AoIR conferences from 1999 to 2008 also revealed the focus in another example of the second mode—Internet studies—was on space, divide, culture, self, politics and privacy phenomena, cultural artifacts and processes. An activist orientation appeared that is rare in the older discourse of Humanities Computing, where the predominant focus is databases, models, resources, systems, and editions.

That said, DH organizations are opening up to new topics. The annual meeting of the flagship Alliance of Digital Humanities Organizations (ADHO) still emphasizes Humanities Computing over new media and cultural interests that find more space in groups such as HASTAC. Yet, a new "Global Outlook" (GO::DH) special interest group has formed to address barriers that hinder communication and collaboration across arts, humanities, and the cultural heritage sector as well as income levels. Scott Weingart's analysis of acceptances to the 2013 ADHO conference reveals that literary studies and data/text mining submissions outnumbered historical studies. Archive work and visualizations also appeared more often than multimedia. That said, despite being small, multimedia beyond text was not an insignificant subgroup. Gender studies also had a high acceptance rate of 85 percent, and the program included a panel on the future of undergraduate Digital Humanities. Traditional topics of text editing, digitization, computational stylistics, and curation are still invited for the Australasian Association's hosting of the 2015 conference, but so are arts and performance, new media and Internet studies, code studies, gaming, curriculum and pedagogy, and critical perspectives.

Locating

The history of Digital Humanities is painted both in broad strokes, revealing shared needs and interests, and in thin strokes, revealing distinct sub-histories. Like linguists, classicists have invested in making digital lexica and encyclopedias, and they have benefited from advances in graphic capacity and language technologies that facilitate machine translation, cross-lingual information retrieval, and syntactic databases. Like literary scholars, linguists have also created electronic text editions enhanced by the ability to annotate interpretations and hyperlink resources. And, involved as they are in data-intensive work, classicists, archaeologists, and historians have all gained from increased capacity for record keeping and statistical processing. The introduction of Digital Humanities interests often generates a claim of interdisciplinary identity in a discipline. Yet, identities differ. If there is a tight relationship between a discipline and a digitally inflected study object, Patrik Svensson found in mapping modes of engagement, the work may lack strong identity as "digital humanities." A media studies scholar interested in news narratives in online media, for example, may consider this work to be anchored within media studies rather than a separate field. In contrast, if digitally mediated language or communicative patterns in Second Life are incorporated as objects of study, a discipline may change to include digital objects and develop intersections with other disciplines and fields. The changing nature of work practices and perceptions of the role of the digital are evident in the examples of English, history, and archaeology.

Digital Humanities and English have a long-standing relationship which Pressman and Swanstrom attribute to the fact that many groundbreaking projects centered on literary subjects. In an oft-cited essay, Matthew Kirschenbaum identifies six reasons why English departments have been favorable homes ("What is Digital Humanities," 8–9). The beginning reason is not surprising: "First, after numeric input, text has been by far the most tractable data type for computers to manipulate." In contrast, images present more complex challenges of representation. The second reason marks the multidisciplinary scope of English. Subfields of literary and cultural studies, rhetoric and composition, and linguistics have attained separate disciplinary status, but they are still typically housed within the same department. Over time, Pressman and Swanstrom add, conception of the "literary" has expanded beyond traditional texts. In welcoming readers to an online "disanthology" of articles on literary studies in the digital age, the editors called literary studies a "confluence of fields and subfields, tools and techniques." Given that computational approaches come from varied sources, a growing array of methodologies are engaged and practices and methodologies of digital scholarship lead into other fields in humanities as well as computer science and library and information science.

In defining the second reason Kirschenbaum highlights, in particular, the long-standing relationship of computers and composition. Teachers of writing and rhetoric, Jay David Bolter recalls, were among the earliest to welcome new technologies into the classroom, initially word processors and then chat rooms, MOOs, wikis, and blogs. They constituted new spaces for pedagogy, and research on computers and composition expanded eventually from text-based literacy and writing to include new digital media, video games, and social networking ("Critical Theory"). By 2011, the relationship to Digital Humanities was the focus of a featured panel at the annual Computers and Writing conference. Panelist Douglas Eyman called himself a "self-confessed digital humanist," but admitted he is still puzzling over the question of fit for himself and the field of digital rhetoric. On the TechRhet Digest listserv that prompted the session, Dean Rehberger cautioned against equating DH with one area such as composition and writing, or one area subsuming the other. "The trick," he advised, "will be to untangle the points of intersection and interaction."

Throughout its history, composition studies has intersected with multiple disciplines and fields, including literary studies and rhetoric, literacy studies, technology studies, and new media studies. One of those intersections, with rhetoric, is also linked with the field of communication studies. Computer-mediated communication was an early site of studies of behavior in online communities, work that continues in both communications and English departments. In a report on the emergence of "digital rhetoric," Laura Gurak and Smiljana Antonijevic call for a new "interdisciplinary rhetoric" capable of understanding the persuasive functions of digital communications that encompass text, sound, visual, nonverbal cues, material, and virtual spaces. Digital rhetoric, they argue, must assert a new canon that draws on prior constructs while recognizing changes in the 2,000-year-old tradition that constitutes the field of Western rhetoric. "Screen rhetorics," Gurak and Antonijevic add, are not a sidebar to studies of public discourse and public address. They are at the center of what theorists and critics should be studying, and of interest to linguists, psychologists, and others exploring human communication.

The third reason recognizes the link between English departments and converging conversations around editorial theory and method in the 1980s, amplified by subsequent advances in implementing electronic archives and editions. These discussions cannot be fully understood, Kirchsenbaum notes, without considering parallel conversations about the fourth reason—hypertext and other forms of electronic literature. By the 1990s, Bolter recalls, some critics were positioning digital media as an electronic realization of poststructuralist theory. George Landow argued that hypertext had a lot in common with contemporary literary and semiological theories, although it was aligned initially with formalist theory and print continued to dominate ("Theory and Practice," 19–20, 26). The "revolution" envisioned by early theorists of hypertext and electronic modes of authorship beckoned radical restructuring of textuality, authorship, and readership while fostering analysis of digital material culture. It took time, though, for more transformative practices of hypermediation and multimodal remixing to become the object of study.

The fifth reason stems from openness to cultural studies. English departments were early homes for related interests, fostering interactions with other interdisciplinary fields such as popular culture studies, identity fields, and postcolonial studies. The scope of study also expanded with new objects. Once confined to print, the underlying notion of a "text" expanded to include verbal, visual, oral, and other forms of expression. Indicative of this trend, the Texas Institute for Literary and Textual Studies (TILTS), affiliated with the University of Texas English Department, focused on a broadening conception of the "literary" and the "textual." The TILTS 2011 series on "The Digital and the Human(ities)" encompassed traditional works, non-textual forms, and popular genres. Symposium 1—Access, Authority, and Identity—considered older topics of scholarly editing plus social networking, corporatization and Google, and the fracturing of knowledge and undermining of traditional canons. Symposium 2—Digital Humanities, Teaching and Learning—looked at pedagogical innovations and digital mediated learning, new subjects of games and code, student subjectivities, born-digital materials, and multi-media composition. Symposium 3—The Digital and the Human(ities)—included automation, digital vernacular, the changing nature of argument, justice, and rights of students and of citizens. Kirschenbaum's sixth and final reason also recognizes the rise of e-reading and e-book devices, as well as large-scale text digitization projects such as Google Books, data mining, and visualization in distant readings.

The discipline of history also has a long-standing involvement with Digital Humanities. In his report in the Blackwell *Companion*, William G. Thomas identified three phases in historians' use of computing technologies. During the first phase in the 1940s, some historians used mathematical techniques and built large data sets. During the second phase beginning in the early 1960s, the emerging field of social science history opened up new social, economic, and political histories that drew on massive amounts of data, enabling historians to tell the story "from the bottom up" rather than elite perspectives that dominated traditional accounts. The third and current phase is marked by greater capacity for communication via the Internet, in a network of systems and data combined with advances in the personal computer and software. Historical geographical information systems (GIS) also holds promise for enhancing computer-aided spatial analysis in not only history and demography but archaeology, geography, law, and environmental science as well. The number and size of born-digital data collections has increased as well, along with tools that enable independent exploration and interpretive association.

Change, however, stirred debate. During the second phase, cliometrics was a flashpoint, with particular criticism aimed at Robert Fogel and Stanley Engerman's 1974 book *Time on the Cross: The Economics of American Negro Slavery*. Critics questioned lack of attention to traditional methods, including narrative, textual, and qualitative analysis as well as interdisciplinary study of social and political forces. Another initiative launched in the 1970s, the Philadelphia Social History Project, assembled a multidisciplinary array of data while aiming to create guidelines for large-scale relational databases. It was criticized, though, for falling short of a larger synthesis for urban history. Other projects aggregated multidisciplinary materials. *Who Built America?*, for example, compiled film, text, audio, images, and maps in social history. Yet, early products were limited to self-contained CD-ROM, VHS-DVD, and print technology lacking Internet connectivity. As new technology became available, the idea of "hypertext history" arose in projects such as The Valley of the Shadow, which brought together Civil War letters, records, and other materials. Thomas speculates the term *digital history* originated at the Virginia Center for Digital History. In the 1997–98 academic year, he directed the center. He and William Ayers used the term to describe the project. In 1997 they taught "Digital History of the Civil War" and began calling such courses "digital history seminars." Subsequently, Steven Mintz started a digital textbook site named Digital History (Thomas, 57–58, 61–63).

Advances heralded new ways of studying and writing history. However, they also raise new questions about the nature of interpretation. In a 2008 online forum on "The Promise of Digital History," William Thomas cautions that the fluidity or impermanence of the digital medium means scholars may never stop editing, changing, and refining as new evidence and technologies arise. Where, then, do interpretation and salience go in online projects that are continually in motion? And, what impact do technologies have on understanding history as a mode of investigation, meaning and content, and creating knowledge? Douglas Seefeldt joined Thomas in cautioning that expanded access does not answer the question of what history looks like in a digital medium. Production, access, and communication are valuable. Yet, on another level Digital History is a methodological approach framed by the hypertextual power of technologies to make, define, query, and annotate associations in the record of the past and to gain leverage on a problem. The scale and complexity of born-digital sources require more interdisciplinary collaboration and cooperative initiatives, as well as tailored digital resources and exposure for graduate students. Well-defined exemplars, guidelines for best practices, and standards of peer review are also needed. And, the focus must shift from solely product-oriented exhibits or websites toward the process-oriented work of employing new media tools in research and analysis.

Parallel advances are also evident in the third discipline. In his report on "Computing for Archaeologists" in the Blackwell *Companion*, Harrison Eiteljorg II traces the history of computing and archaeology to record keeping and statistical processing in the late 1950s. Early limits of cost and access, however, impeded progress. Punch cards and tape were the only means of entering data, and results were only available on paper. Archaeologists also had to learn computer languages. By the mid-1970s, database software was making record keeping more efficient, expanding the amount of material collected and ease of retrieving information without needing to learn programming languages. By the 1980s, microcomputers and new easy-to-use software were available, and geographical information systems (GIS) and computer-aided design (CAD) programs were enhancing map-making and capturing the three-dimensionality of archaeological sites and structures. Virtual reality systems based on CAD models also promised greater realism, but accurate representations were still limited by inadequate data. Like other disciplines, archaeology also needed more discipline-specific software and standards for use. Furthermore, the increasing abundance of information and preservation of data collections require careful management, doubts about the acceptability of digital scholarship persist, and not enough scholars are trained in using computers for archaeological purposes. Even with notable advances, Eiteljorg concludes, the transformation from paper-based to digital recording remains incomplete.

In a blog posting on "Defining Digital Archaeology," Katy Meyers situates "digital archaeology" historically within the recent rise of "Digital Disciplines." Yet, she reports, archaeologists have not engaged with the most active of them—the interdisciplinary group of Digital Humanities—or the ways technology is changing their work. Digital technologies are widely used and integrated into the discipline to the point that GIS, statistical programs, databases, and CAD are now considered part of the archaeologist's toolkit. Yet, there is no disciplinary equivalent to "digital humanities" that accounts comprehensively for an archaeology of digital materials, including excavation of code, analysis of early informatics, and interpretation of early web-based materials. Or, digital archaeology conceived as an approach to studying past human societies through their material remains, rather than a support tool or method. Meyers also echoes long-standing concerns about the gap between generic approaches and discipline-specific needs, in this case the limits of the Dublin Core standard for metadata. Rather than a separate discipline and approach, the digital may constitute a different specialization such as a focus on ceramics, lithic analysis, or systems theory.

A recently published open-access book, *Archaeology 2.0*, provides an overview of new approaches taking hold in the discipline. It does not explore digital initiatives outside of North America and the United Kingdom, but it does cover a broad range of topics that cut across disciplinary and geographic boundaries. Archaeology, Eric C. Kansa notes in the introduction, has long been considered "an inherently multidisciplinary enterprise, with one foot in the humanities and interpretive social sciences and another in the natural sciences." Technological capacity has increased because of more powerful tools for data management, platforms for making cultural artifacts more accessible, and interfaces for making communication more open and collaboration feasible. Yet, these advances have compounded the challenges of archiving, preserving, and sustaining data, while creating information overload. Even with increased use of themed research blogs and field-based communication devices, the peer-reviewed scholarly journal also remains dominant. And, archeology faces unique challenges in designing computational infrastructure. It deals in longer horizons of "deep time" and complex multidisciplinary projects with data sets for describing complex contextual relations that are generated by different specialists. In addition, it has links to tourism and the marketing of cultural heritage involving commercially controlled mechanisms of communication and information sharing in both professional and public spheres.

Looking back on the trajectory of change in these disciplines, three trend lines stand out: visualization, spatialization, and a computational turn in scholarship. Visualization is not new. Conversations about visuality occur across disciplines and fields. The label *visual culture*, Nicholas Mirzoeff recounts, gained currency because the contemporary era is saturated with images, from art and multimodal genres to computer-aided design and magnetic resonance imaging (1–3). The most striking development for Digital Humanities has been enhanced capacity to visualize information, fostering a "spatial" and "geographical" turn in the field facilitated by technologies of Google Earth, MapQuest, the Global Positioning System (GPS), and three-dimensional modeling. Patricia Cohen, who covers "Humanities 2.0" for the *New York Times*, calls this development the foundation of a new field of Spatial Humanities. Advanced mapping tools, she recalls, were first used in the 1960s, primarily for environmental analysis and urban planning. During the late 1980s and 1990s, geographical historical information systems made it possible to plot changes in a location over time using census information and other quantifiable data. By the mid-2000s, technological advances were making it possible to move beyond restricted map formats and to add photos and texts.

The interdisciplinary character of the spatial turn is evident in three other ways. Visualization in humanities, Burdick et al. report, is based in large part on techniques borrowed from social sciences, business applications, and natural sciences (42). The multidisciplinary scope of materials also renders patterns more visible. A project to create a digital atlas of religion in North America, for example, revealed complex changing patterns of political preference, religious affiliation, migration, and cultural influence by linking them geographically. David Bodenhamer, of the Polis Center, calls the results of capturing multiple perspectives "deep maps" (qtd. in Patricia Cohen). Another project, the Mapping Texts partnership of Stanford and the University of North Texas, allows users to map and analyze language patterns embedded in 230,000 pages of digitized historical Texas newspapers spanning the late 1820s through early 2000s. With one of two interactive visualizations, for any period, geography, or newspaper title users can explore the most common words, named entities such as people and places, and correlated words that produce topic models.

Yet, Drucker admonishes, traditional humanistic skills of cultural and historical interpretation are still needed. Mapping the Republic of Letters is a Stanford-based project that plotted geographic data for senders and receivers of correspondence, making it possible to see patterns of intellectual exchange in the early-modern world. Lines of light expose connections between points of origin and delivery in the 18th century. Drucker cautions that discrepancies of time and flow are disguised by the appearance of a "smooth, seamless, and unitary motion" ("Humanistic Theory," 91). Nonetheless, the project renders networks visible for interpretation. Another Stanford-based initiative, the Spatial History Project, provides a community for creative visual analysis in the organizational culture of a lab environment and a wide network of partnerships and collaborations. Geospatial databases facilitate integration of spatial and nonspatial data, then visual analysis renders patterns and anomalies. These examples underscore the blurred boundaries of data and argument. In the HASTAC Scholars online forum on Visualization Across Disciplines, Dana Solomon calls the practice of information visualization a form of textual analysis with the potential for historicizing and theorizing a technical process. It can also be located within a broader constellation of aesthetic practice and visual representation; in the traditions of statistics, computer science, and graphic design; and in the cultural heritage industry through use of virtual reality and augmented reality in restoration of sites.

The third trend line is signified by the label *computational turn*. David Berry calls it a third wave, extending beyond Schnapp and Presner's first and second waves. The computational turn moves from older notions of information literacy and digital literacy to the literature of the digital and the shared digital culture facilitated by code and software. This development is evident in real-time streams of data, geolocation, real-time databases, Twitter, social media, cell-phone novels, and other processual and rapidly changing digital forms such as the Internet itself. Focusing on the digital component of DH, Berry adds, accentuates not only medium specificity but also the ways that medial changes produce epistemic ones. At the same time, it problematizes underlying premises of "normal" print-based research while refiguring the field as "computational humanities" (4, 15). The translation of all media today into numerical data, Lev Manovich also emphasizes, means that not only texts, graphics, and moving images have become computable but also sounds, shapes, and spaces (5–6).

The names *culturnomics* and *cultural analytics* accentuate the algorithm-driven analysis of massive amounts of cultural data occurring in the computational turn. In the process, Burdick et al. also note, the canon of objects and cultural material broadens and new models of knowledge beyond print emerge (41, 125). The capacity to analyze "Big Data" makes it possible to construct a picture of voices and works hitherto silent or glimpsed only at a microscale and in isolated segments. The project People of the Founding Era, for instance, provides biographical information about leaders along with facts about lesser-known people, making it possible to know how they changed over time and eventually to visualize social networks of personal and institutional relationships. It combines a biographical glossary with group study of nearly 60,000 native-born and naturalized Americans born between 1713 and 1815, their children, and grandchildren.

Like the visual and spatial turns in scholarship, the computational turn in Digital Humanities is indicative of a larger cultural shift. In defining "Digital Humanities 2.0," Todd Presner treats computer code as an index of culture more generally, and the medial changes it affords foster a hermeneutics of code and critical approaches to software ("Hypercities"). At the same time, the computational turn has generated new overlapping subfields of code studies, software studies, and platform studies. At the Swansea University workshop on the computational turn, Manovich dated the beginning of the movement to 2008. The use of quantitative analysis and interactive visualization to identify patterns in large cultural data sets enables researchers to grapple with the complexity of cultural processes and artifacts. New techniques, though, must be developed to describe dimensions of artifacts and processes that received scant attention in the past, such as gradual historical changes over long periods. Visualization techniques and interfaces, Manovich added, are also needed for exploring cultural data across multiple scales, ranging from details of a single artifact or processes, such as one shot in a film, to massive cultural data sets/ flows, such as films made in the 20th century.

Heightened attention to the operations of code and software has also fostered *Critical Interdisciplinarity* in overlapping fields of race and gender studies. Amy Earhart has questioned the ways technological standards such as the Text Encoding Initiative's tag selection construct race in textual materials ("Can Information," 314, 316). Jacqueline Wernimont critiqued the politics of tools and coding practices from a feminist perspective, and Tara McPherson examined the ways early design systems such as the UNIX operating system prioritized modularity and isolated enclaves over intersections, context, relation, and networks. Responding in her blog to the charge of not being inclusive, Melissa Terras addressed the way guidelines in the Text Encoding Initiative assigned sexuality in a document by encoding 1 for male and a secondary 2 for female. As program chair for a Digital Humanities conference, Terras also aimed to widen protocols beyond consideration of disciplines, interests, and geography to include gender equality as well as economic, ethnic, cultural, and linguistic diversity.

The differing modes of engagement and practices reviewed in this chapter affirm Svensson's conclusion: "The territory of the digital humanities is currently under negotiation." It has evolved historically as the body of content expanded, new claims arose, and alternative constructions were asserted. And, as we're about to see, constructions of the field also took root in differing institutional cultures.

Clustered Links for Chapter 2 in Order of Appearance

Julia Flanders, Wendell Piez, and Melissa Terras. "Welcome to *Digital Humanities Quarterly.*" *Digital Humanities Quarterly* 1, no. 1 (2007): ¶3. For overview: ohttp://digitalhumanities.org/dhq/vol/1/1/000007/000007.html http://digital humanities.org/dhq/about/about.html

Lisa Spiro's blog entry on opening of the NEH Office of Digital Humanities: http://digitalscholarship.wordpress.com/2009/02/07/digital-humanities-in-2008-part-i/

Andy Guess's report on opening of the NEH Office of DH: http://www.insidehigh ered.com/news/2008/04/03/digital

Brett Bobley. "Why the Digital Humanities?" Director, Office of Digital Humanities, National Endowment for the Humanities http://www.neh.gov/files/odh_why_the_digital_humanities.pdf. For overview of NEH-ODH: http://www.neh.gov/divisions/odh

Todd Presner and Chris Johanson's March 2009 White Paper on "The Promise of Digital Humanities," http://www.itpb.ucla.edu/documents/2009/Promiseof DigitalHumanities.pdf.

Jeffrey Schnapp and Todd Presner's "Digital Humanities Manifesto 2.0," http://www.humanitiesblast.com/manifesto/Manifesto_V2.pdf

Affiche du Manifeste des Digital Humanities: http://tcp.hypotheses.org/411

Patrik Svensson's typology in "The Landscape of Digital Humanities," *Digital Humanities Quarterly* 4, no. 1 (2010): ¶102 http://digitalhumanities.org/dhq/vol/4/1/000080/000080.html

A Day in the Life of Digital Humanities postings: For 2009–2011, http://tapor.ualberta.ca/taporwiki/index.php/How_do_you_define_Humanities_Comput ing_/_Digital_Humanities%3F#How_do_you_define_Digital_Humanities.3; For 2012: http://dayofdh2012.artsrn.ualberta.ca/dh/; For 2013: http://day ofdh2013.matrix.msu.edu/

Wikipedia entry on DH: http://en.wikipedia.org/wiki/Digital_humanities

Raymond Siemens's talk on "Digital Humanities Curriculum and (Inter)disciplinary Change": http://www.youtube.com/watch?v=9T0_ZaSSxSc&feature=youtube_gdata

Michael Shanks and Jeffrey Schnapp's "Artereality: Rethinking Art as Craft in a Knowledge Economy. A Manifesto." http://documents.stanford.edu/Michael Shanks/Artereality

Douglas Seefeldt and William Thomas III's "What is Digital History? A Look at Some Exemplary Projects." Faculty Publications, Department of History. University of Nebraska-Lincoln. Paper 98. downloadable at http://digitalcommons.unl.edu/cgi/viewcontent.cgi?article=1097&context=historyfacpub

Jacqueline Wernimont's entry on Feminism and Digital Humanities: http://jwerni mont.wordpress.com/2012/02/29/feminism-and-digital-humanities/

Scott Weingart's analysis of "Acceptances to Digital Humanities 2013": http://www.scottbot.net/HIAL/?p=35242

GO::DH Special Interest Group: http://www.globaloutlookdh.org/

Jessica Pressman and Lisa Swanstrom. "The Literary And/As The Digital Humanities." *Digital Humanities Quarterly* 7, no. 1 (2013). http://digitalhumanities.org/dhq/vol/7/1/000154/000154.html

TILTS: http://tilts.dwrl.utexas.edu/symposia/i

William Thomas's comments in online discussion "Interchange: The Promise of Digital History": http://www.journalofamericanhistory.org/issues/952/inter change/index.html

Archaeology 2.0: http://escholarship.org/uc/item/1r6137tb

Katy Meyers's blog posting on "Defining Digital Archaeology." 6 October 2011. http://chi.anthropology.msu.edu/2011/10/defining-digital-archaeology/

Patricia Cohen's column: http://www.nytimes.com/2011/07/27/arts/geographic-information-systems-help-scholars-see-history.html?_r=2

HASTAC Scholars' forum on "Visualization Across Disciplines": http://hastac.org/forums/visualization-across-disciplines

The Computational Turn workshop: https://sites.google.com/site/dmberry/

Melissa Terras's blog entry: http://melissaterras.blogspot.com/2013/05/on-chang ing-rules-of-digital-humanities.html

Mapping Texts project: http://www.neh.gov/divisions/odh/grant-news/mapping-texts-visualizing-historical-american-newspapers

Mapping the Republic of Letters project: http://republicofletters.stanford.edu/

Spatial History Project: http://www.stanford.edu/group/spatialhistory/cgi-bin/site/page.php?id=1

< 3 >

Institutionalizing

Digital Humanities is not some airy Lyceum. It is a series of
concrete instantiations involving money, students, funding
agencies, big schools, little schools, programs, curricula, old
guards, new guards, gatekeepers, and prestige.
—Stephen Ramsay, "Who's In and Who's Out," Position paper for the
"History and Future of Digital Humanities" panel at the 2011 annual
meeting of the Modern Language Association, http://stephenramsay.
us/text/2011/01/08/whos-in-and-whos-out/

In an environment where scholars identify with their
disciplines rather than with their department, and where
significant professional affiliations or communities of interest may transcend the boundaries of scholars' colleges and
universities, centers offer interdisciplinary "third places"–a
term sociologist Ray Oldenburg has used to identify a social
space, distinct from home and workplace.
—Amy Friedlander. "Foreword," in *A Survey of Digital Humanities Centers in the United States*, ed. Diane Zorich (Washington, D.C.: Council
on Library and Information Resources, 2008), vi

**Keywords: institutionalization, critical mass, overt versus concealed
interdisciplinarity, location, migration, leveraging, partnership, infrastructure**

Institutionalization is a process of establishing something within an organization or a social sphere, whether it is an idea, such as democracy, or
an occupation, such as teaching. Categories of knowledge are also institutions, Steven Shapin suggested, not in the conventional sense of buildings

67

and structures but a set of marks constructed and maintained in cultural space. They enable collectivities to instruct their members on where they are and how to conduct themselves (355). This chapter launches a three-part examination of how Digital Humanities is located within the cultural space of the academy through the processes of institutionalizing, professionalizing, and educating. It begins by providing a conceptual framework for thinking about institutionalization of interdisciplinarity. It then identifies patterns of affiliation among scholars and educators, followed by examination of the most prestigious structure, DH research centers, and closing reflections on the challenge of sustainability. This chapter does not present a detailed inventory of examples because the final section of this book, on "Resourcing," offers advice for finding them. Instead, it draws insights from representative models, providing a way of reading all examples through the lens of interdisciplinarity.

Institutionalizing Interdisciplinary Fields

The academic press routinely heralds the rise of new interdisciplinary fields. Their trajectories differ, however. Some develop a shared framework and visible presence, while others have fragmented identities and only limited influence. One question inevitably follows: Where do they fit? The metaphor of "fit," Lynton Caldwell replied in tracking environmental studies, prejudges the epistemological problem at stake in the emergence of new fields: many arose because of a perceived misfit among need, experience, information, and the structure of knowledge embodied in disciplinary organization (247–49). Institutionalizing new fields is a means of securing a place for them. Yet, the topic is hotly debated in humanities.

Ethan Kleinberg called institutionalization a Faustian bargain. "The beauty and utility of interdisciplinary studies," he maintained, "reside not in their institutional strength but their protean nature and their ability to build bridges and make connections" (10). Stanley Fish also contended any strategy that calls into question the foundations of disciplines theoretically negates itself if it becomes institutionalized. As an agenda, interdisciplinarity seemed to flow naturally from imperatives of left culturalist theory, deconstruction, Marxism, feminism, radical neopragmatism, and new historicism. They all critiqued the institutional structures by which disciplines establish and extend territorial claims. Yet, he countered, the multitude of studies and projects do not transgress boundaries through a *revolution tout court.* They center on straightforward tasks requiring information and techniques from other disciplines. Or, they expand imperialistically into other territories. Or, they establish a new discipline composed of a new breed of counter-professionals ("Being Interdisciplinary"). In the ensuing debate, Fish was criticized for perpetuating the dualism of disciplinarity and interdisciplinarity, presuming disciplines are coherent or homogenous, and aligning interdisciplinarity with a quest for ultimate synthesis. He also failed, Alan Liu charged, to offer terms of analysis for the pragmatics of interdisciplinarity. New fields produce protocols, practices, conventions, and closures. Yet, they also facilitate new formulations of knowledge barred by previous configurations (*Local Transcendance*, 173–79).

Facilitating new formulations is neither easy nor simple. When Irwin Feller examined a number of leading U.S. research universities, he found checkered patterns of growth, stasis, and decline in interdisciplinary initiatives, with discernible variations in the willingness of administrators or faculty to accept them. Even where new initiatives take hold, he added, they tend to survive mainly as enclaves or showpieces within the historically determined disciplinary structure of higher education. As a result, they have limited staying power, engendering only marginal changes in performance norms, resource allocations, and outcomes promulgated in strategic plans. Lacking deep roots within core functions of hard money budgets, tenure lines, and space, they remain vulnerable. Even institutions with strong programs face persistent impediments, and uneven development leaves some initiatives at the margins ("Multiple Actors," "New Organizations"). Yet, studies of higher education indicate that institutional cultures are protean by nature.

In an international comparison of research universities, Burton Clark found that modern systems of higher education are confronted by a gap between older, simple expectations and complex realities that outrun those expectations. Definitions that depict one part or function of the university as its essence or essential mission obscure changes that are transforming research and education (155, 246). Trowler and Knight's studies of institutional change shed further light on the gap that Clark identified. The standard model of "contextual simplification" assumes that organizations are culturally simple, fitting into a small number of pigeonholes. Yet, they found, "any university possesses a unique and dynamic multiple cultural configuration which renders depiction difficult and simple depictions erroneous." Viewed from an analytical telescope, differences in values, attitudes, assumptions, and taken-for-granted practices look small. Viewed from an analytical microscope, they loom large (143). Recalling experiments in the 1960s and 1970s, Keith Clayton suggested the "concealed reality" of interdisciplinarity may in fact be greater than the "overt reality." Some activities even flourish most readily when they are not labeled "interdisciplinary" (196).

Turning more specifically to the overt and concealed realities of Digital Humanities, John Seely Brown and Paul Duguid contend the relatively static nature of canonical practices in organizations cannot keep up with the complexity and variability of events on the ground, in the rough terrain missed by large-scale maps and official documents. The dynamic character of knowledge and expertise, they exhort, "drives divergence with the emergence of new ideas, understandings, modes of work, and reinterpretations and reconstructions of tasks, projects, and roles" ("Universities"). Mindful of implications for the future of learning, Cathy Davidson and David Theo Goldberg propose a new definition of "institution" as a "mobilizing network." Institutions develop structures and bureaucracies designed to stabilize, but they cannot contain and constrain all of the energies of individuals who constitute a bureaucracy (*Future*). It takes collective work, however, to channel those energies into sustainable programs.

Anne Balsamo invokes Michel de Certeau's distinction between "place" and "space" (de Certeau, 117). A "place," such as school, has stable boundaries and a fixed location. Space is "a practiced place," created through actions and practices (Balsamo, 143). This conception bridges spatial and organic dynamics through actions and practices that may be likened to a concept in physics. "Critical mass" is the minimum quantity of nuclear fuel required for a chain reaction to start. Elements of critical mass in interdisciplinary fields are grouped roughly by kind:

- adequate number of individuals sharing common interests at the national level
- adequate number of curricular programs and research centers
- adequate inter/national infrastructure for communication and publication
- a scholarly body of knowledge

- full-time faculty lines in a local program, center, or department
- secure location and report line in the organizational hierarchy of a campus
- autonomy in decision making for administration, budget, staffing, curriculum
- coordinated infrastructure and communication across campus
- flexible policies for approval of new programs and courses
- top- and mid-level administrative support of presidents, provosts, deans, chairs

- adequate funding for research and curriculum
- support for student and faculty fellowships
- seed money, incentives, and faculty development opportunities
- adequate space and equipment
- adequate access to library, information technology, computing resources

- recognition in the reward system of tenure, promotion, salary, awards
- guidelines for program review and individual evaluation
- guidelines for research collaboration, indirect cost recovery
- favorable policies for allocation of workload credit in teaching
- awareness of interdisciplinary literature and resources

(Composite of Rich and Warren, 56, 59; Caldwell, 255; Klein, *Crossing Boundaries*, 34–35; Klein, *Creating Interdisciplinary Campus Cultures*, 106)

The magnitude of critical-mass factors checks the unfettered rhetoric of "revolution" and "transformation." The radical model of institutionalization favors Wátzlawick, Weakland, and Fisch's notion of "second-order change." It can shift the paradigm of understanding while allowing space for new thought and action through rapid and discontinuous approaches to existing structures and practices. In contrast, "first-order change" simply "moves the furniture around" (*Change*). Moreover, even though the stature of a field at the national level is a strong factor in its legitimation, the amount of critical mass varies from campus to campus. Institutional specificity matters, Katherine Hayles advises, and is key to deciding which strategies will be more effective and robust (*How We Think*, 52). The possibilities vary by institutional type, administrative culture, research environment, teaching traditions, and distribution of economic and social capital.

Digital Humanities is no exception to this general pattern. Interests may be stalled for lack of resources or resistance to new modes of research and education. Or, spatializing practices might gain traction. At the New York City College of Technology, Digital Humanities has grown from individual projects to a media lab, a graduate certificate, a fellows program in instructional technology, a unified Academic Commons for digital technologies and pedagogies, a conference leading to a dedicated initiative, a role in redesign of general education, and expanding conversations across the City University of New York (CUNY) system (Waltzer, 344–45; Brier, 396–97). At Saint Louis University, DH was one of six areas benefiting from a new High Performance Computing (HPC) research cluster. At Texas A&M University, the Initiative for Digital Humanities, Media, and Culture was one of eight sponsored Landmark Research Areas to receive major funding as part of a master plan. And, at the University of Rochester and the University of North Carolina, support from the Mellon Foundation has been a catalyst for expansion. In North Carolina, a university-wide commitment to a Carolina Digital Humanities Initiative is fostering a transformative practice encompassing research, training, fellowships, undergraduate learning, a Digital Innovation Lab, tenure-track faculty hires and hires in technology and management. Moreover, the new design is linked with UNC's strategic priority for interdisciplinary research and an initiative to create a culture of collaborative work. Promotion and tenure policies are being reviewed as well, to reflect the value of engaged scholarship benefiting the public good, effective use of digital technologies, and interdisciplinary collaboration.

In thinking about specificity, it is helpful to have a fuller picture of the structures and forms that interdisciplinarity typically takes on campuses and are all present in Digital Humanities (adapted from Klein, *Crossing Boundaries*, 56–57):

Interdisciplinary Structures and Forms

Dedicated Sites

- autonomous universities and colleges
- research centers and institutes
- degree programs

- certificate programs, minors and concentrations, independent studies, internships

Visible Interfaces

- joint appointments of faculty
- collaborative research projects and team teaching
- working groups
- cross-listed courses
- shared facilities, databases, instrumentation
- local programming and professional development/training
- alliances with government and industry
- partnerships with local, regional, national, and international groups
- inter-institutional consortia

Boundary-Crossing Activities

- borrowing of tools, methods, approaches, and concepts
- migration of specialists across disciplinary boundaries
- interactions around shared problem domain and topics
- development of new research and teaching interests
- participation in inter/national organizations and networks

"Grassroots" Disciplinary Presence

- new subspecialties in a discipline/department
- jobs for specialists targeting digital and new media interests
- new courses and units in traditional courses
- intersections with interdisciplinary fields
- cross-fertilization between research centers and curricula

The variety of structures and forms becomes further evident when looking at the institutional affiliations of digital humanists.

Affiliating

"The typical digital humanist," Rafael C. Alvarado observes, "is a literary scholar, historian, or librarian—all traditional fields concerned with the management and interpretation of written documents" (51). The affiliations of contributors to the 2004 Blackwell *Companion to Digital Humanities* furnish a fuller picture of locations. Some authors identified with particular subfields, including computational linguistics, Humanities Computing, and computer-mediated communications. Others named interdisciplinary fields, including cinema studies, media studies, digital studies, and hybrid specializations of medieval studies and classics. The largest number of contributors held appointments in departments of history, philosophy, English, music, art history, and Romance languages, with additional individuals in archaeology and mathematics. Some were also affiliated with dedicated centers and institutes, including units for Computing in the Humanities, Literary and Linguistic Computing, and Advanced Technology in the Humanities. And, some held dual titles including English and Digital Studies, a professorship in English and directorship of Media Studies, a position in Humanities Computing and Multimedia located in a school of arts and another in a philosophy department, and a national research chair in Humanities Computing held by an associate professor of English.

The *Companion*'s authors were also active in building the infrastructure of the field. Many worked on major projects, including archives and websites dedicated to William Blake, Dante Gabriel Rossetti, Thomas McGreevy, and Emily Dickinson, as well as the Perseus Project devoted to the classical era, the Civil War–era The Valley of the Shadow, and Forced Migration Online. Some were involved in communication venues for the field, including the Humanist listserv and journals dedicated to Digital Humanities. Others provided leadership in major advances such as the Text Encoding Initiative. Some contributed to the field's professional organizations—including the Consortium for Computers in the Humanities, Association for Computers and the Humanities, Association for Literary and Linguistic Computing, and the Consortium for Computers in the Humanities. And, some were active in networks—such as the Electronic Publishing Research Group and the Open eBook Publication Structure Working Group. Contributors also declared interests in such diverse areas as modeling historical data in computer systems and statistical methods in language processing and analysis, Internet research ethics and intellectual integrity, electronic literature and computer games, performance theory and practice, information visualization, and electronic publishing.

A very recent anthology in the field, Matthew Gold's 2012 *Debates in Digital Humanities*, reflects both continuing and expanding patterns of affiliation. Authors still hold positions in traditional departments, especially English and history, and some are in art, Germanic languages and literatures, philosophy, and anthropology. The most frequently reported professions are librarianship and education, with instructional technology included in the latter. Affiliations with interdisciplinary fields include medieval studies, information studies, cinematic arts, and an increase since the *Companion* in media studies. Centers listed in 2004 also appear, though other sites have gained visibility, including a Culture, Arts, and Technology program, an Interactive Technology and Pedagogy Certificate Program, new appointments focused on scholarly communication/scholarship, the Roy Rosenzweig Center for History and New Media, the University of Nebraska-Lincoln's Center for Digital Research in the Humanities, and the HUMlab at Umeå University in Sweden. In addition, several networks had gained prominence, including HASTAC (Humanities, Arts, Science, and Technology Alliance and Collaboratory) and SHANTI (Sciences, Humanities, and Arts Network of Technological Initiatives).

The location of HASTAC scholars is of particular significance because the majority are graduate students with future career commitments to innovative use of new technologies and media. English and history departments were prominent in the 2010–11 academic year. The scope, though, is wide. Affiliations with English, for example, spanned literary and textual cultures, rhetoric and composition, digital writing and publishing, gaming, race, and new media. The number of co-listings is another indicator of the growing plurality of interests. In English, they included affiliations with women's studies and with education. In history, individuals cited co-affiliation with education and philosophy. A smaller number of scholars were in art and art history, though also listed couplings in visual studies, arts administration, and in a third case triangulating art, engineering, and computer science. Students also listed theater, philosophy co-listed with neuroscience, and computer music. The highest number affiliating with a profession were in library and information science, though several reported education. Affiliations with computer sciences included a coupling with modern culture and new media. And, scholars in communications cited journalism, mass media, comparative media studies, and a combination of technology, communications, and society. The largest number citing interdisciplinary fields were in film/media studies, and visual/cultural studies, plus a co-listing with cinematic arts and critical studies. In addition, individuals identified with American civilization, comparative ethnic studies, comparative literature, and cultural studies. Several also cited social science disciplines as well as human and community development, urban planning, international development policy, leadership, and change.

Hiring is a further index of where Digital Humanities is taking root, based on job listings from 2010 to 2013 identified by a Google Alerts feed for "digital humanities" and ads in the *Chronicle of Higher Education*. Some universities sought DH specialties in traditional disciplines, to develop digital capacity in particular areas and increase use of new technology and media across campus. Given previous findings, it is not surprising to find English prominent. The Cardiff School of English, for example, sought a professor of English with expertise in the history of the book and material culture as well as Digital Humanities, with the expectation of contributing to the Center for Editorial and Intertextual Research. Communications was also prominent, and other positions targeted library and information sciences. The increased visibility of DH in libraries is not surprising. Libraries have long invested in building and curating collections, archives, and corpora. They have been logical locations for DH centers and initiatives, because they serve units across campus and are at the forefront of working with new technologies. In tallying institutional resources for Humanities Computing units, McCarty and Kirschenbaum found that electronic text centers and comparable units have tended to be located in libraries. Moreover, DH and libraries have a common stake in "open access" to information (see also Warwick, "Institutional Models," 194–95).

Even so, in introducing a special issue of the *Journal of Library Administration* on Digital Humanities, Barbara Rockenbach reports that despite a large literature on DH and specialized jobs for librarians, few articles in the library literature and fewer in the DH literature focus on the role of libraries. Echoing early concerns, libraries are also still regarded as service units for departments. One of the most striking recent increases in this sphere is the number of librarians dedicated to DH as part of their existing duties or new positions. One job listing combined an English and DH librarian, and libraries at the University of Illinois and universities at Stanford, Brown, York, Yale, Rutgers, and Ohio State University all advertised for specialists. The DH Librarian at Rutgers, for instance, was expected to support faculty and students in integrating digital and traditional resources and approaches, while also being a liaison for departments, strengthening core infrastructure, and fostering collaborations among stakeholders across campus. The DH Developer at Stanford Library was charged with general Digital Humanities support along with developing and supporting digital library efforts and strengthening collaborations across units of the libraries system.

Prestigious positions were also on the market, including McGill University's Canada Research Chair in Digital Humanities and the Alexander von Humboldt Chair of Digital Humanities at the University of Leipzig. Full-time faculty positions were available too, many to lead new initiatives. The University of Western Sydney sought a professor affiliated with the Digital Humanities Research Group. Elsewhere in Australia, the University of Tasmania advertised for a professor or associate professor to lead research, teaching, and creative practice in DH, with the added expectation of facilitating interdisciplinary research. The most powerful development in the interdisciplinary job market has been the cluster hire. Positions typically reside within separate multiple departments but revert to centralized control if vacated, usually the provost's office (Klein, *Creating Interdisciplinary Campus Cultures*, 130–31). Although science and medicine were prioritized in early clusters, DH is becoming more prominent, including hirings at Georgia State University and the University of Maryland. The University of Michigan cluster in Digital Environments/Digital Humanities added faculty in departments of English and Communication Studies, the School of Information, and the Program in American Culture. The University of Wisconsin-Madison's Digital Studies cluster is funded by an undergraduate curriculum initiative including English, communication arts, and library and information studies. The University of Iowa cluster aims to hire six faculty in Public Humanities in a Digital World and the University of Nebraska-Lincoln six tenure-track assistant professors and additional staff.

Lest this snapshot give the impression the Digital Humanities market is booming, when checking the *Chronicle of Higher Education* for jobs in "humanities + technology," Andy Engel found more calls for administrative and technical-service jobs than scholarly positions. The Job Slam at the Digital Humanities 2011 conference included tenure-track positions, but they were outnumbered by administrative and management posts (e-mail, July 13, 2010). Some were in institutions with established reputations in the field. The University of Maryland's Institute for Technology in the Humanities (MITH) sought an assistant director, and the University of Virginia advertised for a "hybrid" humanities design architect for the Scholars' Lab to design and implement digital resources while working with faculty and graduate students across campus. Other positions were in start-up mode. Arizona State University's Institute for Humanities Research (IHR) sought a director of the Digital Humanities Seed Lab, to help develop a campus-wide initiative, build external networks, secure funding, evaluate tools and technologies, provide training, and provide technical support for programs and projects.

The Arizona State example raises a general concern about workload expectations, especially when interdisciplinarity is factored in. The salary level for the director of the Seed Lab, at $45,000–$60,000, was below the magnitude of desired qualifications, including a PhD in a humanities field. The minimum qualifications also included experience in interdisciplinary humanities environments. Comparably, Pennsylvania State University Libraries sought a DH research designer who could "translate and share ideas and concepts effectively across diverse interdisciplinary audiences." The appointment was part of the university's "Humanities in a Digital Age" (HDA) initiative, aimed in part at enriching and promoting cross-disciplinary humanities scholarship and research while building a community of practice. Degree qualifications differ by position, an important determinant of the balance of technology and humanities. The Penn State ad, for example, listed proficiency or fluency with one or more technologies and an advanced degree in a humanities field. In contrast, the DH programmer sought by the University of Rochester could have a degree in software engineering or computer science, or an equivalent combination of education and experience. Knowledge of humanities was not required.

The #alt-academic movement has heightened awareness of alternative careers. Bethany Nowviskie locates this movement transversally across academic and cultural-heritage institutions. In a bleak job market for humanities, #alt-act positions raise hope for employment, including DH specialists at sites as diverse as the American Antiquarian Society and the Extreme Science and Engineering Discovery Environment (XSEDE). Research associate and postdoctoral fellowships are also part of the jobscape, and here too the balance of interests differs. The research associate in East Asian Digital Humanities in the Department of History at King's College

London was expected to conduct research in and publish on a specific project, China and the Historical Sociology of Empire. The postdoctoral scholar at Case Western Reserve University was also expected to work in a specialized discipline but do additional research and teaching in association with the interdisciplinary Culture, Creativity, and Design Project. Echoing the pattern in faculty and administrative jobs, postdocs are also expected to be agents for change. At Dickinson College, the postdoc in DH was required to teach one or two courses a year in a specialty on top of catalyzing faculty innovation in pedagogy, e-learning tools, integrating digital media into teaching and scholarship, guiding and participating in workshops, and working with library and information science staff to train students for research collaborations with faculty.

Centering Digital Humanities

The most prominent institutional structure in advancing Digital Humanities has been the research center. During the 1980s, humanities institutes were established on the model of scientific research institutes, but with far less economic capital (Herbert, 549, n32). The word *center* is ironic, since most are modest in size and reputation. They exist typically on soft money or the largess of their local hosts. They are also primarily places for research, though some offer coursework. Centers provide an "in between" or "shadow" space within discipline-dominated organizations. Classified in organizational theory as "matrix structures" and "ORUs" (organized research units), these enclaves are simultaneously social formations and physical sites that exhibit a "semi-liminal" character, operating partially as countercultures and partially as components of new cultures. They provide interstitial space for boundary crossing and collaboration, bridging gaps between domains while stimulating new alliances, identities, and professional roles (Klein, *Interdisciplinarity*, 123–26). As Friedlander commented in the opening epigraphs, they embody Ray Oldenburg's notion of alternative "third places," fostering ties critical to the life of a community. Oldenburg did not include digital environments, but the analogy holds (vi).

The formation of Digital Humanities centers is an international phenomenon, although Neil Fraistat notes important differences. North American centers, he reports, have been more likely to rise from the bottom up, in contrast to a top-down pattern in Europe and Asia. In North

America, centers have also tended to focus exclusively on humanities and sometimes interpretive social sciences. In contrast, centers in Europe and Asia are more likely to be dispersed through disciplines, or were virtual instead of physically located (283). Diane Zorich's 2008 overview of Digital Humanities Centers (DHCs) in the United States is the most comprehensive study of DHCs. Zorich examined their governance, organizational structures, funding models, missions, projects, and research foci. Based on her findings, Zorich offers a composite definition:

> A digital humanities center is an entity where new media and technologies are used for humanities-based research, teaching, and intellectual engagement and experimentation. The goals of the center are to further humanities scholarship, create new forms of knowledge, and explore technology's impact on humanities-based disciplines. (Zorich, 4)

Zorich classifies DHCs into two general categories: center-focused and resource-focused in virtual space. The former outnumber the latter, with the oldest one founded in 1978 and the mean year of founding 1992. Catalysts differ. A particular event may initiate a process leading to formation of a center, such as a key discussion in a meeting or a casual conversation with administrators or funders. Grants also play a role, and many projects generated other activities subsequently gathered under a single structure for effective management. In addition, individuals who organize centers to meet their personal needs sometimes begin to encompass the interests of others. Some centers have also emerged from campus-wide initiatives focused on humanities or pedagogy, while others began in computing units that evolved over time from being "purveyors" of services to "incubators" and "managers" of projects (1, 8–10). The University of Victoria illustrates the latter model. Efforts began in 1989 with a unit established to support language teaching and research. In 2001, a permanent office was formed, the Humanities Computing and Media Centre. In 2004, an Electronic Textual Cultures Lab and a Digital Summer Institute were added, then in 2012, a Digital L2 Learning Lab and a Maker Lab.

The mission statements of DHCs overlap with the general goals of humanities centers, foremost among them creating a community for humanities work, sharing experiences, providing infrastructure and expertise, offering programs for academic and general audiences, and promoting public and civic engagement. They also address interdisciplinary-specific goals, including providing an environment where members of different disciplines can interact and collaborate, developing new pedagogies and research tools, engaging in experiment and creativity, and advancing emerging fields. The impact of technology varies greatly, Zorich adds, from "prosaic" use of new media in research or teaching to "transformative" developments such as a new products and processes that alter existing knowledge and create new forms of scholarship. The scope of DH-specific missions Zorich identified are regrouped here roughly by kind:

- **Production and Experimentation:** creating tools, contents, standards, approaches, and methodologies; designing innovation; building collections, archives, and repositories
- **Service:** training, networking, and collaborative support for individuals and units; providing technology solutions for departments, information portal, and repository; leveraging networked resources, managing the research process
- **Scholarship:** analyzing and critiquing how digital technologies are changing research and education; advancing new forms of learning, literacy, and media; bridging gaps with science, technology, and social sciences.
- **Programming:** hosting lectures, conferences, seminars, and workshops.

As the last grouping indicates, DH centers provide professional development opportunities. In addition to modeling interdisciplinarity and collaboration, Neil Fraistat also reports, DH centers facilitate mutual learning among graduate students and faculty in the course of working together on projects (281). To illustrate the variety of programming, the Digital Humanities Seminar at the University of Kansas Institute for Digital Research in the Humanities provides a multi-tiered forum, including Digital Jumpstart Workshops with hands-on introductions to tools and practices. The University of Victoria's Digital Humanities Summer Institute covers tools and methods, project planning and management, digitization, digital pedagogy, and databases. The Digital Humanities@Oxford summer school has included combined plenary lectures and work sessions with tutors for a wide audience. And, the Maryland Institute for Technology in the Humanities Digital Humanities Winter Institute offered a weeklong intensive combination of coursework, social events, and lectures. The Humanities High Performance Computing Collaboratory's (HpC) summer institute also offered two five-day workshops, one in collaboration with the University of Illinois' Institute for Computing in Humanities, Arts, and Social Science, and the other at the University of South Carolina's Center for Digital Humanities. In addition to comprehensive education in computation, project design and management, hands-on experience with technical platforms, and work with technical staff, HpC has a yearlong virtual community where scholars support peers in authoring projects.

Although many centers serve similar functions, they have local signatures. To echo Tanya Clement's observation about incorporating multiliteracies into the undergraduate DH curriculum, "Value is clearly dependent on venue" (68). Digital projects in the library may be the focus on one campus, textual analysis or historical research on another, media studies on yet another. The Institute for Advanced Technology in the Humanities (IATH) at the University of Virginia built on its reputation for technical support and advanced computer technology, while the University of Southern California's Institute for Multimedia Literacy has a sustained interest in multimedia literacy and pedagogies now amplified by work on electronic publication. The Center for Textual Studies and Digital Humanities at Loyola University Chicago continues a long-standing commitment to textual studies, while the Center for Public History at Cleveland State University is committed to public history and the Roy Rosenzweig Center for History and New Media (CHNM) at George Mason University is a leader in producing tools and materials for digital history and new forms of digital scholarship and publication.

Centers also tend to host a multidisciplinary range of projects, especially large established sites. Their variety might seem at first blush to be eclectic, with digitizing of an ancient manuscript or 3-D restoring of an archaeological site hosted along with curating electronic literature or gathering oral histories of indigenous peoples. This range is the result of serving the multiple interests of local faculty, external fellows, and partnerships with other centers. A selective snapshot of projects at IATH, for example, includes the Chaco Canyon Research Archive, Virtual Williamsburg, Rome Reborn, Mapping the Dalai Lamas, The Melville Electronic Library, and The Valley of the Shadow Civil War project. Likewise, the Center for Digital Scholarship at Brown University maintains diverse projects, including the signature collection Lincolniana and a close relationship with the Women Writers Project. These examples reaffirm, too, the vital link between centers and libraries. IATH and MITH are both located in libraries, and the Alabama Digital Humanities Center at the University of Alabama is a program of the university libraries providing space and community for over forty faculty across campus.

DH centers also facilitate the laboratory model of humanities. Fraistat describes MITH as an "applied think tank, a place where theory and practice met on a daily and a broadly interdisciplinary basis" (286). The same may be said of other sites. The Digital Scholarship Lab at the University of Richmond has been experimenting with modeling techniques for analyzing data from 19th-century America. And, a jointly organized forum of MIT's HyperStudio and Harvard's metaLAB featured new work in digital musicology. In their presentation on "Listening Faster," Michael Cuthbert and Matthias Röder demonstrated techniques and tools that enable scholars to analyze large repertories of compositions in the time it would take to look at and hear a single work. Together, computational analysis, clustering techniques, visualization tools, and data mining of musical works are fostering a new kind of "wired music scholar." DH centers also illustrate how early projects and resources can be leveraged into robust multidisciplinary portfolios.

Founded in 1994, MATRIX is the Center for Digital Humanities and Social Sciences at Michigan State University (MSU). A self-described "Humanities Computing" center, it began in 1994 when Mark Kornbluh persuaded the College of Arts and Letters to host H-Net, the Humanities and Social Sciences online network. Within two years, MATRIX had obtained two NEH grants for H-Net, and in 1997 hosted a national conference on humanities teaching in the digital age. Over the ensuing years, the center was also able to gain new space and parlay resources from the Provost's office into new projects, external grants, staff, and a stronger infrastructure. Today, the center houses digital library repositories and partners with other units at MSU and external organizations to digitize collections. Its local signature includes a commitment to best practices built on open-source, inexpensive hardware and software that support training initiatives with under-resourced teachers in the Great Lakes region and in Western and South Africa. MATRIX has also built greater "capacitation" with a National Science Foundation Digital Libraries II grant to develop a National Gallery of the Spoken Word. The grant positioned the center within a wider community of science practitioners and a global movement aimed at creating standardized, interoperable digital repositories.

The Simpson Center for the Humanities at the University of Washington (UW) exemplifies the strategy of leveraging in an endowment campaign boosted by a $625,000 NEH Challenge Grant and a $600,000 grant from the Mellon Foundation. The Commons will support innovative and experimental research with three primary objectives: *animation* of knowledge with visualization tools, dynamic databases, and aural tracks; public *circulation* of scholarship; and historical, social, and cross-cultural *understanding* of digital culture. During the academic year, it will augment campus-wide opportunities for graduate students by offering three one-credit courses, bringing a seminal scholar or innovator for an intensive two-day visit, and sponsoring Digital Research Summer Institute (DRSI) workshops and seminars. The centerpiece will be an annual eight-week summer program of fellowships for UW faculty and doctoral students focused on collaborative projects. In advance of the first institute, the center built local infrastructure. "Most important for the long run," Director Kathleen Woodward emphasizes," are the connections and collaborations with other units," including partnerships with the UW Libraries Digital Initiatives Program, Information Technology's Academic & Collaborative Applications, a graduate certificate program in textual studies, and the master of communication in digital media. A session of the fellows program was also devoted to digital humanities, with presenters from English, women's studies, and geography. And, a graduate short-credit course on cultural research and digital collections was taught by members of women's studies, English, and MITH (e-mail, Kathleen Woodward, June 20, 2011).

The Center for Digital Research in the Humanities (CDRH) at the University of Nebraska-Lincoln furnishes added lessons about leveraging. Recalling its creation, Richard Edwards emphasizes that neither initial opportunities nor subsequent successes would have existed without having outstanding digital scholars already on campus. They contributed a vision, commitments to developing the Willa Cather and Walt Whitman Archives, and leadership in pressing for the university's commitment. The quality of their work received national attention from outside funding agencies and the wider scholarly community, and their presence enticed other scholars that Nebraska was attempting to recruit. When the university decided to invest designated funds in selected areas, digital scholarship in humanities was designated as one of nineteen promising "Programs of Excellence." Administrators in charge of information technology, the research office, space allocation, and other pertinent facilities and services were also encouraged to undertake support within their operations and budgets. The university libraries reallocated space to make room for the center, and deans of arts and sciences and university libraries agreed to designate certain vacant faculty lines or assign time of current faculty members to digital scholarship and in some cases directly to the center.

Stepping back from individual examples to assess the overall state of DH centers, Zorich considers their proliferation to be a positive sign. Yet, she raises concern about continuing threats to interdisciplinarity, collaboration, and partnership. Centers have reached a level of maturity, but they face ongoing challenges of sustainability and preservation of content. She also likens them to silos favoring individual projects, resulting in "untethered digital production." Many projects, Luke Waltzer likewise cautions, rarely take steps needed for "generalizable value" or create conditions for "broad adoption" (342). Claire Warwick further cites the contradictory demands of service and research, a tension linked historically to many centers' emergence from service computing. To this day, association with support units of computing service or libraries reinforces the impression that DH is service and the research function thereby vulnerable (194, 196). Moreover, some question whether the "stars" of the system are creating another kind of "digital divide," between the haves and have-nots (282). Karen Sword asks in the *Journal of American History* online forum whether Digital Humanities is genuinely growing or only consolidating at a few institutions. The larger sums of money needed for centers reinforce the Matthew effect of the rich getting richer. Neil Fraistat urges DHCs to become integrated into a larger network to make them more widely known and available, leverage resources and services, and avoid redundancy.

The history of institutionalizing interdisciplinarity furnishes yet another caveat. Experimental programs, William Newell advises in a volume on *The Politics of Interdisciplinary Studies*, are always at political risk. Even when embraced, they may be vulnerable to budget crises or the departure of key supporters. Because they run against the grain of hierarchical discipline-based structures, they are "low hanging fruit" (48). Even when a Digital Humanities center or academic program gains a foothold, it may be subject to the departure of key personnel, shifts in administrative support, and declines in financial support. McCarty and Kirschenbaum cite the closing and radical reformation of several prominent units, including the Humanities Computing Unit at Oxford University and the Center for Computing in the Humanities at the University of Toronto. At Oxford, the unit was based in Computing Services. Organizational changes and budget cuts resulted in reduction of research-oriented activities to instrumentalities of technical support in a reorganization that refocused activities in support of teaching and learning throughout the university and a national humanities hub. At Toronto, humanities evolved from the Faculty of Arts and Science. This type of space, however, did not disturb the existing power structure, no tenure-track positions were created, no new departments set up, and, McCarty emphasized, "nothing done that could not be undone" ("Humanities Computing").

Sustainability, Allen Repko advises in *The Politics of Interdisciplinary Studies*, means "the capacity to function indefinitely" (145). "Indefinitely," however, is not necessarily forever. Even traditional disciplinary departments such as classics and German have learned this painful lesson in recent budget cuts. And, even admired "edge projects" such as the Institute for Multimedia Literacy at the University of Southern California, Balsamo warns, are always in danger of disappearing in the political economy of budget decisions (244, n28). Colleagues and students involved in the ACT Lab (Advanced Communication Technology) at the University of Texas considered being "nomadics" vital to the free play of creativity, practicing a strategy of living under the "institutional radar" and a "codeswitching umbrella." Yet, Sandra Stone admits, the pressure of institutional structuring and "dire necessities" are constant (qtd. in Svensson, "Landscape").

The strength of Digital Humanities at the University of Nebraska-Lincoln is due to a combination of support at top-down, mid-level administrative, and center and individual unit levels. Claire Warwick credits success at the University College London (UCL) to a combination of provost-level strategic development funding, synchrony with the University's Grand Challenge campaign focusing interdisciplinary research on global problems, support from the deans of both Arts & Humanities and Engineering Science, and her own dual role as co-director of UCLDH and vice dean of research for Faculty of Arts and Humanities (210). Matthew Kirschenbaum reminds readers, as well, that institutional structures tend to have "long half-lives." The academic infrastructure of Digital Humanities now includes a major journal, professional organization, and funding support. Moreover, behind these components of infrastructure lie "some very deep investments—of reputation, process, and labor, as well as actual capital" ("Tactical Turn," 416). Even when projects end, they may catalyze change. "What if there is zest in the crevices?" Davidson asks. Projects can prevail in ways that "taunt" and "temper" the institutions housing them, inspiring passion that continues after a project fades and leading to other activities.

At the broadest level, the new alliance between CenterNet and the Consortium of Humanities Centers and Institutes aims to enhance interoperability, accessibility, and sustainability across a wide interconnected grid. Two themes frame the alliance: "Digital Disciplines" focuses on the relation of digital technologies to disciplines, and "Digital Publics" on formation of new collaborations and publics. "Digital Disciplines," in particular, raises several questions central to this book. It asks whether digital techniques and methods should be granted autonomous disciplinary status, to what extent their impact should be distributed in existing or emergent disciplines, to what extent digital practices are affecting how research is performed in humanities and arts, and how relationships between disciplines have been transformed. It also asks how newer disciplines and fields are shaped and enabled, at the same time traditional disciplines and fields are challenged to renew themselves. In order to continue answering those questions, it is necessary to examine the topic of the next chapter: how Digital Humanities is being professionalized.

Clustered Links for Chapter 3 in Order of Appearance

Mellon Foundation support for DH expansion at the University of Rochester: http://www.rochester.edu/news/show.php?id=7752

Carolina Digital Humanities Initiative: http://college.unc.edu/2012/07/06/digital humanitiesmellon/ http://digitalhumanities.unc.edu/about/

St. Louis University DH initiative: http://www.slu.edu/news-rel-research-cluster-grant-417

Texas A&M University's Initiative for Digital Humanities, Media, and Culture: http://idhmc.tamu.edu

Cardiff School of English: http://tinyurl.com/cardiffrarebooks

Willard McCarty and Matthew Kirschenbaum, "Institutional Models for Humanities Computing": Association for Literary and Linguistic Computing (ALLC) founded in 1973 and now under the name European Association for Digital Humanities (EADH): http://eadh.org/

DH Librarian at Rutgers University: http://newjersey.sla.org/2013/08/08/digital-humanities-librarian-rutgers-university-libraries-nj/

DH Librarian at Stanford University: http://library.stanford.edu/news/2013/02/welcome-jacqueline-hettel-digital-humanities-developer

Humboldt Chair of Digital Humanities at Leipzig: http://sites.tufts.edu/perseusup

dates/2013/04/04/the-open-philology-project-and-humboldt-chair-of-digital-humanities-at-leipzig/

Barbara Rockenbach's "Introduction," *Journal of Library Administration* 53, no. 1 (2013): 1–9: link to DOI: http://dx.doi.org/10.1080/01930826.2013.756676 and Taylor & Francis online: http://www.tandfonline.com/doi/abs/10.1080/0 1930826.2013.756676#.UshCOZiJWmA

Ad for Director of Arizona State University Digital Humanities Seed Lab: http://jobs.code4lib.org/job/8276/

Pennsylvania State University's Digital Research Designer: jobs.code4lib.org/job/9002/

University of Rochester's DH Programmer: http://www.library.rochester.edu/digital-humanities-programmer

#alt-academy: http://nowviskie.org/2011/announcing-alt-academy/ http://media commons.futureofthebook.org/alt-ac/

King's College London Postdoc in East Asian DH: http://jobs.lofhm.org/2012/05/16/Kings-College-Research-Associate.html

Case Western University's Postdoctoral Scholar: http://hastac.org/opportunities/digital-humanities-postdoctoral-scholar-case-western-reserve-university-0

DH Postdoc at Dickinson College: http://blogs.dickinson.edu/digitalhumanities/2013/02/12/postdoctoral-fellowship-in-digital-humanities-at-dickinson/

DH at the University of Victoria: http://web.uvic.ca/humanities/aboutus/digital_humanities.php, www.dhsi.org

Digital Humanities Seminar at the University of Kansas: http://idrh.ku.edu/digital-humanities-seminar

Digital Humanities@Oxford Summer School: http://digital.humanities.ox.ac.uk/dhoxss/

Digital Humanities Winter Institute at the University of Maryland: http://mith.umd.edu/announcingdhwi/

Humanities High-Performance Computing Collaboratory: www.dhhpc.org

Institute for Advanced Technology in the Humanities at the University of Virginia: http://www.iath.virginia.edu/

University of Southern California School of Cinematic Arts: http://iml.usc.edu/

Center for Textual Studies and Digital Humanities at Loyola University Chicago: http://ctsdh.luc.edu/

Center for Public History at Cleveland State University: http://csudigitalhumanities.org/

Center for History and New Media at George Mason University: http://chnm.gmu.edu/

Center for Digital Scholarship at Brown University: http://library.brown.edu/cds/

Alabama Digital Humanities Center: http://www.lib.ua.edu/digitalhumanities

UMass Amherst Digital Humanities Initiative: http://digitalhumanities.umass.edu/

Digital Scholarship Lab at the University of Richmond: http://dsl.richmond.edu/

Hyperstudio/Digital Humanities at MIT: http://hyperstudio.mit.edu/

metaLAB at Harvard University: http://metalab.harvard.edu/

MATRIX center at Michigan State University: http://www2.matrix.msu.edu/

Digital Humanities Commons at the University of Washington: http://depts.wash
ington.edu/uwch/programs/initiatives/digital-humanities/digital-humanities-
commons

Center for Digital Research in Humanities: http://cdrh.unl.edu/

Richard Edwards, "Creating the CDRH at University of Nebraska-Lincoln": http://
cdrh.unl.edu/articles/creatingcdrh.php

Karen Sword comment on divide in Digital Humanities: http://www.journalo
famericanhistory.org/issues/952/interchange/index.html

Oxford University computing services: http://www.oucs.ox.ac.uk/internal/annrep/
annrep0001/index.xml?ID=body.1_div.8

Willard McCarty and Matthew Kirschenbaum. "Institutional Models for Humanities Computing," *Literary and Linguistic Computing* 18, no. 4 (2003): 465–89.
http://www.informatik.uni-trier.de/~ley/pers/hd/k/Kirschenbaum:Matthew_
G=

Willard McCarty's "Humanities Computing as Interdiscipline": http://www.iath.
virginia.edu/hcs/mccarty.html

Cathy Davidson's blog comment on "zest in the crevices": http://hastac.org/blogs/
cathy-davidson/sustainability-institutions-prevail-projects-fail

CenterNet alliance with CHCI: http://www.hastac.org/blogs/cathy-davidson/chci-
centernet-future-digital-humanities, http://digitalhumanities.org/centernet

<4>

Professionalizing

"... individual experience is not scalable."
—Comment by Kevin Guthrie to the Commission on Cyberinfrastructure for Humanities and Social Sciences, qtd. in John Unsworth,
"Cyberinfrastructure for Humanities and Social Sciences," University
of Illinois, Chicago. *Microsoft PowerPoint file, Slide 11*, http://people.
brandeis.edu/~unsworth/ECAR/index.xml

The Alliance of Digital Humanities Organizations (ADHO)
promotes and supports digital research and teaching across
all arts and humanities disciplines, acting as a community-
based advisory force, and supporting excellence in research,
publication, collaboration and training.
http://digitalhumanities.org/

**Keywords: professionalization, platforming, communities of practice,
network, partnership, scholarly communication, federation, remixing,
modularity**

Professionalization is a process by which a group establishes and maintains control of a social world. Early learned societies cultivated a wide
range of interests and included members of society outside the academy.
When higher education was restructured around the modern system of
disciplinarity in the late 19th and early 20th centuries, these groups became
outnumbered by new professional organizations dedicated to specialized
subjects. Like the historical guilds that provided workers a social group
for their trades, these organizations met their members' needs while defining and controlling expertise. The most prominent mechanisms of profes-

sionalizing academic domains have been annual meetings, publications, educational credentials, qualifications for career advancement, specialized discourse, norms of conduct, criteria of evaluation, and standards of practice. This chapter examines two major mechanisms of professionalizing Digital Humanities: the formation of communities of practice and scholarly publication.

Communities of Practice

The radical version of interdisciplinarity holds that nothing less than jettisoning the structure of disciplinarity will result in significant change. Yet, in an essay on "The Politics of Disciplinary Advantage," Rodgers, Booth, and Eveline admit that countertactics can never completely overthrow disciplinary hegemony. They advocate getting around rules of constraint by controlling boundaries, establishing methodological and theoretical rigor, formulating recommendations for practice, and creating a self-regulating guild. Through these actions, individuals and groups negotiate the material and representational economy in which interdisciplinarity is deployed, moving within and across disciplinary structure in order to transcend it and thereby "making a difference." Communities of practice are one of the most important means of doing so. The term is associated with Lave and Wenger's studies of craft- and skill-based activities. They examined apprenticeships of midwives, native tailors, navy quartermasters, and meat cutters, though subsequently the concept was adapted in other areas including education, knowledge management, and studies of online communities. The central idea is that people who share a common interest, craft, or profession generate community, establishing common ground through sharing information and experiences. As they learn from each other, they build a repertoire of common knowledge, communal resources, collaborative relationships, shared norms, and best practices (*Situated Learning*).

The repertoires that communities build form the basis for platforming a new field. In the world of computing, *platform* refers to hardware architecture or frameworks that allow software to run. Interdisciplinary fields are neither hardware nor software, but the social architecture for a networked operating system is vital to their strength and sustainability. John Unsworth's description of the shift from Web 1.0 to Web 2.0 provides a way of thinking about this concept. Emphasis shifted with Web 2.0 from the computer as platform to the network as platform ("University 2.0," 227). Networking has played a key role in platforming Digital Humanities. Many campuses began by forming local interest groups, including Denison University, the University of Massachusetts, the University of California at Riverside, Texas A&M, Stanford, Princeton, and Cambridge. In some cases, small beginnings expanded into wider networks, such as the 2011 Digital Humanities Week at the University of Maine, Philly Digital Humanities, the Committee on Institutional Cooperation comprised of Big Ten universities plus the University of Chicago, the Boston DH Consortium, and the Five College Consortium in Western Massachusetts and Tri-Co DH Consortium of Bryn Mawr, Haverford, and Swarthmore. The Digital Humanities Observatory in Ireland exemplifies the national level, building infrastructure in a collaboratory model of services and resources while coordinating distributed networks across national and international platforms.

The process of community building has been bidirectional: simultaneously moving outward toward a wider field and inward toward particular specializations. Some efforts have a narrow focus, such as the session on "Faulkner and the Digital Humanities" at the 2012 Faulkner and Yoknapatawpha Conference. Others serve wider interests. The Association of College and Research Libraries, for example, recently started a Digital Humanities discussion group, and some disciplines have become prominent in serving digital interests at their annual meetings. A "Hands-on Workshop" at the 2011 conference of the American Historical Association (AHA) addressed a range of topics including Teaching with Social Media, Text Mining, Content Management Systems, Digital Publishing, and Digital Storytelling, along with a tour of resources on TeachingHistory. org. DH topics also populate the annual Modern Language Association (MLA) convention in sufficient number to be chronicled regularly in the academic press, and MLA has an Office of Scholarly Communication that includes web-based publishing and networking opportunities.

Archaeology and art history also have a history of serving digital interests. *Computer Applications and Quantitative Methods in Archaeology* was founded in 1973, the *Archaeological Computing Newsletter* appeared in 1984, and by the mid-1980s related sessions were being held at meetings of the discipline's professional societies (Eiteljorg, 22). At the same time, in 1985, art and design historians established Computers and the History of Art (CHArt). This group was initially composed of academics, but they were soon joined by individuals in museums and art galleries as well as managers of visual and textual archives and libraries. In 1982, the Visual Resources Association (VRA) was also founded. Since 1968 it has met at conferences of the College Art Association, and now has its own *Bulletin* serving the needs of image media professionals in educational and cultural heritage settings. Comparable to CHArt, VRA's membership documents the expanding scope of visualization. Members have expertise in not only art and art history but also architecture, information science, museum curation, digital production, and archiving (Greenhalgh, 33).

As DH interests were taking root within discipline-based organizations, new interdisciplinary communities were also forming.

"Strategic knowledge clusters" comprise a generative form of interdisciplinary community. Funded by the Social Sciences and Humanities Research Council of Canada, the clusters are knowledge networks in which scholars can partner with non-academic stakeholders. The Network in Canadian History and Environment (NiCHE), for example, is a self-described "confederation" of researchers and educators working at the intersections of nature and history, with core topics including water and landscapes, geographical regions, and transnational ecologies. Membership is free and open. Because NiCHE includes many prominent environmental historians, it can also provide authoritative peer review for projects and has experimented with an open-source environment. In addition, NiCHE has a new scholars committee and a digital-infrastructure initiative that supports practicing historians by providing online training and materials in a tutorial-based textbook: in addition to being open acccess, *The Programming Historian 2* is community driven and invites feedback from users.

Major projects also generate communities of practice. The project Integrating Digital Papyrology, for instance, is developing a "federated system" of resources to overcome the silo effect of separate projects. Its ultimate aim is to make the entire ancient Greek and Latin documentary corpus available in open form. Integrating textual and material records from many cultures, Gregory Crane advises, places greater importance on interoperability across scholarly cultures and languages. Interlinking enables users to remix content, and a consortial model leverages both traditional peer review and community-based crowd-sourcing (McGann, Stauffer, Wheeles, and Pickard, 135; Crane, 146). Partnership is also important in small fields. Classics, Crane adds, does not warrant a "classical informatics" on the level of bioinformatics. Yet, small fields need to meet their infrastructure needs. Describing the EVIA Digital Archive Project, Alan R. Burdette cites ethnomusiciology as an example of a small discipline that cannot generate resources for library purchases. Yet, being located within the Institute for Digital Arts and Humanities at the University of Indiana, Bloomington, provides a platform for pursuing further funding, means of preservation, and linkages for interdisciplinary teams across units dedicated to information and computer science, library and information science, a Digital Library Program and IT services as well as arts and humanities faculty ("EVIA," 204; Response, 247).

DH communities have arisen in interdisciplinary fields as well. Established in 2003, Digital Medievalist organizes sessions at both medieval congresses and Humanities Computing conferences. This self-described web-based community provides an international network for technical collaboration and instruction, exchange of expertise, and development of best practices. In addition to meetings, the project operates an electronic mailing list and discussion forum, online refereed journal, news server, and wiki. Another initiative, Judaica Europeana, is making available a large online archive of books, documents, visual and audio material related to Jewish history and culture. The organization's "Access to Integration" effort, in particular, is developing a new process for formulating collective solutions to challenges that arise in using digital technologies for studying Jewish history. Both knowledge integration and technological integration, the group's leaders emphasize, are needed.

Collaborative partnerships also form around educational needs. Three graduate Schools of Information (at the Universities of Michigan, Maryland, and Texas-Austin) and three digital humanities centers (at the University of Maryland, University of Nebraska-Lincoln, and Michigan State University) joined forces to enhance education and training opportunities while stimulating collaborative research and generating a syllabus for a DH library and information science course to be taught by one or more iSchool faculty in the project. This effort was aimed at achieving "deep" collaboration. DH centers need graduate students with a strong interest in humanities who are also capable of interdisciplinary research and teamwork. One of their goals, as a result, was to develop cross-disciplinary understanding. Each side needed to become familiar with the other's methods and styles. Close coordination of institutional partners is also crucial for successful partnerships among DH centers and iSchools, along with building and maintaining new digital archives and bolstering technology infrastructure.

The need for standards is also a catalyst for community building. The Text Encoding Initiative (TEI) evolved from recognition of common needs to formation of a professional group. Susan Hockey recalls the emergence of a set of principles from a 1987 meeting aimed at creating a standard encoding scheme for electronic texts. Management of the project was placed in the hands of a steering committee with representatives from the Association for Computers and the Humanities (ACH), the Association for Literary and Linguistic Computing (ALLC), and the Association for Computational Linguistics. TEI was designed primarily by scholars who wanted to be as flexible as possible, so any tag could be redefined and tags added when appropriate. Yet, the philosophy in library and information science differed, prioritizing closely followed standards for ease of finding books. At the time, there was also less input from the library community and the term "digital library" was not in wide use ("The History," 12, 15). Since 1994, though, TEI Guidelines have been widely adopted and are now in a fifth version. Incorporated in 2000, the international TEI Consortium provides a sustained platform for communication and collaboration, with annual meetings, resources and training, and special interest groups in traditional professions such as education and libraries, subject areas such as music or linguistics, and materials such as manuscripts, texts, and graphics.

Borrowing a term from Jerome McGann, "new institutional agents" have emerged as well ("Sustainability," 18). HASTAC (the Humanities, Arts, Science, and Technology Alliance and Collaboratory) is a self-generated community that combines a virtual network with grounded conferences. Its alliance with the MacArthur Foundation's Digital Media and Learning initiative facilitated grants for innovative uses of digital technologies and new media, and its scholars forum engages students in community-based exploration of significant topics in the field. Operating from 2008 to 2012, the cyberinfrastructure initiative of Project Bamboo brought together scholars, librarians, information technologists, and computer scientists in order to develop shared technology services and environments supporting scholarship and curation. Three features of interdisciplinarity stood out: partnership, common language, and collaboration. Working groups addressed topics such as education, scholarly networking, tools and content, and shared services. With support from the Mellon Foundation, the community expanded to an international partnership of ten universities that pledged in-kind institutional resources. One of the challenges they faced was the familiar interdisciplinary problem of finding a common vocabulary. As a result of their cooperative effort, many participants reported that improvements in their ability to talk and think together across domains ultimately helped them with cross-campus communications back home as well.

The professionalizing of a field is most apparent in its flagship organizations, a history Hockey traced in detail. To briefly summarize: the journal *Computers and the Humanities* was founded in 1966, and the first in a series of biennial conferences on literary and linguistic computing held at the University of Cambridge in 1970. ALLC was founded in 1973, the journal *Literary and Linguistic Computing* was established by 1986, and in the mid-1970s a new series of conferences was under way in North America as the International Conference on Computing in the Humanities (ICCH). ALLC and ICCH gradually coalesced around literary and linguistic computing, though ICCH attracted a multidisciplinary range of papers on use of computers in teaching writing and in music, art, and archaeology. Founded in 1978, the Association for Computers and the Humanities (ACH) was an outgrowth of this effort, with the aim of involving a wide range of subjects and communities of practice, including literature and language studies, history, and philosophy ("The History," 6–8, 11). The formation of ADHO also fostered greater networking across ACH and ALLC, joined in 2007 by the Canadian-based Society for Digital Humanities/Société pour l'étude des médias interactifs (SDH-SEMI).

The formation of ADHO raises yet another dimension of "making a difference" in interdisciplinary fields. If the mantra in real estate is location, location, location, in Digital Humanities it is infrastructure, infrastructure, infrastructure. Organizational partnership is key to technical and institutional infrastructure, reinforcing the importance of networking. Project Bamboo, for example, has cooperated with other organizations to build a service-oriented architecture across distributed disciplines, centers, repositories, and infrastructure projects. Its partners have included CenterNet, an international network of DH centers, and a new alliance with CHCI and CHAIN (the Coalition of Humanities and Arts Infrastructures and Networks). CHAIN also facilitates international cooperation by pooling experience in creating and operating digital infrastructure in a shared environment. The cyberinfrastructure of tools, technologies, and methodologies needed for Digital Humanities, however, remains inadequate. A

2011 science policy briefing from European Science Foundation, *Research Infrastructures in the Humanities*, defined multiple challenges requiring interdisciplinary co-development across sectors to achieve a robust research ecosystem.

Not unexpectedly, virtual partnerships and collaboration are playing a role in meeting needs in specialized areas. CLARIN, the Common Languages Resources and Technology Infrastructure, is a Pan-European initiative focused on language resources for both linguists and society in general. Resource and service centers are connected via a grid technology that forms a virtually integrated domain overcoming limits of working across platforms. CLARIN and DARIAH joined forces in 2010 to host an international conference on "Supporting the Digital Humanities." DARIAH, the Digital Research Infrastructure for the Arts and Humanities, is a Pan-European cyberinfrastucture that brings together fourteen partners from ten countries. Describing its "communities of practice," Peter Doorne called DARIAH a virtual laboratory parallel to physical institutions such as libraries and archives. DARIAH maintains the system it develops, but individual member states or international organizations are responsible for data.

"Tweet, Loc.Cit."

"Tweet, Loc.Cit." is both a pragmatic solution and a metaphor for the changing landscape of one of the most important mechanisms of professionalizing a field—its forms and protocols of scholarly communication. Mounting requests prompted the MLA in 2012 to issue guidelines for citing tweets though, Scott McLemee recalls, the American Psychological Association had already introduced a format for citing Twitter and Facebook in 2009, and in 2011 the American Medical Association deemed tweets public discourse. Tweets, long-form blogs, websites, and other nontraditional forms of scholarly communication are the focus of increased attention, along with digital versions of traditional journal and book formats. The advantages include speed of appearance, a larger audience, higher rate of citation due to online access, and less likelihood of going "out-of-print." Yet, digital forms of publication face skepticism and even outright opposition in the conventional peer-review system.

The earliest genres of publication in Digital Humanities were familiar scholarly forms of text editions, indexes, concordances, catalogs, and dictionaries (Hockey, "History," 7–10). Since the mid-1990s, Michael Keller reports, new e-genres have appeared (summarized):

- page images of conventional article and book publications that are passive but might might have a cross-searching feature, such as articles available through JSTOR
- digital compendia, anthologies and complete works that may have expanded descriptions, images of sources, and bibliographies, such as the Matthew Parker online library and papers of George Washington in the digital imprint Rotunda of the University of Virginia Press
- "fluid-text" editions such as Rotunda's publication of the Herman Melville novel *Typee*
- new narratives that consist of streams of texts, media objects, software-based models, and hyperlinks to materials and citations
- "lively monographs" that are conventional but have images and hyperlinked citations
- GIS-based compilations and views such as Richard White and colleagues' Spatial History Project, the David Rumsey Map Collection, and Mapping the Republic of Letters
- image bases such as Artstor and AMICA Library.

(Keller, 377)

The first electronic periodical in humanities appeared in 1990 with the launch of the *Journal of Post Modern Culture*. By 2004, Kathleen Carlisle Fountain recalls, the number of e-journals had grown "exponentially" (47). Older journals were also introducing innovative formats. Differences remain, though. The ADHO-sponsored online journal *Digital Humanities Quarterly* (*DHQ*), for example, is more text-heavy than the more experimental *Vectors*. Launched in 2005, *Vectors* is a self-styled journal in "Multimodal Humanities." It does not publish works that could appear in print, and the editors are dedicated to expanding the nature of academic publication via emergent and transitional media. Calling the journal a "test bed for interdisciplinary digital scholarship," McPherson describes the twofold layering of interdisciplinarity in the production process. First, the content is diverse, bringing together scholars from various disciplines for theme-based issues that create a "sustained space" for experiments with multimodal scholarship by pushing beyond the limited disciplinary relationship of "text with picture." Thematic focus makes it possible to "zoom out to several large questions that cut across multiple fields," while still making close comparisons of separate understandings. Discussions exemplify the second form, a "deep interdisciplinary collaboration" that occurs in development teams.

To illustrate the second form, in producing the issue on *Evidence* scholars from literary studies, sociology, art, and performance co-interrogated the status of evidence in their disciplines. They were also paired with designers and programmers in a weeklong summer workshop that has been a space for rethinking the relationship of form to content. In addition, the fusion of scholarly writing with database practices involves peer evaluation and "scholar-to machine collaboration." And, the design team has learned ways to "scaffold" Digital Humanities through new platforms and tools that can be generalized across humanities. Working in collaboration with scholars, designers developed a relational database better suited to the kinds of evidence they were exploring. The work was bottom-up, emerging from conversations about how scholarship might be reimagined in a dynamic digital vernacular. The outcome is not a predetermined tool for delivery. A middleware package, the Dynamic Backend Generator is an authoring tool and intellectual sketchpad that changes the relationship scholars have to their work and digital environments, while enabling multidisciplinary audiences to construct interfaces to serve their own needs and preferences (McPherson, "*Vectors*," 210).

Monographic publishing was slower to respond. However, by 2009 Christine Borgman declared "a seismic shift toward digital publishing." Series dedicated to Digital Humanities also emerged, including the University of Michigan Press's *Digital Humanities@digitalculturebooks*, the University of Illinois Press's *Topics in Digital Humanities*, Ashgate's *Digital Research in the Arts and Humanities*, and Open Book Publishers' *Digital Humanities*. In addition, other presses have profiles in related areas, including MIT, the University of Minnesota, Routledge, NYU, Sage, and Polity. Interdisciplinarity is not necessarily an explicit goal. However, these forums create favorable environments. Anvil Academic is a scholarly publisher of born-digital and born-again-digital research in humanities. It aims to bring editorial and institutional legitimacy to this new form of scholarship. Speaking as president of the Council for Library and Information Resources, Chuck Henry described Anvil's potential to create a new kind of environment for research as "a linked ecology of scholarly expression, data, and tools of analysis." Korey Jackson, Anvil's program coordinator and analyst, says it is too early to predict payoffs. Yet, "the types of project now being evaluated—ranging from granular GIS maps to interactive timelines and other syntheses of large data sets—all share an interdisciplinary approach to their subject matter." They also appeal to wide audiences, while providing "a credible imprimatur for digital work that transcends disciplinary boundaries" (Korey Jackson, e-mail, June 29, 2012).

Thematic research collections, Carole Palmer proposes, constitute another genre of scholarly publication. Palmer likens many of them to a virtual laboratory where specialized source material, tools, and expertise are brought together to aid scholarly work. Networked technology facilitates aggregation and collocation of materials otherwise distributed across institutional locations, disciplines, fields, and media. Palmer highlights two integrative features of collections in the concepts of "contextual mass" and "interdisciplinary platform." The Rossetti Archive, for example, aims to host all of Dante Gabriel Rossetti's texts and pictorial works complemented by contextual materials including other works of the period, letters, biography, secondary works, and bibliography. The Blake Archive also puts texts together with illustrations, illuminated books, and drawings and paintings, as well as clusters of materials based on medium, theme, or history. And, the Victorian London collection *Monuments and Dust* encourages international collaboration and exchange across literature, architecture, painting, journalism, colonialism, modern urban space, and mass culture. The underlying premise is that aggregation will seed interaction by making it possible to discover new visual, textual, and statistical relationships ("Thematic Research Collections").

These collections could not be created without another aspect of interdisciplinarity in Digital Humanities—inter-institutional collaborations with libraries, museums, and publication venues. Developing a content infrastructure, Ronald Laresen emphasizes, also requires collaboration of research and development involving scientists, technologists, and humanists. Over time, the audience for a collection may also become more multidisciplinary. The digital library Perseus, for instance, was originally narrow even though it provided access to a large body of materials in classics including primary Greek texts, translations, images, and lexical tools. As the project grew, it added collections outside classics and a thematic approach. Digital design makes it possible to structure flexible use. The Tibetan and Himalayan Digital Library (THDL) is a hybrid digital library and thematic collection that takes advantage of internal collocation to create varied structures and perspectives. The Environment and Cultural Geography collection, for instance, organizes texts, videos, images, maps, and other types of materials according to space and time, while thematic and special collections are organized by subject attributes. Thematic collections integrate diverse sources in disciplinary units such as art, linguistics, literature, and music. Subtheme collections are independent projects with their own content and goals, nested within thematic collections. A special collection can focus on an individual as well.

Collocation is also advancing a dimension of interdisciplinarity not widely discussed in the past, the capacity to re/mix materials from different areas and repurpose them in new contexts. In a project to produce a CD-ROM for teaching the film *Birth of a Nation*, called Griffith in Context, Strain and Van Hoosier-Carey demonstrate how "architected meaning" emerges from movement beyond narrow parameters of hypertext. Users can select individual pathways in a hypermediated web of juxtapositions and associations that catalyze humanities and social-science methodologies. The technical architecture of the project creates a new interactive relationship between technology and cultural history that aggregating and hyperlinking materials alone could not produce. Users are able to mix them in new ways, and cross-disciplinary association becomes the platform for interpretation through combinations selected from a range of possibilities.

Interdisciplinarity is further implicated in the changing nature of writing and reading, in several ways Burdick et al. have identified. Visualization and multimodal forms are moving beyond older notions of "writing" to the "design" of argument. Orality is also returning to the mainstream of argumentation, in the form of YouTube lectures, podcasts, audio books, and "demo culture." Together, they are propelling a resurgence of voice, extemporaneous speaking, and embodied performances. Authorship is becoming more "multiplicative" as well, involving scholars and technical experts. Authorial identity shifts from individual voice to a "collaborative, collection, and aggregated voice." Moreover, the design of an interface, data structures, and database becomes part of collaborative argumentation (7, 10–12, 36, 56, 89–90). The concept of *authorship* is more complex in digital environments because it entails the composite work of compiling and archiving, editing and curating, and making or adapting tools for searching, indexing, annotating, and collaborating. Web 2.0 elements, authors of the European Science Foundation's report on *Changing Publi-*

cation Cultures in the Humanities also note, make multidisciplinary view-points more possible. A sociologist is unlikely to author a formal review of a book in history, but might contribute sociological expertise on a site that could prompt discussion, collaboration, or borrowings across disciplines.

Presner characterizes his own collaborative project Hypercities as a "generative" model of Digital Humanities 2.0. Hypercities integrates visual, cartographic, and time/space-based narrative strategies in digital constructions of ten world cities. The platform facilitates a "connective tissue" for mapping projects and archival resources across distributed databases held in common by "geo-temporal argument." Developed by a team of scholars, librarians, community partners, and programmers, the platform went through several iterations in a participatory open-source environment. Collections other than historical base maps are stored in curated groupings of media objects and interpretative narrative owned and controlled by their creators, though they can be made public. In the Tehran subproject more than 1,000 media objects including YouTube videos, Twitter feeds, and Flickr photographs were deployed to trace the history of protests in the streets of Tehran and other cities following elections. Original archival collections remain intact but can be nested to create a large project within a single "collection." HyperCities is distinct from Google Earth/Maps because it enables browsing both space and time through integration of "time-layers." Moving from simple aggregation to an integrative platform, it is a new mode of publishing and archiving in a social network for creating, accessing, editing, and sharing content ("Hypercities").

Developments in scholarly communication have also fostered new periodizations of the field. Tara McPherson situates the historical base of *Humanities Computing* in the early work of building tools, infrastructure, standards, and collections. This work continues, but a second category of *Blogging Humanities* emerged from networked media and peer-to-peer writing. A new breed of digital humanists is porting words and monographs of scholarship into networked spaces of conversation and dialogue. Text often remains the lingua franca of expression, and their work is still discounted in the academic reward system. However, it fosters connections and peer-to-peer conversation. A third category of *Multimodal Humanities* is now bringing together tools, databases, networked writing, and peer-to-peer commentary while leveraging the interdisciplinary potential of visual and aural media ("Introduction"). Implications follow for one of the mainstays of publication—editing.

In a fourfold periodization, Johanna Drucker tracked shifts over time. Web 1.0 was characterized by static display and navigation. Web 2.0 afforded greater interactivity within structured sites, and Web 3.0 facilitated collaborative content development by users, aggregation in real time, and on-the-fly analysis. The prospect of Web 4.0 is now unfolding in increased customization of web-based resources and intensified attention to the design of conditions and use (*SpecLab*, 198). The impact of praxes and technologies of new media critical work and scholarly editing, Martha Nell Smith emphasizes, are not just advances. They are necessities that mark a "profound shift in humanities knowledge production." New materialities of editing make it possible to examine documentary evidence once hidden from view, recording and storing feedback in manageable formats of dynamic databases, and manipulating forms in ways not possible in print (307, 316–19). The boundaries separating authors, editors, and technical professions also blur in the process. In the Canterbury Tales Project, Peter Robinson reports, traditional divisions of transcribing, editing, and reading dissolve in mergers of text- and edition-based work (172). Jack Dougherty and Kristen Nawrotzki's book *Writing History in the Digital Age* also illustrates the changing relationship of authors and editors with readers and reviewers, publishers, and libraries and repositories.

One of Dougherty and Nawrotzki's goals in editing a born-digital collection was to find out if new technologies could counter limits of the traditional publication process, including solitary writing, secretive peer review, and slow production. The project began in 2010 and unfolded during an eight-week period in fall of 2011 with open peer review resulting in over 940 online comments on essays selected from a call for ideas, including reviews by four anonymous external experts invited by the University of Michigan Press. A final version appeared in print in 2013, and a free web version is hosted on a server at Trinity College. One of the editors' challenges in this experiment in development editing was performing the traditional role of content expert while encouraging participation, managing public discussion, and serving as website designers and code-writers, human spam-filters and troubleshooters, and guides for authors unfamiliar with WordPress (Nawrotzki and Dougherty; Doughtery, Nawrotzki, Rochez, and Burke).

Doughterty and Nawrotzki's project also documents expanding commitment to open access and participation in scholarly communication. In proposing a set of shared set of values for Digital Humanities, Josh Honn and Geoff Morse combined being *Open & Accessible*, citing public forms ranging from pre- and post-publication peer review of Twitter and blog posts to Creative Commons licensed publications, curated archives, and interactive projects. Written collaboratively in 2013, the "Berne DH Summer School Declaration on Research Ethics in Digital Humanities" is a draft set of guidelines that reiterates commitment to open access software while calling for broad-based inclusion of gender, disabilities, and global access. Burdick et al. further situate Digital Humanities within a broader form of "open-source culture production" that combines approaches and perspectives in multiple ways including collaborative authorship, multiple versioning, more flexible attitudes toward intellectual property and the notion of a peer, as well as multiplying communities (77).

The social nature of editing in open environments results in another form of boundary crossing. As research is being shared increasingly through social media, Geoffrey Rockwell observes, the lines between professional expert and amateur blur in an expanded form of distributed knowing and decentering of authority (151–52). The Electronic Textual Cultures Lab at the University of Victoria, to cite one example, is developing a social edition of *The Devonshire Manuscript*, a verse miscellany dating from the 1530s and '40s. Anyone will be able to adapt, update, and add information in a pooled wiki-style knowledge base, thereby collaborating in the process of building. The current online version offers transcriptions with scholarly apparatus, as well as contextual, textual, and bibliographic material. The final version, to be published by *Medieval and Renaissance Texts and Studies*, will reassert authorial control. Two projects at University College London's Centre for Digital Humanities also model public engagement.

Transcribe Bentham uses crowdsourcing to facilitate transcriptions of the manuscript papers of philosopher and reformer Jeremy Bentham, in a project aimed at creating a new authoritative edition of his collected works. After users submit transcriptions they are checked for textual accuracy and encoding then, if completed satisfactorily, locked to prevent further changes (Causer, 29–31; see also Jones, 92–93). Indicative of the changing affordances of technologies, Melissa Terras recounts, the Bentham Project has developed from a simple web page to an interactive Web 2.0 environment, and from MS Word to TEI-encoded SML texts, and from an inward-looking academic project to an outward-facing community-building exercise. The practice of "post-moderation" in cultural heritage institutions also crosses the boundary of academe and the public. UCL's

QRator Project facilitates co-creation of museum content using mobile devices, social-media software, and an interactive digital labeling system for displaying public comments and information next to actual museum objects (Ross, 37–39). The Social Interpretation (SI) project at the Imperial War Museum also turns museum objects into "social objects" by allowing the public to comment on, collect, and share them through social media channels of their choice.

Experiments are not without risk. However, new platforms continue to be built and older ones enhanced. The University Press Consortium book collections, which are integrated with Project MUSE's electronic journal collections, enable individuals to create their own formats, interact with others, mine the database, and annotate works. Highwire Press, in concert with Stanford University Press, offers web-hosting services and platforms for managing digital content. And, Cengage Learning's platform Artemis is an integrated research environment that will enable users to search across Gale's Digital Humanities collections. After moving the Eighteenth Century and the Nineteenth Century Collections Online into one platform, Gale will make literary resources and criticism searchable through another portal. The publisher also plans to offer collaboration tools. The experiment PressForward also continues to combine scholarly review with open web-based peer-to-peer interactivity. The growth of these and other resources, though, raises the next topic for consideration–learning how to use them effectively and in an interdisciplinary manner. Education is key across all stages of the career life cycle, from the student years to ongoing professional development.

Clustered Links for Chapter 4 in Order of Appearance

Kevin Guthrie comment to the Commission on Cyberinfrastructure for Humanities and Social Sciences, qtd. in John Unsworth, "Cyberinfrastructure for Humanities and Social Sciences," University of Illinois, Chicago. *Microsoft PowerPoint file, Slide 11*, http://people.brandeis.edu/~unsworth/ECAR/index.xml

Alliance of Digital Humanities Organizations (ADHO) http://digitalhumanities.org/

Steve Rodgers, Michael Booth, and Joan Eveline. "The Politics of Disciplinary Advantage." *History of Intellectual Culture* 3, no. 1 (2003). http://www.ucalgary.ca/hic/issues/vol3/6

Digital Humanities Observatory, Ireland: http://dho.ie/

Faulkner and Digital Humanities: hastac.org/opportunities/cfp-faulkner-and-digi
tal-humanities

American Historical Association meeting: http://blog.historians.org/annual-meet
ing/1531/digital-humanities-a-hands-on-workshop

American Historical Association and Modern Language Association meetings: http://
connect.ala.org/node/158885;   http://digitalhumanitiesnow.org/2011/12/edi
tors-choice-digital-humanities-at-the-mla-and-aha-meetings/

Modern Language Association meeting: http://www.mla.org/

Computers and the History of Art (CHArt): http://computersandthehistoryofart.
org/

Network in Canadian History and Environment: http://niche-canada.org/about

The Programming Historian 2: http://programminghistorian.org/

Digital Medievalist: http://www.digitalmedievalist.org/

Judaica Europeana: www.judaica-europeana.eu

iSchools and DH Centers project: http://www.ischooldh.org/

Text Encoding Initiative: http://www.tei-c.org/index.xml

HASTAC: http://hastac.org/

Project Bamboo: http://www.projectbamboo.org/

The Association for Computers and The Humanities: http://www.ach.org/

Coalition of Humanities and Arts Infrastructures and Networks: http://mith.umd.
edu/chain/

European Science Foundation policy briefing on Research Infrastructures in the
Digital Humanities. downloadable at http://www.esf.org/publications/science-
policy-briefings.html

CLARIN: http://www.clarin.eu/external/index.php

DARIAH (Digital Research Infrastructure for the Arts and Humanities. https://
www.dariah.eu/

Scott McLemee. "Tweet, Loc. Cit." *Inside Higher Education*, March 7, 2012. http://
www.insidehighered.com/views/2012/03/07/column-twitter-and-scholarly-
citation

Rotunda, University of Virginia Press: http://rotunda.upress.virginia.edu/index.
php?page_id=About

Christine Borgman. "The Digital Future is Now: A Call to Action for the Humanities." *Digital Humanities Quarterly* 3, no. 4 (2009). http://www.digitalhuman
ities.org/dhq/vol/3/4/000077/000077.html

Anvil   Academic: http://www.insidehighered.com/news/2012/02/13/anvil-aca
demic-aims-provide-platform-digital-scholarship

Ronald L. Larsen. "On the Threshold of Cyberscholarship." *Journal of Electronic
Publishing* 11, no. 1 (2008). http://quod.lib.umich.edu/j/jep/3336451.0011.10
2?view=text;rgn=main

European Science Foundation report on Changing Publication Cultures in the Humanities: downloadable at http://www.esf.org/publications/humanities.html

Todd Presner, "Digital Humanities 2.0: A Report on Knowledge": http://cnx.org/content/m34246/1.1/

Hypercities: http://www.hypercities.com

Honn and Morse's talk on "Digital Humanities": http://acrl.ala.org/dh/2013/03/27/digital-humanities-101/?utm_source=feedburner&utm_medium=feed&utm_campaign=Feed:+DHNowUnfiltered+(DH+Now++»++Unfiltered

"Berne DH Summer School Declaration on Research Ethics in Digital Humanities." https://docs.google.com/document/d/1A4MJ05qS0WhNlLdlozFV3q3Sjc2kum5GQ4lhFoNKcYU/edit#heading=h.fbfb3vwicb5

The Devonshire Manuscript: http://earlymodernpost.wordpress.com/2012/03/04/digital-humanities-the-devonshire-manuscript-and-social-knowledge/

Melissa Terras's full account of the Bentham Project: http://melissaterras.blogspot.com/2010/07/dh2010-plenary-present-not-voting.html

Tim Causer's comment in "Building A Volunteer Community: Results and Findings from *Transcribe Bentham*," *Digital Humanities Quarterly*, 6, 2 (2012). http://www.digitalhumanities.org/dhq/vol/6/2/000125/000125.html

QRator and the Grant Museum: QRator, http://www.ucl.ac.uk/dh-blog/2012/05/17/award-for-qrator-and-the-grant-museum/, http://www.qrator.org/

Social Interpretation project at the Imperial War Museum: http://www.guardian.co.uk/culture-professionals-network/culture-professionals-blog/2012/apr/13/social-interpretation-imperial-war-museum

GALE Cengage Learning: gale.cengage.com

Connexions: http://cnx.org/aboutus

Highwire Press, Stanford: http://chronicle.com/blogs/profhacker/the-printing-press-of-the-digital-environment-a-conversation-with-stanfords-highwire-press/39520

< 5 >

Educating

Providing the foundation for the development of skills of
creative and critical synthesis is one of the most important
learning affordances offered by the university to those whose
learning emerges through their travels across media flows,
among distributed learning sites, and in dialogue with contradictory sources of disciplinary authority.
—Anne Balsamo, *Designing Culture: The Technological Imagination at
Work* (Durham, NC: Duke UP, 2011), 147

The CMS approach is characterized by radical interdisciplinarity: our goal is to encourage students to mix and
match approaches taken from the humanities and the social
sciences in search of answers to driving questions about the
cultural and social impact of media on the world around us.
—"Comparison Across Disciplines," Academic Program Overview of
the Comparative Media Studies Program at MIT," formerly http://
cmsw.mit.edu/about/

**Keywords: context, balance, tractability, relationality, interplay, par-
ticipatory, interplay, remixing, intentionality**

Research centers have been more prominent in the institutional profile of
Digital Humanities than educational programs. In the Blackwell compan-
ions to *Digital Humanities* and *Digital Literary Studies*, Brett Hirsch reports, "pedagogy" and its synonyms appear far less often than "research."A
survey of recent literature also indicates a trend toward "bracketing" that
relegates teaching to an afterthought and even outright exclusion (4–5).

And, in a survey of article titles in *Digital Humanities Quarterly* and abstracts of NEH Digital Humanities Start-Up Grants, Stephen Brier found that "research" appears far more often than "teaching," "learning," "pedagogy," and "classroom" (390–99). This hierarchy of values is not unique to Digital Humanities. Katherine Harris calls teaching "invisible labor" (341), and Brier dubs pedagogy, curriculum development, and scholarship of teaching and learning "the ugly stepchildren of the university" (344). The number of DH courses and programs is increasing. The pattern is uneven, however, and claims need to be weighed against generic indicators of strong programs in interdisciplinary studies. After examining the nature of the DH curriculum, this chaper turns to the particularities of introductory courses, balance of humanities content and technological skills, and role of theoretical and critical analysis. It then defines pedagogies that promote interdisciplinary learning and attendant skills. Taken together, the findings suggest a definition of digital teaching and learning as *interdisciplinary* practice. The chapter closes by comparing strategies in different institutional settings and factoring in continuing professional development.

Curriculum

Digital Humanities is one of many forms of *interdisciplinary studies*, an umbrella term for programs as varied as integrated approaches to general education, interdisciplinary fields, and professional training. Strong programs share several traits: they have a clear intellectual agenda, required core courses, their own full-time faculty, a supportive infrastructure, partnerships with other units, a clear report line to an upper-level administrator, and a voice in policy, budget, staffing, and curriculum (Klein, *Creating Interdisciplinary Campus Cultures*, 105–7). Many programs fall short of these criteria, however, and few offer all undergraduate and graduate degrees. There is no comprehensive collection of Digital Humanities syllabi, but several sources yield a general picture. The CUNY Digital Humanities website has a volunteer sampling, Tanya Clement compiled a list of DH-inflected undergraduate programs from a survey on the Humanist listserv, and the Zotero Digital Humanities Education group also has volunteer samples. Most degrees, Hirsch found, have support from DH research hubs (9), and most Humanities Computing programs, Melissa Terras reported, have been offered at the master's level. The new MA in

Digital Humanities at Carleton College, for instance, is an outgrowth of experience in the Hypertext and Hypermedia Lab, Carleton Immersive Media Studio, and Great Lakes Research Alliance for the Study of Aboriginal Arts and Cultures.

Terras's own study drew on multiple sources, including a conference on the Humanities Computing curriculum, literature review, interviews with ten scholars, and comparison of the MA in applied computing in the humanities at King's College, master's courses in Humanities Computing at the University of Antwerp, Digital Resources in the Humanities at University College London, and Digital Humanities at the University of Illinois at Urbana-Champaign. Although they are located in different units—a center for computing in humanities, an English department, and schools of library and information studies—they bear similarities. Most courses focus on techniques to produce, manipulate, and deliver e-text. A significant amount of groupwork and assessment occurs in projects or take-home exams demonstrating both implementation of technology and the theory behind it. Digital text is a common focus, along with theory, tools, and techniques for markup and analysis. And, reading lists are similar ("Disciplined").

Like other interdisciplinary fields, Digital Humanities exhibits a range of offerings (see fig. 2), from specialized courses and degrees to digitally inflected approaches that do not concentrate on DH but expand the presence of new technologies and media across the curriculum. Spiro's analysis of 134 syllabi in the Zotero DH Education group collection provides an overview of courses taught after 2005. They were all written in English, and most were from the United States, although the collection includes some submissions from Canada, Great Britain, New Zealand, and Belgium. Undergraduate courses outnumbered graduate ones (sixty-six versus fifty-one, though in eight cases appearing at both levels and in nine cases unclear). English was the most frequently represented discipline (thirty-seven versus twenty-two in history, with a separate category for rhetoric and composition tallying four). The areas typically categorized as *interdisciplinary* included media studies (twenty-one), Digital Humanities (sixteen), interdisciplinary studies (fifteen), and visual studies (three). In addition, submissions came from library and information science (seven), computer science (four), and communication (two), as well as the disciplines of anthropology (two) and philosophy (one). At the time of Spiro's analysis the collection did not have entries from classics, linguistics, and languages, though other reports document increased attention to digital technologies in related classrooms. Spiro's SEASR ngram captures the key-word landscape of syllabi.

Looking more deeply at content, Spiro analyzed the reading lists of fifty-one courses. The most frequently reported assignment is the Blackwell *Companion to Digital Humanities*. Many courses focus on text, although other forms of media include video, audio, images, games, and maps. The most common defining concepts include *data* and *database*, *openness* and *copyright*, *network*, and *interaction*. Arriving at preliminary conclusions from this "Big Tent" collection, Spiro highlights several shared features. The courses tend to link theory and practice, underscoring the orientation toward methodological interdisciplinarity observed in earlier chapters. They tend to produce projects and are collaborative in nature, also affirming movement away from the traditional lone-scholar model of humanities research. And, they engage the topic of social media as well as reflections on contemporary topics such as copyright. (Spiro's results and the ngram are available in a PowerPoint presentation for the June 2011 Digital Humanities conference "Knowing and Doing: Understanding the Digital Humanities Curriculum.")

Representative examples in three areas sketch an even fuller picture of the interdisciplinary contours of DH curricula and teaching.

Introductory Courses

Introductory gateway courses are crucial, because they are the moments when a field and its core content and methods are defined. Without a clear understanding of the field and relationship between courses in a program, students and even faculty lack a sense of its disciplinary and interdisciplinary contours. Introductions to DH appear across a broad range of contexts, from general education and traditional disciplines to programs training DH professionals. Generally speaking, introductory courses have a multidisciplinary tendency, because they must provide an overview of content, methods, and tools. The balance and focus vary, though, depending on curricular goals, student population, and local infrastructure.

The MA/MSc degree in Digital Humanities at University College London (UCL) illustrates a strong technical-professional mandate. Housed within UCL's Department of Information Studies, the MA/MSc prepares

Fig. 2. Lisa Spiro's Word Cloud of Digital Humanities syllabi

students for work as project managers, information specialists, or researchers in the cultural and heritage industry and in publishing and digital environments that require constructing computational systems. All students take five modules during the first two of three terms: Digital Resources in the Humanities, Internet Technologies, Introduction to Programming and Database Querying, Server Programming and Structured Data, and XML. The program culminates in a dissertation and work placement at a London-area library, archive, or museum. The claim to being "truly interdisciplinary" is trifold. First, teaching units are linked structurally with computer sciences and modules in arts and humanities, social and historical sciences, engineering sciences, and the Bartlett Faculty of the Built Environment. Second, the gateway Digital Resources course aims to "familiarize" students with computing technologies and applications in humanities research and teaching, preparing them to make "informed" decisions about design, management, and use of resources. Third, foundational knowledge and decision-making capacity are integrated into understanding how access, manipulation, and analysis of resources can benefit both humanities and the cultural and heritage sector.

In contrast to the full degree program at UCL, David Michelson's undergraduate "Introduction to Digital Humanities" was housed in a history department at the University of Alabama. The course covered three areas: definition of Digital Humanities, readings and guest visits with project directors, and development of a digital element in individual projects. The focus was primarily on the relationship of DH research to the disciplines of history and literature, although the course also considered questions of interest to humanities in general and the limits and constraints of technology. This combination is typical in introductory courses, bringing together preliminary definition with core readings and/or guests then culminating in projects that allow students to situate digital technologies and new media within their own interests. The choice of readings and guests, as well as the range of projects, usually reflects the disciplinary or professional setting of the course. Even in the same discipline, though, focus may vary.

In English, for example, John Unsworth's English-listed course on Digital Humanities at Brandeis University introduced students to the history and range of DH with a focus on literacy studies. Seated at the intersection of humanities and information technology, the course covered extensible markup language, text mining, and social media, along with hands-on work with tools. In contrast, Alexander Huang's English seminar on Digital Humanities featured themes such as race, gender, access, disability, and diversity, as well as visual and print cultures, canon formation, and reading strategies. In further contrast, Adeline Koh's "Introduction to Digital Humanities" combined introduction to basic concepts and debates in the field with hands-on lab work on a specific project, Digitizing Chinese Englishmen, and participation in a distributed online MOOC on "The Future of Higher Education" (Adeline Koh, e-mail, July 12, 2013). My own graduate seminar in DH moved from initial definitions to an overview of implications in the three major areas of the local department: literary and cultural studies, composition and rhetoric, and (film and) media studies. Because the majority of students did not have advanced technical skills, their final work was more thematic but with a required digital component and short "lightning talk" accompanied by a handout.

Given the proliferation of digital technologies and new media, it is not surprising to find a growing presence in general and liberal education. When John Theibault taught "Introduction to Digital Humanities" at Stockton College, it was offered in the undergraduate General Arts and Humanities curriculum. Accessible publicly online for a limited time, the course introduced students to ways the computer and Internet are transforming research and teaching in disciplines such as literature, history, art, and music history. Theibault incorporated computer methods and digital media into the study of traditional topics, while also applying humanities methods to studying products made possible by new media. Theibault's sense that the field is strongly connected to project-based work was evident in the combination of exemplary projects and students' own final work. It is not unusual to find similar readings across contexts, especially the Blackwell *Companion to Digital Humanities* and more recently Matthew Gold's *Debates in Digital Humanities*. From there, however, lists are tailored to context. Theibault's required readings, for example, included the Blackwell *Companion to Digital Humanities* and Dan Cohen and Roy Rosenzweig's *Digital History*. In an English department, Matthew Kirschenbaum's essay "What is Digital Humanities and What's it Doing in English Departments?" is more likely to be assigned and chapters from the *Companion to Digital Literary Studies*.

Like DH research centers, curricula also have institutional signatures. Loyola University Chicago's three-credit "Introduction to Digital Humanities Research" prepares students for careers in conjunction with local expertise in textual studies. The targeted areas are archiving, digitizing, editing, and analyzing, as well as interface and web design, and presentation skills. The course, though, also takes up broad social and ethical questions surrounding media and contemporary culture. In contrast, the Media and Cultural Studies major at Macalester College is aligned with a local commitment to internationalism, multiculturalism, and community service with a focus on history and critique. The introductory course on "Texts and Power" establishes a history of cultural analysis that frames continuing debates in media studies. In addition to other courses and a capstone seminar centered on an independent project, the major requires one advanced course in media/cultural theory, two courses on race or gender/sexuality and the media, one in analyzing or making media, and two approved electives in media studies.

The Balance of Humanities Content and Technological Skills

All interdisciplinary fields grapple with the challenge of achieving a balance of their disciplinary parts. In Digital Humanities, balance is compounded by the added involvement of occupational professions, though the most contentious point of debate is the proper weight of technology and humanities content. William Turkel expressed dismay when meeting people who describe themselves as digital humanists but do not do programming or master some of the technologies. On the opposite side of the debate, others worry about depth of content knowledge. In a 1986 article based on a workshop about teaching computers and humanities, Susan Hockey reported no consensus on whether programming should be taught ("Workshop," 228), although a search of the word *undergraduate* in the journal *Literary and Linguistic Computing* revealed a prevalent view that undergraduate curricula are skill based rather than research based (Clement, 371). Here again, context matters.

Theibault's "Introduction" did not require special programming skills, and Michelson's "Introduction" did not stipulate prior technical literacy because it is open to students at all levels. In contrast, the "Proseminar in the Digital Humanities" in the School of Information at UC Berkeley expects students to contribute to designing, analyzing, and evaluating a new software tool. Yet, while information- and computer-science students are expected to bring experience or backgrounds in designated technical areas, humanities students are only expected to "have an open mind and a passion to learn about new techniques." The MA in Humanities Comput-ing at the University of Alberta, faculty members Rockwell and Sinclair recall, was also designed with the realization that it would include a broad range of students from humanities, social sciences, and arts. Students need to deepen expertise in particular domains and be trained in technical skills as soon as possible. But, the program avoids limiting them to particular software packages and methodologies. It emphasizes, instead, understand-ing fundamental techniques and broad implications of technologies for manipulating digital images. In addition, students have the option of de-veloping an interdepartmental specialization and pursuing a joint MA/MLIS that confers degrees in both academic arts and professional library and information science ("Acculturation," 191–92).

Because it is preparing students for professional careers in academic settings, cultural institutions, and web-based professions, UCL's MA/MSc program places a high priority on technical capacity. Yet, it also enrolls students with differing backgrounds: those in humanities needing to ac-quire skills in digital technologies, and those with technical backgrounds needing to learn about scholarly methods. Comparably, the MA in Digital Humanities at Loyola University Chicago has two converging tracks: one for students with a background in computer science and the other for students from humanities. Everyone takes six courses in common, but in order to achieve balance students in the humanities track must enroll in an "Introduction to Computing" course, with hands-on experience in basic coding, and do a practical computing project or a research paper related to the history and contexts of computing. For their part, students in the computing track take an approved graduate-level course in literature or another humanities discipline pertinent to their particular background and needs. To illustrate, a student in the Computer Science track working toward a career in libraries might take History 482: "Archives and Records Management." A student preparing to work in communications might take English 415: "Media and Society" instead.

Like UCL, the collaborative master's in Digital Humanities at Carlton University in Canada also takes advantage of its location for practicum components of the degree. At Carlton, students can enhance their exist-ing degree programs in both disciplines (anthropology, art history, English language and literature, history, philosophy, and sociology) and in inter-disciplinary areas (applied linguistic and discourse studies, film studies, French and Francophone studies, music and culture, public history, and

Canadian studies). Regardless of background, they undertake a piece of original research, while engaging with students and faculty from across the university. A practicum component allows them to take advantage of nearby public and private-sector organizations engaged in digital media production, game development, digital start-ups, the entertainment industry, and digitization projects in local libraries, archives, and museums.

Even with differing balances of technology and content, faculty in all contexts are mindful of the danger that technology becomes an end rather than a means. Students also need knowledge of humanities methodology and vocabulary. Only then, Joshua Sternfeld advises, is it possible "to preserve or create contextual layers." Advanced subject knowledge at the graduate level may not be possible, but students need to be trained in basic practices and terminology. Moreover, they need to know that every decision—whether about formal design elements or which information to include—involves an act of interpretation. Recalling a course on digital historiography that was taught twice at UCLA, on "History, Media, and Technology," Sternfeld reports the solution to the challenge of a diversified student audience was to limit historic thematic material in order explore the methodological nature of historiography in greater depth. Representations were narrowed to two periods: the Holocaust and the Cold War, though the framework could be adapted to any period or region with a body of digital or new media work (268, 270–71, 279–80).

Others weighed the question of balance at an online forum on "The Promise of Digital History." Amy Murrell Taylor contends the most important skill in teaching students to do digital history is "thinking in bold and creative ways about how the technology can serve the interests of history." Dan Cohen reports he does not even begin with technical skills. Instead, he prods students to ask questions about overall intent, the audience, ways to tailor a website or digital tool to their needs and expectations, and the genre of a digital resource such as an archive, a learning module, or a collaborative space. Students also need to consider what else has been done with respect to a particular project. Technical literacy matters, especially at an advanced level. Yet, a comprehensive vision of what a student or a practicing historian is trying to accomplish also matters. Details about web design, appropriate technologies, and other concerns follow from this initial framework. Sternfeld's observations coupled with insights from the Digital History online forum underscore Mahony and Pierazzo's caveat: "Skills training is not research training" (224). A more comprehensive orchestration of the relationship of technology, content, and critical thinking is needed.

The plan for a program that was never offered posits a metaphor for the means-end relationship. The defining image of interdisciplinarity in the proposed master's in Digital Humanities at the University of Virginia (UVA) was tractability, achieved through a dialogue of content and technological competence. Concentration Electives would have insured in-depth coursework in a humanities subject, making content "tractable" to computational methods. A student with a background and interests in medieval literature, for example, might select electives in medieval literature, history, and linguistics, then intern with a project in medieval studies and design a thesis that applied Humanities Computing tools and techniques to a problem in a particular text. Reflecting on why the course was not offered, John Unsworth reports the proposed model did not conflict with library science, journalism, and communication programs because UVA lacked such units. Many worthy projects also existed at Virginia, but more in parallel than with the coalescing force that led to a degree program at King's College (Unsworth and Tupman, 235).

Theoretical and Critical Analysis

One of the most frequent words in descriptions of Digital Humanities programs is *application* of computing to materials and problems of humanities, affirming the prominence of *Methodological Interdisciplinarity*. Yet, *Theoretical* and *Critical Interdisciplinarity* also play important roles in two ways: epistemological reflection on the nature of technology and critique of its impact in the mode of cultural studies.

The word *application* implies instrumentality but, echoing the discussion of theory in chapter 1, the relationship is not a dichotomy. It is important to learn to make things, James Gottlieb acknowledges, but coding in and of itself should not substitute for understanding how projects are to be structured, built in order to share code and data with other projects, and constructed in ways others find compelling and influential. The MA program at King's College emphasizes the capacity "to think with and against the computer," not use it merely as a tool. The epistemological question of how we know what we know is developed throughout the program as a prompt for critical thinking about "combining" divergent perspectives of computing and humanities. Reflection on both the capacities and limits of tools also bridges formal methods and techniques and the implications of applying them to source materials and problems of humanities. The PhD program, which focuses on a research problem in the primary discipline of a student's bachelor's degree, considers methodological, second-order knowledge that is discovered or created in the process of modeling a problem computationally.

Although a PhD is rare in this field, several lessons from King's College London's doctorate have generic value. In order to prepare students for handling more advanced technical needs, the Department of Digital Humanities offers technical courses in formats ranging from one-day immersion training to a twenty-credit master's module and a weeklong course (Mahony and Pierazzo, 218–22). Recalling the experience of creating the degree program, Willard McCarty reports the newness and "high interdisciplinary" nature of the program meant students needed significant help in developing their proposals before making formal application. Because the British PhD is more research-based than its North American counterparts, McCarty and his colleagues also concluded they needed to introduce formal instruction in research skills the first year, although by design they have continued to allow for a range of instrumental uses of existing tools in speculative or theoretical projects ("The PhD"). In programs claiming to be "interdisciplinary," explicit attention must also be paid to integrative process. Lack of explicit definitions and guidelines has been a longstanding weakness of individualized programs, especially, which often turn out to be more multidisciplinary or focused on the disciplinary specialization of a student's advisor.

Other programs combine technological skills with cultural studies and critique. "Re-envisioning Diasporas" was a collaborative seminar between Swarthmore College and Ashesi University in Ghana. The primary themes included globalization, nationality, and the nature of identity in a diaspora. Students examined experiences of communities separated from their homelands and ways they are represented through historical, visual, aural, and literary sources from Turkey, Latin America, and West Africa. In the process, they also gained skills of using Skype for cross-cultural communication and technological tools of production and editing. In a different context, Katherine Harris conceptualizes DH as a way of bridging past and contemporary cultures. In studying 19th-century British literature, her students explore gaming as a way of discussing the technological upheaval of the printing press in the early 1900s. They use tools not only to assess the 19th century but also create content that serves as a reflexive critique of the use of Twitter, Moodle, ClassSpot, and technology-enhanced teaching facilities (postings to "Day of Digital Humanities," 2009 and 2010).

Georgia Institute of Technology's School of Literature, Communication and Culture (LCC) exhibits a different balance of technical and cultural study. The school is the result of a bold interdisciplinary restructuring of an English Department with emphasis on cultural studies of science and technology. LCC offers a BS in science, technology and culture and a BS in computational media, an MS in digital media, an MS in human-computer interaction (HCI), and a PhD in digital media. The chair of LCC, Kenneth Knoespel, described digital media as a "common ground on which humanities scholars can use their special skills in interpretation, critical theory, close readings, and cultural studies to enhance and codirect projects with their colleagues in the sciences, engineering, and social sciences" (qtd. in Hayles, *How We Think*, 45). The master's in human-computer interaction illustrates how components are integrated. It is offered collaboratively by three Schools: Interactive Computing, LCC, and Psychology. A combination of fixed and flexible coursework in a studio- and seminar-based curriculum places design within technical, cultural, aesthetic, and historical contexts. In addition to a common core, summer internship, and a master's project, students take courses in their specializations (e.g., computing, digital media, or psychology), and electives (e.g., architecture, industrial design, cognitive science, computing, management, or policy studies). Design is configured as both a creative and an intellectual challenge. The keyword of interdisciplinarity in the program is *interplay*: between technology and culture and between critical analyses and design.

Pedagogy and Learning

"The term 'digital pedagogy,'" Aaron Santesso contends, "has now achieved the same status as 'interdisciplinarity' or 'entrepreneurial scholarship.' We express enthusiasm about it publicly, while privately confessing that we don't exactly know how to do it." Despite uncertainty, though, descriptions abound. Steven Mintz's periodization of stages of engagement in the discipline of history provides an overview of the changes that are occurring. Stage 1.0 consisted of communication and course-management tools, such as e-mail, online syllabi, Web-CT, and Blackboard, supplemented by websites such as History Matters, Lincoln/Net, and his own Digital History site. They provided a rich storehouse of documents, music, historic images, and film clips. Stage 2.0 was marked by hands-on inquiry- and problem-based projects designed to let students actually "do" history. Using Richard B. Latner's Crisis at Fort Sumter, for instance, they could read information available to President Lincoln at the time of his election and compare decisions they make with decisions he made at critical junctures in his presidency. In the current Stage 3.0, active learning, collaboration, and enhanced interaction are being emphasized in the digital landscape of wikis, blogs, mash-ups, podcasts, tags, and social networking. Stage 4.0 lies on the horizon but is foreshadowed by three-dimensional virtual-reality environments that allow students to navigate and annotate lost historical settings, such as the 1893 World's Columbian Exposition in Chicago.

Cathy Davidson suggests that new modes of learning might be called Learning 2.0 and, along with David Theo Goldberg, articulates ten principles for redesigning learning institutions in the digital age (summarized):

(1) *Self-learning* through browsing and scanning occurs when working with multiple sources of knowledge and information.

(2) *Horizontal structures* have moved away from top-down instruction to collaborative learners capable of multitasking and working together on projects.

(3) *The move from presumed authority to collective credibility* shifts traditional reliance on authorities or certified experts to collaborative and interdisciplinary learning.

(4) *De-centered pedagogy* encourages collaborative knowledge-making and collective pedagogy based on collective checking, inquisitive skepticism, and group assessment.

(5) *Networked learning* shifts from competitive to cooperative forms in a vision of the social that stresses cooperation, interactivity, mutual benefit, and social engagement.

(6) *Open-source education* moves from copyright-protected publications to networked learning in an "open source" culture.

(7) *Learning as connectivity and interactivity* reinforces networking through file sharing, data sharing, and seamless communication.

(8) *Lifelong learning* acknowledges the speed of change in a digital world

that requires individuals to keep learning anew, face novel conditions, and adapt at a record pace.

(9) *The conception of learning institutions as mobilizing networks* shifts from learning as a bundle of rules, regulations, and norms governing actions within a structure to networks that mobilize flexibility, interactivity, and outcomes.

(10) *Flexible scalability and simulation* means being open to various scales of learning possibilities, from the small and local to wide and far-reaching constituencies.

(Davidson and Goldberg, 26)

Although it is not named specifically, interdisciplinarity is implicated throughout this list. (2) *Horizontal structures* flatten older boundaries, facilitating integrative learning while also refiguring the teacher-student relationship to broaden expertise. (5) *Networked learning* stresses cooperation, interactivity, mutual benefit, and social engagement. (7) *Learning as connectivity and interactivity* reinforces networking through file-sharing, data sharing, and seamless communication. (8) *Lifelong learning* acknowledges the speed of change in a digital world that requires individuals to continue grappling with novel conditions and adapt quickly. (9) *The conception of learning institutions as mobilizing networks* shifts from learning as a set of rules, regulations, and norms within a structure to networks that mobilize flexibility, interactivity, outcomes, and, we can add, respond more quickly to emergent fields. (10) *Flexible scalability and simulation* means being open to multiple scales of learning possibilities, from the small and local to wide and far-reaching constituencies.

Digital and interdisciplinary learning share other traits as well. They are both active and dynamic. Group work and projects are common and, echoing the constructivist theory of learning, students build new knowledge through exploration and the actual "doing" of a subject rather than passive receipt of predetermined meaning. Innovative pedagogies are common as well, including collaborative-, inquiry-, discovery-, and problem-based learning. And, a shift from "teaching-" to "learner-centered" classrooms occurs as the traditional model of telling, delivering, directing, and being a "sage on the stage" is expanded in the roles of a mentor, mediator, facilitator, coach, and guide (Klein, "Introduction," 13–15). Davidson cites the example of Mobile Musical Networks, a course at Princeton University led by two professors from music composition and computer science. They worked with students to co-develop networked portable musical laptops so musicians could co-compose, improvise, perform online simultaneously, and customize laptop instruments together. As they rethought the common problem of time tag in musical composition and in engineering audio transmission, the hierarchies placing science over art and teacher over student flattened, performance and writing code combined, and thinking and doing merged ("Humanities and Technology," 209, 214–15).

The prominence of project-based learning underscores the active nature of Digital Humanities. The definition of *project* in the syllabi that Spiro examined is wide, including a research paper, video, digital history resource, collaborative multimedia, and grant proposal (69). In addition, many courses involve hands-on learning, leading discussion, and peer review. Collaboration was also an explicit learning outcome in roughly fifteen courses, and many courses required blogging. Sternfeld's account of UCLA's course on "History, Media, and Technology" affirms this variety, with final projects ranging from documentaries, geospatial visualizations, and a virtual museum exhibition to children's literature, board games, and film (275). In the undergraduate DH minor at UCLA students work in teams doing research with real-world applications, using tools and methodologies such as 3-D visualization, data mining, network analysis, and digital mapping. Students in the MA program at Loyola University Chicago also engage in hands-on training in workshop- or seminar-based classes, gaining skills of text editing and text encoding, e-publishing and platforms, programming, interface design, project management, and archive construction. Moreover, collaborative learning is encouraged at every stage.

The opportunities digital environments afford, Burdick et al. emphasize, also expand what qualifies as knowledge and methods for producing it in student assignments: "This implies that the 8-page essay and the 25-page research paper will have to make room for the game design, the multiplayer narrative, the video mash-up, the online exhibit and other new forms and formats as pedagogical exercises" (24). Stefan Sinclair's graduate seminar combined reflective weekly blog entries (30 percent of grade); individual presentations using a digital technology (15 percent); individual mini project write-ups of efforts to digitize, prepare, and analyze a textual corpus (15 percent); a group project with a significant digital component (30 percent); and individual seminar participation (10 percent). Mark L. Sample also integrates public writing into his classes in lieu of traditional essays (404–5). Trevor Owens treats blogging as a genre of public writing with greater visibility than traditional essays (409). And, in a unique collaboration centered on the poetry of Walt Whitman, Matthew Gold and Jim Groom participated in a four-university experiment in creating "loosely networking learning spaces." This approach, they found, reimagines possibilities for working on related projects in separate places through an "open and porous learning ecosystem" (406–7).

In addition, interdisciplinary studies and Digital Humanities cultivate similar skills. The fundamental learning actions in Clarke and Agne's account of *Interdisciplinary High School Teaching* are asking questions and constructing answers in a process that entails grappling with uncertainty, working with multiple criteria, and arriving at nuanced judgments and interpretations. In college, Klein and Newell highlight exploration and question posing, experiential learning, decision making and problem solving, comparing and contrasting different perspectives, then synthesizing them (407–8). Teachers also report evidence of increased motivation and ability to deal with complex issues, a more reflective stance, greater creativity, and enhanced critical thinking. At higher levels, students become more reflexive about the nature of disciplines. And, they are able to locate and to work with pertinent information, to compare and to contrast different methods and approaches, to clarify how differences and similarities relate to a task, to discern patterns and connection, and to create an integrative framework and holistic understanding of a theme, question, or problem.

Digital Humanities places a greater burden on learning how to use tools. However, Wosh, Hajo, and Katz contend, students must also master the core skill sets of relevant knowledge domains. In NYU's Archives and Public History Program that meant an interdisciplinary combination of historiographical content, museological approaches, and information theory (81). Although contexts vary, DH courses typically combine an introduction to the field with particular tools and methods—whether text editing or visual presentation—in order to work in a designated area—whether history or performance art. Since answers to questions and solutions to problems are typically dependent on context, off-the-shelf approaches are insufficient. Some DH courses also include training in team skills. "Digital thinking," Davidson exhorts, "is a mode of thinking together."

Taken together, the characteristics that have been identified produce a set of outcomes in DH teaching and learning as *interdisciplinary* practice:

- *technical competence*: to use pertinent tools and programming languages, to write code as needed, and to engage with data, databases, and platforms
- *navigation*: to identify and use relevant sources of knowledge and information from multiple disciplinary, professional, or interdisciplinary sources as well as textual, visual, and aural modalities
- *evaluation*: to weigh the relevance and adaptability of multiple contents, tools, methods, modes of presentation, and interpretive approaches
- *integration and synthesis*: to achieve a working balance of technological and humanistic components, and to create a new design, analysis, or interpretation that addresses a complex question, problem, topic, or theme
- *critique*: to employ higher-order critical thinking skills and conduct critical analysis of media content, the impact of new technologies, and the design process
- *collaboration*: to work in teams, involve consultants when needed, manage projects, and negotiate institutional resources, infrastructure, and sustainability.

These are not separate items on a checklist. In teaching Digital Humanities in an English department, Jentery Sayers found that students needed to be simultaneously *strict* (in text encoding) and *flexible* (in project development), *abstract* (in creating data elements or categories for data modeling) and *concrete* (in data gathering), *technical* (in computation) and *critical* (in literary and cultural studies). In his graduate seminar on digital literary studies, the focus was multimodal scholarly communication. The course blended multiple media (maps, video, audio, graphs, code, images, and text) with varied modes of attention (close listening, distant reading, distraction, computer vision, and repeated watching). Students also combined knowing and doing when responding to prompts for multimodal method exercises.

Much has been written about the learning style of the *born digital* generation, a term for youth born after 1987. They were the first generation, Balsamo recalls, to grow up in a world of portable computers, networked communications, and creative graphics applications. By the time they were reaching school age they were experiencing daily life as a scene of constant shifts among networked contexts and performing creative synthesis in data mining, remixing, and modding. Moreover, they were learning outside of school, and as "just-in-time learners" finding something by mining their digital and social networks. In the process, they cross knowledge communities, synthesizing from disparate sources (138–41). Rob Clark, dean of the Hajim School of Engineering and Applied Science at the University of Rochester, describes today's college students as "less interested in boundaries between disciplines." Davidson concurs in describing the mobilizing features of interdisciplinarity in HASTAC as "revaluing, replaying, and remixing across, between, and among opposite areas." Today's youth do not intuitively distinguish between "art" and "science" in everyday and information learning. Someone might be writing code for a multiplayer game or for a better interface on a MySpace page then in the next moment design a new avatar for Second Life ("Humanities 2.0," 214).

Optimism, however, is checked by limits. Wosh, Hajo, and Katz found the assumption that a new generation of "digital natives" has superior technological skills was not borne out in survey data for restructuring NYU's Archives and Public History Program. Students lacked familiarity with digitization methods, standards, and basic terms such as *metadata*, and their experience with social-networking tools was uneven (82–83). They need to know, Balsamo adds, how to critique the information flows they remix when working with multiple modalities, networked and physical spaces, and open and collaborative environments (139–57). In his book on *Teaching History in the Digital Age*, T. Mills Kelly recounts the cautionary tale of a student who "fixed" newsreel footage of the Nuremberg trials. He removed most of the original triumphalist music and substituted new audio, including the famed bass notes from the movie *Jaws* and parts of Mozart's *Requiem*. After discussing why the original source was more appropriate, Kelly reports, as much as half the class still sided with the student's argument that his mash-up was "better." That said, Kelly urges, it is important to meet students where they are at while teaching them how to use sources critically (2–3, 51).

Recalling Davidson and Goldberg's principles for redesigning learning institutions, *Self-learning* through browsing and scanning is easier today because of powerful tools for locating knowledge and information. *Open-source education* is making a wider range of materials and interpretations accessible on a global scale, and *the move from presumed authority collective credibility* has broadened the notion of expertise. Yet, Jill Vickers cautions, new tools for navigating and collaborating reinforce the need for guidelines to determine what constitutes reliable knowledge in interdisciplinary work. Ease of access does not guarantee quality of use ("Diversity"). Moreover, even the best of "federated" search engines, tailored thesauri, RSS feeds, adaptive filters, spiders, and tools for sharing do not automate the process of integration.

Strategies

Weighing the importance of institutional structures for the future of Digital Humanities, Katherine Hayles identified two strategies: assimilation and distinction:

> Assimilation extends existing scholarship into the digital realm; it offers more affordances than print for access, queries, and dissemination; it often adopts an attitude of reassurance rather than confrontation. Distinction, by contrast, emphasizes new methodologies, new kinds of research questions, and the emergence of entirely new fields.
> (Hayles, *How We Think*, 46)

The King's College Department of Digital Humanities (formerly the Center for Computing in the Humanities [CCH]) illustrates the strategy of assimilation. CCH evolved from an undergraduate teaching major into a research unit and graduate degrees. Hayles attributes its success to embedding collaborative projects within historically oriented humanities research. The center also has its own robust funding profile, so does not compete with traditional units for financial support. In contrast, the School of Literature, Culture, and Communication (LCC) at the Georgia Institute of Technology employs a strategy of distinction anchored in preparing students for careers in media research in the academy and industry. LCC also operates in a technical institution with strong engineering and computer science departments. And, digital media is viewed as a separate field rather than an integral part of humanities research. Neither strategy, Hayles cautions, should be considered superior to the other without considering specificities of local context. Assimilation and distinction are two ends of a spectrum. Hybrid programs also exist: including the program in electronic writing at Brown University; Design Lab at the University of Wisconsin-Madison; Virginia Commonwealth University's PhD program in media, art, and text; the Maryland Institute for Technology in the Humanities at the University of Maryland; and the Institute for Advanced Technology in the Humanities at the University of Virginia (*How We Think*, 46–53).

Institutional niche also plays a role in shaping strategies. The advance of Digital Humanities in liberal-arts institutions, Bryan Alexander and Rebecca Frost Davis (2012) report, has been "uneven" and "partial." DH is usually taught within disciplines, although it is part of a humanities program at the University of Puget Sound. Smaller institutions typically lack the social capital and infrastructure needed to mount and sustain DH centers that anchor community building, expertise, advocacy, and team-based projects. DH centers have formed in liberal-arts settings, though, including the Digital Scholarship Lab of the University of Richmond, the Digital Humanities Initiative of Hamilton College, and the Center for Digital Learning and Research at Occidental College. When centers emerge in this sector of higher education the liberal-arts signature is evident. At Hamilton and Occidental, for example, there is a strong pedagogical focus. Liberal-arts institutions, Alexander and Davis also find, highlight the effectiveness of "unbundled" practices and integration into existing structures that centralize support for computing and information access.

To illustrate: at Wheaton College, Willamette University, Lewis and Clark College, Occidental, and Puget Sound the library is that structure. All students in DH courses, Alexander and Davis also remind us, will not become "digital humanists." The value of the field for their careers and civic engagement is grounded in the learning values of liberal arts. Borrowing a term from software development, they suggest we may be "witnessing a fork in the digital humanities development path": "Liberal arts campuses have taken the digital humanities source code and built a different application with it than their research university peers are currently constructing" (383). Instead of research and products, they emphasize teaching and learning. At the same time inter-institutional projects provide research support, evidenced by Swarthmore College's collaboration with the University of Pennsylvania on the Early Novels Database project. William Pannapacker also notes other areas for collaboration including curricular innovation, regional networking, resource sharing, professional development, collaborative projects, and enlarging the concept of "digital humanities" to "digital liberal arts."

The absence of a tradition of Digital Humanities requires other strategies. When Lazslo Hunyadi and his colleagues tried to establish DH at the University of Debrecen in Hungary, they learned how difficult that can be without an established history in a country, recognition as a discipline, and formal accreditation. Moreover, they had to counter suspicion they were doing information science, not humanities-oriented teaching and research integrated with information technology. Individuals were teaching subjects with some applied computational methodology. However, collaboration and professional relationships were lacking. After weighing options, Lazslo and his colleagues decided to establish a virtual Center for Digital Humanities relying on existing teaching positions with established departments, while also offering a service running courses in Humanities Computing. They selected two specializations of broad interest for the MA in Digital Humanities: cultural heritage preservation and language technology. Students can enter the MA program with an undergraduate degree in modern or classical languages and literatures, or in history and ethnology. Once enrolled, they encounter disciplines spanning classical humanities, information science, music, architecture, and sciences ("Collaboration").

Even though lack of a center creates a disadvantage, with no central place for networking, Wosh, Hajo, and Katz found that a curricular project has the side benefit of reaching out to identify "kindred souls" and similar projects. For NYU's Archives and Public History Program that meant connecting with other humanities departments and the Information Technology Service. They were able to leverage the history department's experience in archival management and public history. Then, when a professional development grant from the National Historical Publications and Records Committee ended, the library started a Humanities Computing interest group. The radical stance on interdisciplinarity demands nothing short of transformation. Yet, Saklofske, Clements, and Cunningham advise, change might be accomplished more easily if presented as "an evolutionary, rather than revolutionary, process." They suggest starting small, gaining momentum through collaborative activities, resource building, integrating DH into existing courses, modifying existing program requirements, and other opportunities for modeling cross-disciplinary conversations. Digital Humanities, they contend, is not a discipline or end in itself. It is a means of scholarship and pedagogy (323–29).

The local political economy of a campus may also require adjusting strategies. When Ryan Cordell assumed a new position at St. Norbert College, he submitted a course proposal for "Introduction to Digital Humanities." However, the curriculum committee rejected it, deeming the proposed course "a methodological mishmash." One of the lessons Cordell drew is that colleagues "understand 'interdisciplinary' from the perspective of their disciplines." His revised proposal, "Technologies of Text," recast the proposal as a "literature course" by incorporating insights that helped them see "lines of disciplinary intersection." It was approved and eventually taught. This form of "interdisciplinarity," as Cordell calls it, is an incursion into a curriculum resistant to DH methodologies. It is a "'pandemic' curriculum reform" capable of reshaping institutions beyond DH centers, by foregrounding the traditional disciplinarity of a course while building new methodologies into practice. Proponents of radical interdisciplinarity are dismissive of embeddedness, branding it an accommodationist strategy. Yet, Cordell and others reply, even as DH grows "the vast majority of its practitioners will work within institutional structures formed by traditional humanities categories."

That said, more radical change occurs on other campuses, akin to the transdisciplinary refiguration of Georgia Tech's English department. Launched in 1998 with seed money from the NEH, the Transcriptions initiative in the Department of English at the University of California, Santa Barbara, integrates curriculum, a research agenda, a technology model, support resources, and special events. Directed by Alan Liu, Transcriptions is modeling a humanities department of the future. The undergraduate specialization in Literature and Culture of Information asks students to grapple with the information culture both intellectually and practically, while working in new spaces for advanced information technology. The underlying metaphor of *transcription* signifies the multiple integrations that occur: between past and present understanding of what it means to be a literate, educated, and informed person; and between information culture and literary history. The project also advances understanding of the way information technology remolds interrelationships and methods of existing academic fields through collaborative work modes, themes of information technology, and research activities that transect the academy and professional sectors of business and private industry.

Regardless of strategy, it is important to be explicit about interdisciplinarity. The Comparative Media Studies program at MIT was based on a sixfold comparative approach: *across media* (including multi-modal relationships), *across national borders* (including cross-cultural dynamics, the political economy of global culture, and new media styles and genres), *across historical periods*, and three other comparative frames fundamental to this book. *Comparison Across Disciplines*, in particular, engages "radical interdisciplinarity" by encouraging students to mix and match approaches from humanities and social sciences in search of answers to questions about cultural and social impacts of media. It brings together a humanistic tradition of thinking about media content, genre, storytelling, and pedagogy with a qualitative social science tradition of analyzing media context, culture, society, and community. *Comparison Across Making and Thinking* bridges theoretical knowledge and hands-on learning in producing and critically evaluating tangible products. *Comparison Across Perspectives* invokes trans-sector *transdisciplinarity* as students encounter "front-line perspectives" on current media change in dialogue with representatives of industry, government, education, arts, and public institutions.

Drawing lessons from the field of cultural studies, Goodwin and Woolf caution that the limits of individual competence are "the weak link in the chain of cross-disciplinary reasoning." As students move beyond coursework to dissertations, the problem of expert advice arises. For all the anti-disciplinary talk of dismantling specializations, in the absence of expertise the risk of dilettantism looms. "There are no short cuts to knowledge," Goodwin and Woolf admonish (138–40), for teachers and students alike. Short-term certificate programs are becoming more popular for picking up DH training, along with new minors. However, the capacity for "informed decision making" at the heart of the master's program at University College London does not result from short courses and modules. Students need sustained experiences in selecting tools and content for a particular task then designing an integrated approach that is greater than the simple sum of the parts. Moreover, Claire Warwick admonishes, without a core teaching program, Digital Humanities will continue to struggle to claim status as a discipline (208), and, we can add, an interdisciplinary field with a strong institutional foothold.

Speaking on the topic of "Becoming Interdisciplinary" at the 2013 meeting of the Alliance of Digital Humanities Organizations, Willard McCarty contended discussions of the ontological meaning of interdisciplinarity and the nature of collaboration do not help individuals understand what the work entails. To argue that the interdisciplinarity is poorly understand, as he does, sidesteps a sizable body of work on integrative process and dynamics of communication. Yet, related insights are underutilized in DH curricula. Reframing interdisciplinary research as a way of acting, Mc-

Carty argues, is more helpful than the abstract noun "interdisciplinarity." It shifts attention to finding suitable pidgins for negotiating the "trading zone" between a discipline and computing, understanding how disciplines operate while being alert to their refiguration, and honing skills of interdisciplinary navigation. In his own teaching practice, McCarty highlights an ethnographic direction, treating disciplines as "epistemic cultures" that need to be explored to understand their perspectives from a "native's" view, while realizing what one's own discipline has to offer.

No discussion of education would be complete without factoring in the growing number of professional development opportunities for scholars and teachers who are already employed. Earning another degree is one way of gaining expertise. However, the more typical means are short-term events for learning new skills and content. DH centers and workshops at the conferences of DH organizations are key sites, along with THATCamps, hackathons, and special sessions at annual meetings of discipline-based organizations. Formats range from introductions to the field and project demonstrations to hands-on workshops on project design and implementation and training in particular technologies and programming languages. Online services such as DH Answers are further sources of help, and DevDH.org offers support for projects and grant writing in a multimodal repository of training materials, lectures, readings, examples, links, and other resources. In recent years the number of summer institutes and schools has also increased. Older forums such as the Digital Humanities Summer Institute at the University of Victoria are now joined by the European Summer School in Digital Humanities, the Digital Humanities Summer School in Switzerland, and initiatives such as the Postcolonial Digital Humanities Summer School's collaborative online course (#dhpoco) and Brown University's conference on "Teaching with TEI."

Inter-institutional partnerships constitute a further source of professional development. Ithaka S+R, a service of the non-profit organization ITHAKA, provides resources and services to help the academic community and other organizations operate in online environments. The DH training network links efforts across summer schools, and the Praxis network administered by the Scholars' Lab at the University of Virginia Library connects graduate and undergraduate programs at several colleges and universities. Preliminary surveys for the Praxis network indicated that many graduate programs were not preparing professionals adequately for current jobs, including skills of project management, collaboration, and functioning in related work cultures. Local programs have unique features, but they share a common focus on practical skill training, interdisciplinarity, and, a focus of the next chapter, collaboration.

Clustered Links for Chapter 5 in Order of Appearance

CUNY DH syllabus collection: http://cunydhi.commons.gc.cuny.edu/2011/06/06/digital-humanities-syllabi/

Tanya Clement's list of DH-inflected undergraduate programs: http://tanyaclement.org/2009/11/04/digital-humanities-inflected-undergraduate-programs-2/

Zotero DH Education group: http://www.zotero.org/groups/digital_humanities_education

Lisa Spiro, "Making Sense of 134 Syllabi": http://digitalscholarship.wordpress.com/2011/06/20/making-sense-of-134-dh-syllabi-dh-2011-presentation/, http://digitalscholarship.files.wordpress.com/2011/06/dheducationpresentation2011-revised.pdf

UCL (University College London) master's degree: http://www.ucl.ac.uk/dh/courses/mamsc

David Michelson's *Introduction to Digital Humanities* course site: http://introtodigitalhumanitiesspring2011.digress.it/

Alexander Huang's DH seminar: http://www.inthemedievalmiddle.com/2013/01/digital-humanities-gw.html

John Unsworth's DH seminar: http://www.brandeis.edu/now/2013/january/new courses.html

John Theibault's *Introduction to Digital Humanities* course offered at Stockton College in spring 2011, though the original link is now dormant: http://wp.stockton.edu/gah3223spring2011/about/

Loyola University Chicago's Center for Textual Studies and Digital Humanities: http://www.ctsdh.luc.edu/?q=ma_digital_humanities

Carleton College's MA in Digital Humanities: http://www6.carleton.ca/dighum/about/

Macalester College's Media and Cultural Studies major: http://www.macalester.edu/academics/mcs/

William J. Turkel's comment in Interchange online discussion in the *Journal of American History*: http://www.journalofamericanhistory.org/issues/952/interchange/index.html

Plan for master's in DH at University of Virginia: http://people.lis.illinois.edu/~unsworth/laval.html

James Gottlieb's comment on coding: http://www.jamesgottlieb.com/2012/03/coding-and-digital-humanities/

King's College London's Department of Digital Humanities: http://www.kcl.ac.uk/artshums/depts/ddh/study/index.aspx

Swarthmore College and Asheshi University's collaboration: http://www.swarth
morephoenix.com/2012/02/02/news/swatties-re-envision-the-meaning-of-dias
pora

Postings for A Day in the Life of Digital Humanities postings: For 2009–2011,
http://tapor.ualberta.ca/taporwiki/index.php/How_do_you_define_Humani
ties_Computing_/_Digital_Humanities%3F#How_do_you_define_Digital_
Humanities.3F; For 2012: http://dayofdh2012.artsrn.ualberta.ca/dh/; For 2013:
http://dayofdh2013.matrix.msu.edu/

Georgia Institute of Technology's School of Literature, Media, and Communication: http://www.lmc.gatech.edu/

Aaron Santesso's comment on digital pedagogy: http://chronicle.com/article/Deep-
Digital-Pedagogy-and/131657/

Steven Mintz's description of stages of digital history teaching in online Interchange
on digital history. http://www.journalofamericanhistory.org/issues/952/inter-
change/

Cathy N. Davidson's definition of digital thinking, "Crowdsourcing Grading: Fol-
low-Up." HASTAC, August 9, 2009: http://www.hastac.org/blogs/cathy-david
son/crowdsourcing-grading-follow

Jentery Sayers's comments and courses in digital learning: http://scalar.usc.edu/
maker/english-507/index, http://www.jenterysayers.com/2009/498/, http://
www.jenterysayers.com/2012/dh2012/

UCLA's Digital Humanities minor: http://www.cdh.ucla.edu/instruction/dhminor.
html

Stefan Sinclair's graduate course in DH: http://stefansinclair.name/llcu-601–1/

Thomas DiPiero's comment on students today: http://www.rochester.edu/news/
show.php?id=4064

Ryan Cordell's posting on DH, Interdisciplinarity, and Curricular Incursion: http://
ryan.cordells.us/blog/2012/02/20/dh-interdisciplinarity-and-curricular-incursion/

Transcriptions at University of California, Santa Barbara: http://transcriptions.en
glish.ucsb.edu/index_netscape.asp

MIT's Comparative Media Studies/Writing: http://cmsw.mit.edu/

Digital Humanities Questions and Answers: http://digitalhumanities.org/answers/

Development for the Digital Humanities: http://www.devdh.org

#dh poco Summer School: http://dhpoco.org/blog/2013/05/20/coming-soon-dh-
poco-summer-school/

European Summer School: http://www.culingtec.uni-leipzig.de/ESU_C_T/
node/97

Digital Humanities Summer Institute: http://dhsi.org/

Willard McCarty's address on "Becoming Interdisciplinary": http://dh2013.unl.
edu/abstracts/ab-107.xml

Ithaka S+ R at ITHAKA. http://www.sr.ithaka.org/

The Praxis Network: https://news.virginia.edu/content/uva-digital-humanities-
training-program-establishes-new-network

‹ 6 ›

Collaborating and Rewarding

Collaboration—literally a shared work—is always understood to carry with it some kind of sacrifice, a trade-off between autonomy and synergy. In our collaborative relationships, we intensify the concessions we make to the demands
of the social contract, and we voluntarily submit to norms of
behavior and constraints on our freedom of action in order
to gain the benefits of a group undertaking . . .

—Julia Flanders, "Collaboration and Dissent: Challenges of Collaborative Standards for Digital Humanities," in *Collaborative Research
in the Digital Humanities*, ed. Marilyn Deegan and Willard McCarty
(Farnham: Ashgate, 2012), 67

Properly so called an interdiscipline is not just another
administrative entity with its budget, chair and department
members, difficult as this is to carve these days out of existing turf; it isn't an institutionally sanctioned kind of poach-
ing. Rather it is an entity that exists in the interstices of the
existing fields, dealing with some, many or all of them. It
is the Phoenician trader among the settled nations. Its existence is enigmatic in such a world; the enigma challenges us
to rethink how we organize and institutionalize knowledge.

—Willard McCarty, "Humanities Computing as Interdiscipline,"
http://www.iath.virginia.edu/hcs/mccarty.html

**Keywords: collaboration, trading zones, interactional expertise, as-
sociative thought processes, negotiation, mutual learning, hybridity,
culture of recognition, interdisciplinary paradigm shift, triple efficacy,
aggregate activity**

This book has explored a wide range of topics, signaled by keyword clusters at the head of each chapter. It closes by considering two final topics that are essential to prospects for interdisciplinarity in Digital Humanities: collaboration and a culture of recognition. The chapter begins by defining characteristics of interdisciplinary collaboration, common problems, dynamics of integration in trading zones of expertise, the role of conflict and mutual learning, interdisciplinary work practices, and an ethics of collaboration. It then identifies parallels in efforts to legitimate interdisciplinary and digital scholarship and teaching in the academic reward system, countering impediments with authoritative guidelines for equitable inclusion. The chapter closes by returning to the question that prompted this book in the first place: Is Digital Humanities an interdisciplinary field? Three concepts come together in a final answer. A triple efficacy is unfolding across the "circuit of work" that constitutes the field: across disciplines, interdisciplinary fields, and professions; within and across their institutional locations; and within and across all organizations and groups that are grappling with implications of the digital and new media. Individuals and teams are leveraging change through a plurality of "strategic tractions" in particular contexts that have, at the same time, multiplicative effects in the "network aggregate university" of Digital Humanities.

Collaboration

Collaboration is not a typical mode of work in humanities. It occurs, and many believe teamwork is a necessity in Digital Humanities. Yet, the legacy of the lone scholar persists. The literature on interdisciplinary collaboration grew exponentially over the past several decades because of the heightened profile of teams in science-based fields of international competition, including biomedicine and pharmaceuticals, computer sciences, manufacturing, and high technology. Interdisciplinary collaboration is also a prominent focus in the Science of Team Science network and in transdisciplinary research on complex problem solving. John Unsworth cautions against adopting structural models from science, since the size, scale, and needs of humanities projects differ (Unsworth and Tupman, 232). Yet, DH teams face similar challenges, so can benefit from comparative understanding of insights in the wider literature on interdisciplinary collaboration.

Janet Nelson identified three kinds of collaboration in Digital Humanities:

- "intradisciplinary" work within a particular hybrid specialization, such as Anglo Saxonism;
- "interdisciplinary" interactions of technologists and subject specialists in fields that are not usually involved;
- "administrative" collaboration within and across universities.

(Nelson, 129–31)

Although more attention has been paid to the third kind in science and industry, one of the recommendations in Williford and Henry's report on projects supported by the NEH Big Data Challenge underscores the importance of administrative collaboration in humanities as well. Exhorting readers to "Embrace Interdisciplinarity," they call for greater organizational flexibility and restructuring, partnerships between scholars and professionals, and collaborations of project managers across different approaches (3, 13). There is no universal formula for success. However, in an overview of team science, Stokols et al. identified collaborative-readiness factors that influence prospects for success. The range of interpersonal, environmental, and organizational factors includes leadership skills, individual commitments to teamwork, shared space, electronic connectivity, and prior experience working together (476–77, 490).

One of the most important early considerations is discussion of goals, roles, authorship, and obligations, encapsulated in interdisciplinary health research in a Collaborators' Pre-Nup (Ledford). Veterans of Digital Humanities projects also urge advance measures. In identifying core administrative competencies, Burdick et al. urge clarification of resource allocation, report lines, job descriptions, goals, and outlines of responsibility in a memorandum of understanding (133). Comparably, Melissa Terras recommends formulating a "charter" that stipulates modes of communication among stakeholders, expected roles, means of conduct, and means and modes of publication. The "Collaborators' Bill of Rights," developed at a Digital Humanities workshop in Maryland in 2011, also includes a comprehensive model of credit, coupling group outcomes with descriptions of individual contributions, while allowing "soft" ownership of collaborative work to continue even when individuals change institutions or projects.

Even advance measures, though, do not guarantee success ("Being the Other").

Because of the many challenges that arise, collaboration places a high priority on leadership. Leaders must not only tend to structural and financial tasks but also broker cognitive connections and the process of information flows across epistemic cultures (after Gray). When leaders of NEH Digital Humanities Start-Up Grants awarded between 2007 and 2010 were asked about difficulties they encountered, personnel emerged as their number one challenge. Many realized projects required library professionals and other support staff, but assistance was not always timely or forthcoming. They also had to cope with conflicting work cultures among artists, librarians, and humanities scholars. "If there is a single lesson we have learned," one director concluded, "it is the need for a clear development structure with a concrete time commitment from the academic project participants." Technical issues must be addressed as well, especially learning how to navigate between priorities of humanities scholars and technical personnel. Another director recommended preliminary training courses for faculty. Yet another suggested engaging "technology translators" who have a grasp of both complex technical issues and practical solutions for achieving overall goals.

Conflict is another major concern associated with both technical and interpersonal issues, including turf battles over ownership of research problems, mistrust of others, and resistance to innovation. Status is an especially tenacious problem. Following Mitchell McCorcle's definition, an interdisciplinary team is an open, rather than a closed, system. It has a heterogeneous but interconnected membership driven by the presence of individuals from different fields. Heterogeneity is a source of strength, because diversity taps differing capacities over time. Capturing this quality, Cathy Davidson describes the management and intellectual style of organizations such as HASTAC as "collaboration by difference." Yet, heterogeneity is also a source of conflict. The theory of "status concordance" holds that organizational success is related to matched and equal factors. Rarely, though, do perfect matches occur, resulting in tensions around disciplinary and professional pecking orders, quantitative versus qualitative approaches, academic rank, gender, race, and cultural background (Klein, *Interdisciplinarity*, 127–28).

Interdisciplinary Work Practices

Projects comprise a primary focus for thinking about interdisciplinary work practices in Digital Humanities because they are, Burdick et al. contend, a "basic unit" in the field. Projects are both nouns and verbs in a form of scholarship that requires not only design but ongoing management, negotiation, and collaboration (124). McCarty depicts collaboration in Digital Humanities as a "spectrum of work-styles" ("Collaborative Research," 4). Variances occur because teams differ in agenda, structure, size and scale, duration, physical proximity of their members, and the mix of disciplines, professions, and fields. Degrees of interaction also vary, a dimension of work style Lisa Spiro recognized in distinguishing tightly coupled from loosely coupled forms in the digital project Orlando: Women's Writing in the British Isles. The space in which project work occurs may be likened to a concept in science studies. Peter Galison borrowed the idea of "trading zone" from anthropology in order to explain how physicists from different paradigms collaborated with each other and with engineers on common problems and shared interests, in this case developing particle detectors and radar. The core idea is that dissimilar subcultures can find common ground through exchanges, such as bartering fish for baskets. Exchanges were possible between incommensurable subcultures of theory and experiment, and across different traditions of making instruments and subcultures of theorizing (*Image and Logic*).

Subsequently, Collins, Evans, and Gorman combined the concepts of trading zone, interactional expertise, and interdisciplinary collaboration ("Trading Zones"). Trading zones vary along two axes: collaboration-coercion and homogeneity-heterogeneity. If there is high collaboration and high homogeneity an Interlanguage Trading Zone may develop, producing a new merged culture. The combination of high coercion and high homogeneity produces a Subversive Trading Zone, such as imposition of the authority of one culture on another or a dominant operating system such as Microsoft Windows. High coercion coupled with high heterogeneity is associated with an Enforced Trading Zone such as slavery, an imposed ideology, or a central planning model that ignores indigenous expertise. The combination of high collaboration and high heterogeneity is associated with two kinds of Fractionated Trading Zones. The first, Boundary Object

Trading Zones, is mediated by material culture, usually without linguistic exchange. The classic example is the collaboration of scientists, trappers, amateur collectors, and academic administrators in providing and cataloging specimens for the Museum of Vertebrate Zoology at the University of California, Berkeley. The second form, Interactional Expertise, is of greater interest for Digital Humanities because it involves linguistic exchange that generates interlanguage and interactional expertise.

The Speculative Computing Laboratory (SpecLab) is a striking example of the second form. *SpecLab* is a composite name for projects that emerged in 2000 at the University of Virginia. The theoretical shape of SpecLab, Johanna Drucker recounts, was not clear at the beginning. Working together in an environment akin to a studio lab or design shop, participants embarked on an ambitious reading program across humanities, social sciences, informatics, natural sciences, and visual design. Pushing theoretical ideas and insights gained from reading and dialogue, they learned on the job, figuring out how to work in teams and non-hierarchical relationships within a collaborative space. As they engaged in modeling and creating tools, design came to the forefront of intellectual activity. Recalling the process, Drucker reflects, "Making things, as a thinking practice, is not only formative but transformative." The Ivanhoe game, based on Walter Scott's novel of the same name, demonstrates transformative thinking as well as the reciprocal relationship between *Methodological* and *Theoretical Interdisciplinarity*.

Ivanhoe was both a "toy" and a "tool" for testing how digital media might be used to provoke critical modes of reading in literary studies. Earlier projects tended to be oriented to systems for administering and delivering materials in library and information management. The game was premised on different principles. Within its creative space players could assume and rework the role of a character. Every text generated was an alternative to the original that deformed or transformed it. The interdisciplinary moves involved in making Ivanhoe bridged aesthetic work and empirical analysis while making production and reception of a document part of its social history. The design space also challenged the secondary status of graphic form, exposing emergent, generative, iterative, procedural, and transformative activities that are properties of digital media. Visual form *does* something, Drucker emphasizes, not simply dresses something else. Relationality was also a core principle, reawakening awareness of associative thought processes. And, the narrow meaning of "text" was replaced by a broader notion of "work" in a field of shifting elements that constitute it. Iteration, manipulation, and dialectical engagement were key to refiguring the meaning of an object or artifact at the "intersection of aggregate activity" (*SpecLab*, xii, 31–40, 46, 52, 66–75, 93, 97).

SpecLab also illustrates the role of interlanguage in interdisciplinary work. The quality of outcomes, Wilhelm Vosskamp admonishes, cannot be separated from the development and richness of a shared language culture ("Crossing"). In an early study of interdisciplinary communication, Gerhard Frey reported discussions typically occur on a level similar to a popular scientific presentation. They become more precise as individuals acquire knowledge of other disciplines and, at a higher level of conceptual synthesis, a shared metalanguage may develop from the mixing of separate approaches ("Methodological Problems"). Algorithms may be combined with linguistic analysis or cultural critique. Or, big data mining may be combined with close reading of selected individual texts or objects. This process depends in no small part on negotiating the meaning of words. The SpecLab group, Drucker recalls, had to develop a new specialized vocabulary of concepts and principles. Raymond Siemens et al. had a similar experience in the HCI-Book-Consultative Group and the INKE Research Team. They were using the same words in different ways, even basic terms such as *book*, *text*, *reading*, *authority*, and *prototype*. In order to collaborate, they had to work through different meanings to achieve the common ground of shared vocabulary (180).

The metaphor of bilingualism is a popular characterization of interdisciplinary work, but it is not an accurate description of what typically happens. Galison identified three types of "in-between" vocabularies in trading zones. The simplest is a "jargon." A "pidgin" is a more complex interim interlanguage. A "creole," such as biochemistry, is a new language that can be taught to new generations (Collins, Evans, and Gorman, 8). The formation of interlanguage requires Schmithals and Berhenhage's notion of a "cooperation and communication culture." Careful attention needs to paid to interfaces: to points where the work of one individual is necessary for the work of another and where participants must coordinate effectively (cited in Bergmann, Knobloch, Krohn, Pohl, and Schramm).

A new common culture, though, will not remain static. Boix-Mansilla, Lamont, and Sato's model of *socio-cognitive platforms for interdisciplinary collaboration* shows that platforms change over time as individuals and groups gain communicative and collaborative capacity. Micro-social networks also realign, with growing "deliberative competency" and cognitive gains such as the ability to provide constructive feedback ("Cognitive-Emotional Interactional Platforms," "Successful Interdisciplinary Collaborations"). Other studies highlight the value of peer editing, reviewing assumptions on a recurring basis, and revisiting provisional conclusions in light of feedback (Klein, *Crossing Boundaries*, 212, 222–23). O'Donnell and Derry liken the challenge interdisciplinary teams face to Krauss and Fussell's concept of the "'mutual knowledge' problem." Experts in the same discipline typically share a "common referential base" that aids in communication. In contrast, interdisciplinary teams must negotiate a shared knowledge base (73, 76–77).

Teams must also, Anne Balsamo urges, go beyond facile divisions of labor: relegating scientists to studying conditions and providing methodologies, engineers and computer scientists to designing new devices and applications, artists to creating performances and new modes of expression, social scientists to assessing impacts and analyzing effects, and humanists to conducting critique. Individuals have distinct contributions and roles, but everyone must learn new skills, methods, practices, and frameworks (158–62). "Deep interdisciplinarity," Shanks and Schnapp emphasize, requires experts to alter their disciplinary practices by adopting new media and modes of communication, learning to speak new hybrid languages, having an experimental attitude, being willing to learn from experience, and flattening hierarchy in project management.

The values espoused in studies of teamwork are reinforced in Balsamo's ethical principles for multidisciplinary collaboration in Digital Humanities (summarized):

The first two principles highlight requirements for individuals. Collaboration is often treated as a collective phenomenon, but responsibility for self is crucial:

> *Intellectual generosity*: Sincere acknowledgment of the work of others expressed explicitly to them and in citation practices. Showing appreciation in face-to-face dialogue and throughout the collaborative process sows seeds for intellectual risk-taking and courageous acts of creativity.
> *Intellectual confidence*: The understanding that one has something important to contribute to the collaborative process. Individu-

als must be accountable by being reliable and thorough while eschewing shortcuts and intellectual laziness.

The second two principles move from individual to group responsibility in a form of intersubjectivity. Reflexive self-awareness of one's own values is a crucial step in this process. Socialization in disciplinary worldviews creates underlying assumptions about truth in the form of the "right" methods, tools, concepts, and theories. Differences in worldview and the meaning of the same words must be recognized and mutual learning occur through listening to others and developing respect for their approaches, rather than defaulting to orthodox disciplinary expertise.

> *Intellectual humility*: The understanding that one's knowledge is always partial and incomplete and can be extended and revised by insights from others. Team members need to be able to admit they don't know something without suffering loss of confidence or a blow to self-esteem.
> *Intellectual flexibility*: The ability to change one's perspective based on new insights from others. This quality entails the capacity for play and reimagining the rules of reality, suspending judgment and envisioning other ways of being in the world, and other worlds to be within.

An overriding principle of integrity emerges from the foregoing principles that fosters movement from secondary- to primary-group relations. Young IDR teams, Anthony Stone found, lean toward secondary-group relations that are protective of the individual. Older teams shift consciousness from "I" to "we," forging primary-group relations dedicated to a common task and shared cognitive framework (355).

> *Intellectual integrity*: The habit of responsible participation that serves as a basis for developing trust among collaborators. This quality compels them to bring their best work and contribute their best thinking to collaborative efforts.
> (Balsamo, 163; Balsamo and Mitcham, 270)

Ethics of collaboration are not limited to the project level. Julia Flanders cites the example of encoding standards: "they presume the need and the desire to co-ordinate shared work, to generalize individual insights to a community, and to support extension, critique, and reuse of ideas and techniques." When two people work together on a digital edition of the same manuscript they need to agree on a shared encoding system for transcription and editing, so their efforts add up to a consistent whole. They establish "a collaborative vector" mediated by using a common standard, a process that also occurs internationally through indirect contributions. As a community-driven standard, Flanders adds, TEI is rare in taking dissenting voices seriously, generating ongoing recommendations for improving digital representations. Consensus is not achieved by fiat: "The challenge—as with human language—is to achieve mutual intelligibility while still being able to say what is worth saying. Collaboration, too, walks this precarious line between egoism and altruism, between private insight and public communication, between local nuance and common ground" ("Collaboration," 71, 73, 79).

Transformational research in Digital Humanities, Balsamo adds, also has the capacity to refigure the nature and structure of collaboration in universities (158). The experience of working in a space such as SpecLab, Drucker recounts, "provided a way to integrate imagination and intellect, design and theory, individual vision and collaborative work within a variety of professional and institutional settings." It modeled possibilities for interdisciplinary work in digital environments, incubating subsequent and future projects (*SpecLab*, 199). "True collaboration" over a period of time, McCarty cautions, is rare ("Collaborative," 2–13, 22–23). Yet, the emergence of Digital Humanities has heightened awareness of the need for institutions to cooperate in creating antecedent conditions for collaboration. It has also heightened awareness of the need for change in the reward system.

A "Culture of Recognition"

In a report titled *Research Infrastructures in the Humanities*, the European Science Foundation called for a new "culture of recognition" (ESF). Even with viable communities of practice, research centers, educational programs, new forums of scholarly communication, and the recent emergence of guidelines from professor organizations, individuals still find their work discounted in the academic reward system. Core references for interdisciplinarity include a report of the Council of Environmental Deans and

Directors (CEDD) on *Interdisciplinary Hiring and Career Development*, a special issue of *Research Evaluation* on interdisciplinary quality assessment, and two chapters in *The Oxford Handbook of Interdisciplinarity* on navigating the career life cycle (Pfirman and Martin; Graybill and Shandas). Key works in Digital Humanities include guidelines issued by the American Historical Association and the Modern Language Association (MLA), a special section of MLA's 2011 *Profession* on "Evaluating Digital Scholarship," a link on tenure and promotion on the University of Nebraska-Lincoln's Center for Digital Research in the Humanities website, the Networked Infrastructure for Nineteenth-Century Electronic Scholarship (NINES) Summer Institute Guidelines to Evaluating Digital Scholarship, 18th Connect's report on new forms of publishing, and the fall 2012 issue of the *Journal of Digital Humanities* on "Closing the Evaluation Gap."

Interdisciplinarity is not the only topic in discussions of rewarding digital work in humanities, and it is more often implicit than explicit. Yet, it is strongly implicated, especially credit for individual contributions and appropriate criteria of evaluation. Interdisciplinary scholars in general, Pfirman and Martin found, must often negotiate their own process and structure at the same time they are trying to navigate them. Both interdisciplinarity and Digital Humanities fall outside conventional criteria of evaluation, or are only partially covered at best. When evaluators are uncertain about what counts as an acceptable form of knowledge production in a field, they often default to counting proxy measures of publication, presentations, grants, patents, and citations. Furthermore, both interdisciplinarity and Digital Humanities cannot be accounted for by a single model of research and teaching assessment, and *measurement* is too narrow a term to account for the wide range of *evaluation* techniques being used. The literature on interdisciplinary quality assessment includes an expanded range of indicators that may be combined with factors for evaluating interdisciplinary dimensions of digital scholarship and teaching.

- broadened scope and conceptualization of research topics
- new methodological and empirical analysis
- new research hypotheses and conceptual models
- greater explanatory power providing feedback to and outcomes for a "home" discipline as well as other disciplines and fields
- new integrative frameworks
- new expertise and the ability to work in more than one discipline or field

- increased collaborative capacity in projects and programs
- changing career trajectories in new appointments and affiliations in other areas
- co-mentoring students in other departments
- recognition outside original discipline, and service on multidisciplinary advisory or review groups
- contributions to new journals and other communication forums central to the field
- contributions to multi-authored works.

(composite of Boix-Mansilla, 2006; Boix-Mansilla, Feller, and Gardner, 2006; Klein, "Evaluation ")

When situating generic indicators within the particularities of Digital Humanities, several parallels stand out. Resistance to new forms of scholarly work is a major stumbling block and, Schreibman, Mandell, and Olsen report in *Profession*, new forms have been relegated to the lower status of "service" work or "teaching" pedagogy rather than scholarly "research." Relying on print versions when judging digital work also shortchanges it. Geoffrey Rockwell suggests in the same issue that candidates doing experimental or technically difficult work provide "cribs" for evaluators, such as narratives with screenshots, descriptions, and explanations of the nature of the scholarship. Even so, he cautions, cribs should never substitute for experiencing the work in its original form. Process is a further consideration. Once a book or article appears in print, it is considered "done." In contrast, digital work often develops in an iterative environment that may continue after "publication" or commercial availability. Indeed, this topic is the focus of an entire section of *Digital Humanities Quarterly* 3.2 (2009). Josh Honn and Geoff Morse identify *Iterative & Experimental* as a shared value of DH, but individuals often pay a price for experiments that take longer to produce results, require refiguring, and depend on others for completion. Moreover, it takes extra time in interdisciplinary work to learn new content, methods, and skills, and collaboration often results in a slower rate of productivity.

In her guest columns in the ProfHacker section of the *Chronicle of Higher Education*, Adeline Koh identifies four major issues that parallel challenges of evaluating interdisciplinary work. They arose in a preconference workshop on tenure and promotion for digital scholarship at the MLA conference, the third in a series begun in 2008. The first parallel is "Educate Your Audience." Scholars with digital projects often need to not only explain their work but also justify the field. Peter Lange, provost of Duke University, offers parallel advice for doing so in the *Research Evaluation* publication on quality assessment of interdisciplinarity. Candidates must define what constitutes an interdisciplinary field and its problem space, scholarly community, genres of scholarship, venues of publication and funding, and awards. For journals that are unfamiliar to evaluators, Laura Mandell, suggests in the *Journal of Digital Humanities'* special issue on evaluation, appropriateness and status can be established using traditional measures such as rejection statistics, contributors' profiles, composition of the editorial board, and circulation statistics or other evidence of centrality. Because projects vary and may not "look" like traditional scholarship, Todd Presner also advises in the same issue, rigor must be defined on the basis of alignment with the state of knowledge in a field, the nature of the knowledge created, and the methodology used. Moreover, it is important to explain how the intellectual work of Digital Humanities entails not only new content but new ways of organizing, classifying, and interacting with it.

Even in a new field, the benchmark of "best practices" also applies. In his "Short Guide to Evaluation of Digital Work," which appears in the *Journal of Digital Humanities* special issue, Rockwell urges that a best-practice approach consider both content and technology. In the case of digitization, the TEI Guidelines and Getty Data Standards and Guidelines provide authoritative criteria. In many instances, though, candidates will be educating committees, curbing the tendency to default to generic measures that do not completely address the nature of work in a new field. Mindful of this problem, other groups have devised criteria for evaluating interdisciplinary scholarship, teaching, and program review, including the American Studies Association, the Women's Studies Association, and the Association for Interdisciplinary Studies. In Digital Humanities, Rockwell stresses, it is important to provide an explanation for decisions informed by traditions of digital scholarship, to indicate why and how engagement and collaboration with other areas is necessitated by the nature of the work, and to define technological requirements of a project. DH work, Burdick et al. also note in their guidelines, often crosses two other sets of boundaries. It may have an impact on multiple fields, institutions, and the general public. It also often crosses boundaries of research, teaching, and service. Consequently, impact needs to be defined broadly (128–29).

Mark Sample and Kathleen Harris provide helpful models for presenting a candidacy in the fall 2012 special issue on evaluation in the online *Journal of Digital Humanities*. Describing his case at George Mason University, Sample explains how he met two conventional criteria—impact and evidence—in multiple contexts with unconventional outcomes. The contexts were literature, new media, and videogames. The outcomes included collaborative writing, computer code, peer-reviewed essays in e-journals, remixes of others' scholarship, and blog posts subject to post-publication peer review. Describing her strategy at San Jose State University, Harris shares her "Candidate's Statement" with a full explanation of the nature of the field and her work as a self-identified Digital Humanist and scholarly editor engaged in recovering unknown literature by women, blogging and tweeting, and other new forms of scholarly communication verified by evidence of impact outside conventional notions of peer review. Harris also anchored her case in MLA's professional endorsement of online scholarly electronic editions and its guidelines.

The second issue Koh identifies in the MLA workshop is "Understand that Digital Projects are Diverse." New technologies and electronic publication are more familiar in the sciences, Deborah Lines Andersen emphasizes in *Digital Scholarship in the Tenure, Promotion, and Review Process* (7–8, 12, 19). In contrast, digital scholarship is unfamiliar to many humanists. Introducing the MLA's special section on "Evaluating Digital Scholarship," Schreibman, Mandell, and Olsen cite metadata, text encoding, programming, tools, databases, interface design, a digital archive or edition, and a Web 2.0 resource. More specifically, Koh explains, DH projects might focus on "digital tools (e.g., geospatial mapping and literary tools), or tools for fine textual analysis (e.g., Carnegie Mellon's *Docuscope*, which helps scan literary texts for irregular patterns commonly missed by the human eye), video-books (e.g., 'Learning from YouTube,' published by MIT Press), and blogging for scholarship (e.g., Jason Mittell's (@jmittell) blog *JustTV*)." Others suggest using the tool *Anthologize* to create e-books out of blog posts and present scholarly blogs in a more traditional looking format.

The third issue in the MLA workshop, Koh reports, is "Document Your Role in Collaborative Projects." Josh Honn and Geoff Morse include *Collaborative & Distributed* in their proposed set of core values for Digital Humanities. Yet, Zach Coble comments when considering the need for evaluation guidelines in the library profession, the collaborative nature of DH work often complicates definition of individual responsibilities and contributions. Preparing a tenure and promotion case becomes an act of boundary work. In addition to Rockwell's suggestion of providing "cribs" for committees to comprehend individual contributions, Bethany Nowviskie cites INKE, a multinational interdisciplinary project on Implementing New Knowledge Environments in the context of digital transformations of the book. The Praxis Program at the Scholars' Lab at the University of Virginia, she reports in MLA's *Profession*, has emulated the INKE charter for negotiating questions of credit, authorship, and intellectual property in advance. Its "corporate authorship convention" often results in the group being listed as author in publications and presentations, though individuals can still be acknowledged and linked.

Both interdisciplinarity and Digital Humanities are also confronted by the Holy Grail of academic legitimacy—peer review. Lange stresses the importance of identifying experts who fit the problem space of a candidate's work. The task is easier in established fields such as women's studies and American studies. It is more difficult in emerging areas where criteria of excellence have not been developed, the epistemic community and literature are less well defined, and the pool of qualified peer experts is smaller. The fourth issue in the MLA workshop follows: "Explain Changing Forms of Peer Review." The fall 2010 and fall 2011 issues of *Shakespeare Quarterly*, Kathleen Fitzpatrick's 2011 book *Planned Obsolescence*, and the journal *Kairos* opened peer review to a wider audience, and "altmetrics" are based on social web tracking of impact beyond preselected databases. The *Journal of Digital Humanities* also filters the best work posted online in a strategy aimed at "catching the good" based on interest, transmission, and community response. Starting with Editors' Choice selections at *Digital Humanities Now*, items go through evaluation, review, and editing. NINES and 18thConnect provide external review for digital work as well, and the recently emerging MESA for medieval studies, REKn for Renaissance/Early Modern, and ModNets for Modernists.

The MLA's *Guidelines for Evaluating Work with Digital Media in the Modern Languages* further recommend that work in digital media be evaluated in light of changing institutional and professional contexts, and redefinitions of traditional notions of scholarship, teaching, and service. MLA also urges local committees to "Seek Interdisciplinary Advice" of experts in other disciplines, though they mean "multidisciplinary" inclusion. The risk in evaluating any interdisciplinary candidate is that parts will be reviewed piecemeal rather than evaluated by someone with interdisciplinary exper-tise or integration of the parts of a dossier. The *Guidelines* go on to urge candidates to make results, theoretical underpinnings, and the intellectual rigor of their work explicit, including descriptions of how it overlaps or redefines traditional categories and collaborative relationships necessitated by new technologies and media. Presner also advises candidates to explain how digital work engages with a problem specific to a discipline or group of disciplines, reframes that problem or contributes a new way of under-standing it, and advances an argument through its content and presenta-tion.

Two years after MLA issued its *Guidelines*, the Council of the American Historical Association (AHA) endorsed its own *Suggested Guidelines for Evaluating Digital Media Activities in Tenure, Review, and Promotion*. The document was prompted by a survey of tenure, review, and promotion policies regarding technology-related activities at more than 650 history departments. Negative findings, including ignorance of and discrimina-tion against digital scholarship, led members of the executive council of the affiliate American Association for History and Computing (AAHC) to work with MLA and the American Political Science Association on appro-priate guidelines. Comparable to CEDD and MLA, AAHC emphasizes the importance of developing local written guidelines and proportioning credit for work in more than one area. The *Guidelines* also urge committees to review work in its proper medium and, following MLA, "seek interdis-ciplinary advice" when engaging reviewers. AAHC recommends as well that candidates explain how their work overlaps or redefines traditional categories of the discipline and the collaborative relationships required by work in digital media.

In 2008, the University of Nebraska-Lincoln's Center for Digital Re-search in the Humanities (CDRH) issued yet another set of guidelines, "Promotion & Tenure Criteria for Assessing Digital Research in the Hu-manities." This document is framed from the outset by interdisciplinar-ity, explaining that DH crosses boundaries between computer science and humanities disciplines, arts, and the profession of library science. Digital work is often by necessity collaborative as well. Paralleling other guide-lines, CDRH urges candidates to explain the nature of their scholarship, alternative forms of publication, and the originality of digital components and implications for multiple audiences. In addition to having committees review work in the medium in which it was produced, CDRH recommends delineating responsibilities of review committees throughout the early career life cycle. More generally, Lange recommends the composition of search committees for all interdisciplinary candidates replicate the anticipated committee structure for pre-tenure and tenure review as much as possible. The MLA workshop also urges candidates to negotiate projects as part of tenure plans as soon as possible, to create a hospitable environment for their work. And, CEDD provides models for annotating CVs and negotiating a letter of agreement at the hiring stage.

The bottom line of comparison for interdisciplinarity and Digital Humanities is that standards, authoritative guidelines, and models for presenting work not only exist but should be actively deployed in the evaluation process. Yet, both professional organizations and individuals need to be proactive. The profession of librarianship, Coble reports in the special issue of the *Journal of Digital Humanities*, lacks a coordinated approach to Digital Humanities, though a 2011 report by the Association of Research Libraries acknowledges that DH projects often call on librarians for consultation and project management, technical and metadata support, instructional services, and resource identification. An organized approach will be crucial to enhancing incentives, resource support, institutional backing, and a network of colleagues. Coble also urges librarians to link up with the standards and evaluation projects of other organizations.

The Triple Efficacy of Digital Humanities

Given the plurality and complexity witnessed throughout this book, what is the future of Digital Humanities? In a series of blog postings in the *New York Times*, Stanley Fish sounded alarm about a "new insurgency" in humanities, based on upwards of forty sessions devoted to Digital Humanities at the 2012 MLA conference. The span of interests under the DH umbrella made it "the new 'Everything.'" Burkdick et al., though, suggest the era of DH may already be coming to an end (101). Katherine Hayles reports the term is morphing as emphasis turns from text encoding, analysis, and searching to multimedia practices (*How We Think*, 25). James O'Donnell predicts it may eventually fall out of use (99). Joshua Sternfeld imagines a future when digital history has become so integrated into the traditional curriculum the qualifier "digital" disappears (278). And, Terras predicts the "ecological bedrock of digitization" will keep shifting and user expectations changing ("Digitization," 57).

Even in the midst of differing assessments, Balsamo contends the emergence of Digital Humanities marks a paradigm shift with the potential to transform the core of the academy by refiguring the labor needed for institutional reformation. Balsamo likens doing interdisciplinarity to "shift work." Unlike shifts that begin and end by punching a clock, shifts from one framework to another require ongoing boundary work. She also suggests that formal educational programs have a "double efficacy." They disseminate disciplinary knowledge, with its traditional literacies and knowledge bases. At the same time they evoke new literacies and knowledges (135–38, 149–50, 177). Patrik Svensson identifies a parallel "double affiliation." The term *digital humanities* accommodates a wide range of organizational relations by maintaining links to the heart of disciplines, while engaging broadly with the digital in an identifiable field. Yet, individuals should not depend on departments and disciplines "to make things happen." A center, for example, may be needed for new positions in areas that are not of immediate interest to departments. At the same time, a broader form of "strategic traction" leverages interests and resources across the academic landscape, thereby increasing visibility, development, and impact ("Envisioning," 21, 2–26).

Ultimately, Svensson concludes, "There is no single model or size that fits all." He configures the field as a trading zone and a meeting place ("Envisioning," 24). The boundary work of contextualizing will also continue to prompt differing conceptions. Whitney Anne Trettien, for instance, describes her born-digital thesis for MIT's comparative media studies program as "a media archaeology" that excavated the history of text-generating mechanisms. This kind of web-based scholarship differs from the work in labs at the University of Virginia and George Mason University, and from database-oriented resources such as NINES and scholarly aids such as Zotero. The "literary-critical-digital humanities scholars" who produced them provided valuable collections, artifacts, and tools. Yet, Trettien's thesis differed: "It is critical, individualistic, and self-aware of its methodology and its historical moment." It has more in common with the journal *Kairos*, though ultimately found a home in the arts community. Trettien proposes a radical "anti-disciplinary" break with university structures. In contrast to the DH community that formed around institutions, labs, and the economy of grants and funding, her model is "lower-case and personified," fostering micro-revolutions that reframe intersections with new media as points of connection and collaboration. She is not alone in endorsing a radical break. Mark Sample dubs Digital Humanities "an insurgent humanities." Calling for release of humanism from "its turtlenecked hairshirt," Ian Bogost exhorts humanists to embrace the world of things that computing has revealed. And, Lisa Nakamura critiques preoccupation with silo-ed work and preservation over engagement with everyday life, media studies, and cultural studies critique (qtd. in Svensson, "Envisioning," 6–7).

After nearly sixty-five years of work in an evolving field, the promise of Digital Humanities also remains greater than the uneven realities of practice and institutionalization. Lynne Siemens's survey of Canadian humanities and social science communities revealed familiar concerns about tenure, funding, training, and infrastructure. One respondent called for more "hybrid" individuals at home in two cultures and committed to building a new hybrid culture in the academy. Students and younger scholars completing the survey were less likely than associate professors to present their research results at discipline-specific and digital-focused conferences, or to publish them. And, only a small percentage are members of DH associations, with less than a third having attended institutes, workshops, or courses for skill development. Even so, Siemens's respondents are actively involved across the spectrum of Digital Humanities. They are creating and applying methods, technologies, and resources. They are grounding research in both traditional humanities and social science approaches and within new fields such as virtual worlds, interface design, and gaming. And, they are using digital methods, tool, and resources to facilitate and enhance collaborations. Respondents also believe digital approaches will become more widely adopted with increased collaboration, broader questions, and "cross-discipline work."

Given the proliferation Siemens reports, predictions of the growth of Digital Humanities are not unfounded. Burdick et al. contend we are living in a rare moment of opportunity for humanities, comparable to other eras of cultural-historical transformation such as the shift from the scroll to the codex, the invention of moveable type, encounters with the New World, and the Industrial Revolution. In a networked information age, communities of practice have become more fluid, and the questions being addressed cannot be confined or reduced to one genre, medium, discipline, or institution. Moreover, a global, transhistorical, and transmedia approach to knowledge and meaning making is unfolding (vii). In the midst of this complexity, Balsamo's notion of "double efficacy" and Svensson's "double affiliation" may be extended to signify a triple efficacy of Digital Humanities that is unfolding: within and across disciplines, professions, and interdisciplinary fields; within and across centers, programs, and departments; and within and across DH organizations, discipline- and profession-based associations, and interdisciplinary groups.

The complexity of triple efficacy is evident in the work that has continued to appear since submission of the manuscript of this book for print publication. Increasing attention is being paid to not only launching but also sustaining projects and programs, marked by the appearance of a Sustainability Implementation Toolkit. Jobs ads continue to appear. Increasing attention is being paid to data mining and visualization, marked by the new *Journal of Data Mining and Digital Humanities*. Professional development opportunities and THATCamps abound. *Digital Humanities Now* continues to track expanding discourse, projects, and programs. And, recent publications bridge earlier and current theory and practice: including a special issue (#5) of *New American Notes Online* on the relationship of public humanities and digital humanities; a new anthology of essays on *Transmedia Frictions: The Digital, The Arts, and The Humanities* (Kinder and McPherson, 2014); and an overview of the humanistic project of thick mapping in *HyperCities: Thick Mapping in the Digital Humanities* (Presner, Shepard, and Kawano, 2014). In a forthcoming edited collection, *Deep Maps and Spatial Narratives*, David J. Bodenhamer is also extending his earlier work on the concept of spatial humanities (2010, 2014). In a posting to the 2011 Day of Digital Humanities, D. C. Spensley called Digital Humanities "a network aggregate university." Individual institutions are slow to change, he acknowledged, but "the networked body consisting of DH individuals from many different universities can combine to evolve an educational ecosystem that thrives on change, embraces technology, plurality and open doors, while benefiting from the support of traditional educational organization." Yet, echoing Balsamo, individuals will continue to be differently positioned across the "circuit of work" in the field. Networking across the "aggregate university" will be essential to defining overlaps, intersections, and divergences. It will occur in flagship communities that represent Digital Humanities at large. But, it is occurring just as much in the boundary work of claiming "the digital" and "new media" in local institutions, disciplinary and professional practices, and interdisciplinary fields.

Clustered Links for Chapter 6 in Order of Appearance

Willard McCarty, "Humanities Computing as Interdiscipline," http://www.iath.vir ginia.edu/hcs/mccarty.html

NEH Summary of Findings of Digital Humanities Start-Up Grants (2007–2010). http://www.neh.gov/files/summary.report.odh_.sug_.pdf

Cathy Davidson' blog entry on "Collaboration by Difference and Affinity," February 15, 2008: http://www.hastac.org/blogs/cathy-davidson/collaboration-differ ence-and-affinity

Lisa Spiro's comment in presentation on "Exploring Collaboration in Digital Scholarship": http://digitalscholarship.files.wordpress.com/2013/04/casewesterncol laborationfinal.pdf

Shanks and Schnapp's manifesto of Artreality: http://documents.stanford.edu/mi chaelshanks/270

European Science Foundation report on Research Infrastructures in the Humanities. Downloadable at http://www.esf.org/publications/humanities.html

Fall 2012 special issue *on Closing the Evaluation Gap in the Journal of Digital Humanities*: http://journalofdigitalhumanities.org/1-4/

Digital Humanities Now: http://digitalhumanitiesnow.org/

MLA's "Guidelines for Evaluation Work in Digital Humanities and Digital Media": http://www.mla.org/guidelines_evaluation_digital

MLA's workshop on "Evaluating Digital Work for Tenure and Promotion": http:// www.mla.org/resources/documents/rep_it/dig_eval

American Association for History and Computing's "Tenure Guidelines": http:// quod.lib.umich.edu/j/jahc/3310410.0003.311/--aahc-suggested-guidelines-for-evaluating-digital-media?rgn=main;view=fulltext

The collection of articles on "Evaluating Digital Scholarship" in the 2011 issue of MLA's *Profession:* http://www.mlajournals.org/toc/prof/2011.

University of Nebraska-Lincoln CDRH's "Promotion and Tenure Criteria for Assessing Digital Research in the Humanities": http://cdrh.unl.edu/articles/pro motion_and_tenure.php

NINES' guidelines on peer review: http://www.nines.org/about/scholarship/peer Review.html

IDHMC Comment/press document on "Promotion and Tenure for Digital Scholarship": http://idhmc.tamu.edu/commentpress/promotion-and-tenure/

Collaborators' Bill of Rights: http://mith.umd.edu/offthetracks/recommendations/

Office of Digital Humanities, National Endowment for Humanities, Summary

Findings of NEH Digital Humanities Start-Up Grants (2007–2010). http://www.neh.gov/files/summary.report.odh_.sug_.pdf

Special issue of the *Journal of Digital Humanities* on evaluation: http://journalofdigitalhumanities.org/1–4/closing-the-evaluation-gap/

Honn and Morse's talk on "Digital Humanities": http://acrl.ala.org/dh/2013/03/27/digital-humanities-101/?utm_source=feedburner&utm_medium=feed&utm_campaign=Feed:+DHNowUnfiltered+(DH+Now++»++Unfiltered

Adeline Koh's guest posting at ProfHacker on MLA Preconference session on "Evaluation Digital Work for Tenure and Promotion": http://chronicle.com/blogs/profhacker/the-challenges-of-digital-scholarship/38103

altmetrics: http://altmetrics.org/about/

Issue of *Digital Humanities Quarterly* on "Done: Finishing Projects in the Digital Humanities": http://www.digitalhumanities.org/dhq/vol/3/2/000037/000037.html

Digital Humanities Now: http://digitalhumanitiesnow.org/how-this-works/

Stanley Fish's blog postings in the *New York Times*: "The Old Order Changeth," http://opinionator.blogs.nytimes.com/2011/12/26/the-old-order-changeth/, "The Digital Humanities and the Transcending of Mortality," http://opinionator.blogs.nytimes.com/2012/01/09/the-digital-humanities-and-the-transcending-of-mortality/, and "Mind Your P's and B's: The Digital Humanities and Interpretation," http://opinionator.blogs.nytimes.com/2012/01/23/mind-your-ps-and-bs-the-digital-humanities-and-interpretation/

Patrik Svensson. "Envisioning the Digital Humanities." *Digital Humanities Quarterly* 6, 1 (2012). http://www.digitalhumanities.org/dhq/vol/6/1/000112/000112.html

Whitney Anne Trettien's posting on her dissertation, "Digital Humanities vs. the digital humanist." 26 April 2010 on Hyperstudio blog. http://hyperstudio.mit.edu/blog/thoughts/digital-humanities-vs-the-digital-humanist/

ITHAKA. Sustainability Implementation Toolkit. http://sr.ithaka.org research-publications/sustainability-implementation-toolkit

Special issue on Digital Humanities, Public Humanities in *New American Notes Online* (2014). http://www.nanocrit.com/issues/5/introduction-digital-humanities-public-humanities

Resourcing

Andy Engel

To ask for a map is to say, "Tell me a story."
—Peter Turchi, *Maps of the Imagination: The Writer as Cartographer*
(San Antonio: Trinity UP, 2004), 11

Keywords: contours, scatter, scale, strategies, aggregators, taxonomy vs. folksonomy, degree of specialization, depth vs. breadth, timeliness, purpose

In advising interdisciplinary scholars and educators on how to find materials, Klein and Newell propose a new way of thinking about *resources*: not as a noun—as things, data, and products—but as the verb *resourcing*—as methods, strategies, and processes (140). The shift from *resources* to *resourcing* presents a particular challenge for individuals who are entering new or emerging fields. The problem is not simply one of information overload. Knowledge and information are also scattered across disciplines, occupational professions, and interdisciplinary fields. By developing savvy searching strategies to cope with "overload" and "scatter," researchers align themselves with Peter Turchi's notion of the writing process: "at some point we turn from the role of Explorer to take on that of Guide." This process requires striking a balance between efficiency and coverage while becoming self-reflexive about the tools and strategies needed for identifying both large-scale patterns and fine-grained details.

High degrees of scatter in interdisciplinary fields complicate the speed of research. For instance, running a search for *digital humanities* in Google generates 1.3 million hits, so reducing results to a manageable number is the first and most significant hurdle. The inclusion of Boolean logic in search strings—*and, or, not*—can reduce the blunt instrument effect of Google. Searching instead for *digital humanities-AND-English-AND-degree programs-NOT-centers* reduces returns to less than 5,000. That number is still too large, but can be shrunk further with additional *and* as well as *not* terms. Beyond using Boolean searches to tackle the problem of scatter, researchers can engage other strategies—in the form of spectra—for developing savvy approaches to the overabundance of online research materials. This final section of the book is aimed at helping researchers cope with the problem of scatter by providing *links to resources* (CATEGORIES) and *strategies for resourcing* (SPECTRA) to meet their continuing and future needs. In the course of doing so, they will evolve from being DH explorers to guides in their own right. Their efforts will be aided greatly by the aggregators below, which are themselves guides to the field.

This chapter is not meant to be exhaustive. Instead, it is a representative sample of Digital Humanities scholarship and community based on robust starting points. Links to resources appear in two annotated categories, Aggregators and Keeping up to Date, and unless otherwise noted entries have a three-part structure: a brief description, links, and unique features. Five resourcing spectra frame these categories and help individuals develop personal research and teaching frameworks by making sense of the abundance of available materials. These framing strategies are particularly necessary online, where formal statements of purpose on websites are not always clear and media of publication are not traditional, so not readily captured by conventional database searching.

Aggregators

Aggregators draw together the highest quantity of resources in the smallest amount of space. All aggregators are not created equal, however, so users should weigh quantity of relevance against time invested. Many aggregators in the list below are broad-based sources. Others are selective, but they all have the common goal of identifying multiple resources. Spectrum 1, "Taxonomic vs. Folksonomic," is evident in differences in how aggregators are organized, managed, and maintained. At one end of the spectrum, sites such as the Alliance of Digital Humanities Organizations (ADHO) take hierarchical approaches and have structured, centralized forms of site maintenance, and conventional categories of sorting. Although easy to navigate, such a top-down approach can be restrictive and leave out some of the emergent richness of the Web. At the other end of this spectrum, sites such as Humanities, Arts, Science, and Technology Alliance and Collaboratory (HASTAC) are run by a community of users and have organizational structures built on user-generated tagging. HASTAC is a flexible and dynamic model, though without careful moderation a tag-based system can become so decentered that locating information can be difficult.

Many aggregators are also excellent places for keeping up to date. Those with the greatest potential for frequent updates are flagged with an asterisk (*), along with ones that tend to collect more broadly across knowledge boundaries. The methods by which scholars organize aggregations or syntheses of a field exhibit a permeability of boundaries that can make some sites, and especially aggregators, difficult to classify. With this complication in mind, spectrum 2, "Degree of Specialization," sharpens the search for and use of particular sites by highlighting their disciplinary specificity while recognizing that no single aggregator can cover everything. Site specificity is continually being reinforced, expanded, or challenged by virtue of

TABLE 1. Searching Strategies

RESOURCE CATEGORIES (annotations)	RESOURCING SPECTRA (parameters)
• **Aggregators:** sites that cast the widest net and have the largest quantity of information. • **Keeping up to date:** sites to return to for regular updates: Library Guides, Blogs & Forums, and Networks & News	• **Taxonomic vs. Folksonomic:** organization, management, and maintenance useful for weighing reliability and credibility • **Degree of specialization:** boundaries between disciplines continually reinforced, expanded, or challenged by virtue of the types of sources included/excluded • **Depth vs. Breadth:** quantity of resources with which a site tries to engage and the disciplinary variety of those sources • **Timeliness:** recognition of how often and by whom sites are updated for determining their role in research • **Purpose:** a reminder to be savvy about a site's owners by examining its construction and range of resources

the types of sources that are included and excluded. With the exception of the largest sites such as the Association for Computing and the Humanities (ACH), which has a global reach, many smaller sites rely on particular disciplinary, professional, or interdisciplinary homes. "NINES" is a homebase site with a network of disciplinary and interdisciplinary interests catering to period studies. Another example, the Digital Classicist, serves the interests of a decentralized community of scholars and students who are focused on digital tools and methods for researching the ancient world.

Spectrum 3, "Depth vs. Breadth," helps researchers assess bibliographic strengths and weaknesses by highlighting the range and quantity of resources a site collects and the level of disciplinary detail for each resource category. The most concentrated traditional sources for identifying further readings and other resources online are bibliographies and library guides (Lib Guides). Some aggregators, such as arts-humanities.net, have in-depth bibliographies focusing on a single medium—in this case, primarily books and articles in print. DH Lib Guides, which are growing in popularity, exhibit differing degrees of development and types of media. Some are rudimentary, while others, such as the DH Café at Harvard University, collect DH materials across multiple categories. Lib Guides are not included in this initial category of aggregators, though, because they do not tend to have the scope of the following examples.

* Alliance of Digital Humanities Organizations (ADHO) (http://digitalhumanities.org). A large umbrella organization working across arts and humanities disciplines. Includes: Publications, Initiatives, Conference, Awards, Committees, and News. Unique feature: includes member-organized Significant Interest Groups.

arts-humanities.net (http://arts-humanities.net). An extensive collection of resources for almost twenty humanities disciplines and fields. Includes: Projects, Methods, Tools, Library, Centers, Community, and News. Unique feature: organized by category.

* Association for Computers and the Humanities (ACH) (http://www.ach.org). A major professional organization dedicated to a computer-assisted approach to research, pedagogy, and design in humanities disciplines. Includes: Activities, Conferences, News, and Publications. Unique feature: hosts DH Answers Q&A discussion board.

Bamboo DiRT (Digital Research Tools) (http://dirt.projectbamboo.
org/). A site for finding a wide range of resources as varied as content management systems and music OCR. Includes: resources for working with
data, texts, and collections, as well as brainstorming, networking, sharing
information, transcribing, annotating, and other functionalities. Unique
feature: provides support for tools such as statistical analysis and mind-
mapping software difficult to find elsewhere.

Computer-Assisted Language Instruction Consortium (CALICO)
(https://calico.org). A group working at the intersection of computer technology and language learning. Includes: Scholarship, Awards, Sister Organizations and Journals, Publications, and Conference. Unique features:
hosts a book series and special interest groups (SIGs) that foster communities in areas including Gaming, Teacher Education, Virtual Worlds.

CUNY Academic Commons: Digital Humanities Resource Guide
(http://commons.gc.cuny.edu/wiki/index.php/The_CUNY_Digital_
Humanities_Resource_Guide). A collaboratively produced guide where
contributors can link to items using social media. Includes: Online
Communities/Discussion Forums, DH on Twitter, Blogs to Follow,
Journals, Conferences & Events, Training/Professional Development,
Scholarships/Fellowships, Funding/Awards/Competitions, Centers,
Organizations/Associations, Tools & Methods, DH Syllabi, Jobs, Tips,
and Other Resources. Unique feature: has a wide scope and invites con-
tributions.

The Digital Classicist (http://www.digitalclassicist.org). A user-centered
initiative focusing on digital technologies to engage with the ancient
world. Includes: Projects, Tools, FAQ, Resources, Discussion List, Blog,
and Seminar. Unique feature: a decentralized international community
collective that also links to partner sites.

*** The DH & Digital LAM Daily*** (http://paper.li/retius/dh-and-lib-folks).
A site collecting DH-related news including accounts in popular news
media such as the *New York Times* and the *Chronicle of Higher Education*. Includes: Headlines and Topics of Education, Stories, Technology,
Leisure, Society, and Art & Entertainment. Unique feature: resource head-
ings change depending on available stories when updated.

Digital Humanities Now (http://digitalhumanitiesnow.org/). A collection of informally published DH scholarship and resources from the open web. Includes: links to Submit Your Work, Editor's Choice, and News. Unique features: continues to refine internal processes for gathering and reviewing and is affiliated with the *Journal of Digital Humanities* (see below).

European Association for Digital Humanities (http://www.allc.org). An organization founded as the Association for Literary and Linguistic Computing with emphasis on literature and language now expanded to a wider scope of disciplines. Includes: News, Elections, Publications, Conferences, Education, Support, and Awards. Unique feature: has archived conferences from 1989 to the present.

Digital Humanities Wiki (http://digitalhumanities.pbworks.com). A collaboratively constructed wiki with many useful resources despite not being updated since 2008. Includes: Blogs, Wikis, Portals, Centers, Conferences, Funding Sources, Journals, and Bibliographic Resources. Unique feature: generated productive discussions about DH conditions in the academy.

Resource Center for Cyberculture Studies (University of San Francisco) (http://rccs.usfca.edu). A network providing infrastructure and extensive resources for teaching, researching, and supporting cybercultural studies. Includes: Introducing Cyberculture, Book Reviews, Courses in Cyberculture, Events and Conferences, and Featured Links. Unique feature: although not updated since 2009, provides an archive of discussions between reviewers of scholarly work and authors.

Spatial Humanities (http://spatial.scholarslab.org). A community-based approach to the spatial humanities, GIS scholarship, and spatial technologies. Includes: definitions of the Spatial Turn, Projects & Groups, and Resources. Unique feature: includes a step-by-step series of peer-reviewed tutorials and guides for teaching and research.

A Survey of Digital Humanities Centers in the USA, a publication, by Diane M. Zorich (http://www.clir.org/pubs/reports/pub143/contents. html). Online version of an authoritative comprehensive study of DH Centers published in 2008. Includes: survey results for thirty-two centers and a detailed explanation of selection criteria highlighting distinctions between centers and other DH communities and organizations. Unique feature: "Appendix F: Tools for Humanists" emphasizes roles that tools play in humanities research and their capacity to act as "extensible assets" in the DH community.

Voice of the Shuttle (VOS) *(*http://vos.ucsb.edu*).* A long-running online collection that began in 1994 and hosts a wide range of web-based resources for humanities disciplines. Includes: Academe, Teaching Resources, Libraries & Museums, Reference, Journals & Zines, Publishers & Booksellers, Listservs & Newsgroups, Conferences, and Travel. Unique feature: serves general humanities needs as well as specific disciplines and fields.

Keeping up to Date

Spectrum 4, "Timeliness," addresses the challenge of keeping up to date and the addition of new information that expands and reshapes a site over time. Researchers can better determine the role sites play in their research by tracking the frequency and types of updates (news, blog posts, projects, etc.) and the credentials of those doing the updating. Once identified, relevant sites with a higher frequency of updates can be treated as "check first" for recent news and information. Surprisingly, lack of timeliness can play a productive role in identifying strata of time on the Web. For example, Digital Humanities Wiki has not been updated since 2008, but it provides a snapshot of time that would be more difficult to determine if a site is constantly updated and reformatted as well. Despite not being updated since 2009, the Resource Center for Cyberculture Studies also remains a valuable starting point for this subfield.

In addition to observing the timeliness of sites' resource catalogs, researchers engaged in interdisciplinary work also need to be attentive to the goals of individuals and groups who are building these sites. Spectrum 5, "Purpose," is less of a spectrum than a reminder to be savvy about the intentions of site owners by examining their method of site construction and range of resources they include. Awareness of this spectrum means that, if necessary, researchers can seek out other sites with resources that compensate for the various limits site owners set for their resource catalogs because of their unique purposes.

Keeping up to Date (Library Guides)

Library Guides have many qualities approximating aggregator sites because they draw together a wide range of materials across a variety of media. They are particularly relevant because librarians have extensive experience confronting the problem of scatter. The selected examples below will be especially helpful for those new to DH because of their high percentage of introductory materials, and they are good models for campuses wanting to build their own counterpart Lib Guides. The annotations do not have a "unique features" component because this resource genre follows a fairly standardized template, though with some variety in local categories and materials.

Digital Collections and Digital Humanities Projects-English and American Literature LibGuide at New York University (http://nyu.libguides. com/content.php?pid=34183&sid=2731247). A guide for collections at the intersection of digital media and humanities research. Includes: open-access DH Collections and Projects.

Digital Humanities Café LibGuide (Harvard University) (http:// guides.hcl.harvard.edu/digitalhumanities). A comprehensive guide that is updated. Includes: Conferences, Workshops, and Seminars as well as Events, Quick Links and Reads, Past Conferences, and a Twitter feed, plus sections on Introductions, e-Scholarship/Open Access, Scholarly Communication, and Collections.

Digital Humanities and Cornell University: A Research Guide (Cornell University) (http://guides.library.cornell.edu/digitalhumanities). Another comprehensive guide. Includes: Definitions, Associations plus Blogs and Journals, local and other Projects, Tools, New Books, and Visualization.

Digital Humanities LibGuide (Boston College) (http://libguides.bc.edu/ digitalhumanities). A guide focusing on collaborative and technical resources. Includes: Projects, Centers and Organizations, Published Resources, Technical Resources, and DH Conferences/Workshops as well as Definitions and Introductions to the Field.

Digital Humanities LibGuide (Catholic University of America) (http://guides.lib.cua.edu/digitalhumanities). A guide for users who are beginning research in DH. Includes: Books, Journals & Articles, Associations and Centers, Projects, Tools & Tutorials, plus Courses and Introductory Readings.

Digital Humanities LibGuide (Duke University) (http://guides.library.duke.edu/digital_humanities). A reading and resource guide for participants in Duke's Haiti Humanities Lab (http://www.fhi.duke.edu/labs/haiti-lab). Includes: Defining DH, Associations, Journals & Blogs, Projects, More Readings, and Textmining Tools as well as Introduction and Good Practice Guides.

Digital Humanities LibGuide (University of California, Los Angeles) (http://guides.library.ucla.edu/digital-humanities). A guide with links to local activities and help for Getting Started. Includes: Reference, Publications, Centers, Programs, Projects, Tools, Community, and Workshop.

Digital Humanities LibGuide (University of Central Florida) (http://guides.ucf.edu/content.php?pid=185689). A guide for scholars and students orienting them to the field and key topics. Includes: Archives, Projects, Books/Articles, Resources, News/Blogs, Organizations, Text & Technology, Scholarly Communication, and Open Access.

Digital Humanities LibGuide (University of Virginia) (http://guides.lib.virginia.edu/digitalhumanities). A guide with special emphasis on professionalization and evaluation. Includes: Tools & Texts, Worth Following, Copyright & IP, Organizations, Funders, and Promotion & Tenure.

Digital Humanities LibGuide (University of Washington) (http://guides.lib.washington.edu/digitalhumanities). A guide for DH resources with a particular focus on English and American literature. Includes: Resources, Projects-Centers-and-Tools, and Associations & Groups with a link to the English Lib Guide.

Digital Humanities LibGuide (Western Michigan University) (http://libguides.wmich.edu/digitalhumanities). A guide that emphasizes the emergence of the field and provides tools for users. Includes: Defining the Digital Humanities, How Digitizing Works, Text Mining Tools, Resources at WMU, and Examples of Projects.

Mass Media & Pop Culture LibGuide (Yale University) (http://www. library.yale.edu/humanities/media). A guide oriented toward pop culture with a specific focus on mass media technologies. Includes: Mass Media in General, General Research Resources, Topic-Specific Resources, News, Journalism & The Press, and Related Research Guides.

Keeping up to Date (Blogs & Forums)

Many online publications have high timeliness quotients, as do blogs maintained by individuals, groups, and organizations. Like the Library Guide listings, the annotated blogs in this category of resourcing do not include "unique features" since this genre tends to be more sharply focused than aggregators. Readers can choose sites or authors based on the topics covered and/or the types of links included. They can also scour their immediate interest areas for blogs with an orientation to Digital Humanities. The Junto: A Group Blog on Early American History, for instance, provides an introductory set of resources and a space for sharing experiences in digital pedagogy (http://earlyamericanists.com/2013/04/22/the-future-of-the-past-is-now-digital-humanities-resource-guide/). In addition, the following selected sites are useful for keeping up to date.

20 Best Blogs in the Digital Humanities (Online College.org) (http:// www.onlinecollege.org/2011/07/10/20-best-blogs-in-the-digital-human ities-2). An excellent starting list for discussions about DH scholarship, practices, and news. Includes: scholarly and popular blogs and other sites.

100 best blogs for new media students (Associates Degree.com) (http:// www.associatesdegree.com/2009/08/24/100-best-blogs-for-new-media-students). A wide-ranging list of links in the field of new media studies. Includes: Academic Blogs, Social Media, New Media Arts, New Media and Culture, New Media Business, Technology, Politics and Policy, Media Censorship and Freedom Issues, New Media Working for Social Change, Gaming Technology, and News and Popular Culture.

2cultures.net: humanities + computing (Craig Bellamy) (http:// www.2cultures.net). A site that syndicates real-time blogs and other sites around the world, and is searchable by topics with links back to authors' original sites.

Cathy Davidson's Blog (http://www.hastac.org/blogs/cathy-davidson). A personal blog maintained by the co-founder of HASTAC (Humanities, Arts, Science, and Technology Alliance and Collaboratory), covering a wide range of topics with emphasis on learning in the digital age.

CUNY Digital Humanities Initiative (CUNY Academic Commons Wiki) (http://cunydhi.commons.gc.cuny.edu). The blog of the CUNY DH initiative aimed at building momentum and community. Includes: Recent Posts and Comments, links to the CUNY initiative as well as Bloggers, Journals, Digital Organizations, and Instructional Technologists, along with an archive of past postings.

dancohen.org (Dan Cohen) (http://www.dancohen.org). A robust personal blog maintained by Dan Cohen, a historian and executive director of the Digital Public Library of America. Includes: Publications, Best of the Blog selections, and Twitter, Podcast, and RSS features.

Digital Digs (Alex Reid) (http://www.alex-reid.net). A personal blog focused on digital media and culture, with particular interest in rhetoric and composition practices, maintained by Alex Reid at the University of Buffalo. Includes: Research, Teaching, and The Two Virtuals link for reflecting on shared space between the traditional and the virtual.

Digital Scholarship in the Humanities: Exploring the digital humanities (Lisa Spiro) (http://digitalscholarship.wordpress.com). A rich personal blog maintained by Lisa Spiro, Executive Director of Digital Scholarship Services at Rice University's Fondren Library. Includes: a wide range of topics and Spiro's presentation materials.

Network for European Digital Media Arts and Cultural Heritage Studies (EuroMACHS) (http://euromachs.fl.uc.pt/blog). A network blog at the intersection of Digital Media and Cultural Heritage Studies, with emphasis on European contexts. Includes: Events, EuroMACHS Network, Podcasts, and Projects.

Hyperstudio (Digital Humanities at MIT) (http://hyperstudio.mit.edu/blog). A blog maintained by the Hyperstudio DH laboratory at MIT. Includes: Basic Research, Events, News, Thoughts, and Visualizations along with scroll-bar links to Popular Posts.

Matthew Huculak (http://matthuculak.com/digital-humanities). A personal blog maintained by Matthew Huculak of the University of Victoria. Includes News/Blog, Publications, Teaching, Projects, and answers to frequently asked questions at the first link in the Resources section.

ProfHacker (Chronicle of Higher Education) (http://chronicle.com/blogs/profhacker). A multi-authored blog on current topics with news updates and tips for teaching.

Scholarly Electronic Publishing Weblog (Charles W. Bailey Jr.) (http://www.digital-scholarship.org/sepb/sepw/sepw.htm). An accumulation of articles, books, e-prints, and technical reports pertinent to scholarly e-publishing on the Internet that is updated bimonthly.

Stunlaw (David Berry) (http://stunlaw.blogspot.com/). A personal blog maintained by David Berry at the University of Sussex. Includes: Books and Blog Archive, with sections on Research, Selected Publications, and Student Feedback and Drop-In Sessions

Wiki Wrangler (CUNY Academic Commons Wiki) (http://wikiwrangler.commons.gc.cuny.edu). A blog providing a collaborative space for sharing resources, investigating ways of integrating blogs with group forums, and showcasing wiki pages, maintained by the CUNY Academic Commons.

Networking forums are also fruitful sites for getting a sense of the people and organizations that are actively fostering community in Digital Humanities. In addition to the aggregators listed above, groups identified in chapter 3 on "Institutionalizing" and chapter 4 on "Professionalizing" are worth checking periodically. Their newsletters, online bulletin boards, and listservs are excellent sources for news. So is Fibreculture, a forum for information technology, policy, and new media (http://fibreculture.org), and Culture Machine, a forum for cultural studies and cultural theory (http://www.culturemachine.net). One of many historical-period based groups, Networked Infrastructure for Nineteenth-Century Electronic Scholarship (NINES) is also exemplary in serving the needs of its users by providing a peer-reviewing body and on-line space for groups and exhibits for research and education (http://www.nines.org). The following additional sites are useful as well.

Digital Humanities Education Library (Zotero) *(*https://www.zotero.org/groups/digital_humanities_education*)*. A Zotero-based resource collection for DH education with syllabi, curriculum planning documents, and articles on a range of pertinent topics.

Digital Learning Network (DLnet) *(*http://digitallearningnetwork.net*)*. A forum for sharing ideas and practices in digital learning in the cultural heritage sector, including museums, archives, and libraries.

Humanities, Arts, Science, and Technology Alliance and Collaboratory (HASTAC) *(*http://hastac.org*)*. A user-generated international network of individuals and institutions committed to innovative uses of technology in learning, with collaborative space for Groups as well as Blogs, Topic forums, News and Events, and Competitions.

New Media Consortium (NMC) *(*http://www.nmc.org*)*. An international locus of expertise in educational technology engaged in research and publications, symposia and workshops, community building, and communication forums.

Spotlight on Digital Media & Learning *(*http://spotlight.macfound.org*)*. An online publication covering stories at the intersection of technology and pedagogy and learning both inside and outside the classroom, with a StudentsSpeak and Videos section.

THATCamp *(*http://thatcamp.org*)*. A central site for identifying non-hierarchical, collaborative, and real-time "unconference" formats that addresses issues relating to the humanities and technology.

Next Steps

New tools for discovering, sorting, and dealing with the scatter of online resources appear on a weekly and sometimes a daily basis. Many of these tools fall into a category called "distant reading," which Franco Moretti describes as *"a condition of knowledge*: it allows you to focus on units that are much smaller or much larger than the text: devices, themes, tropes—or genres and systems" (57). Two tools that employ aspects of distant reading to address the problem of scatter stand out:

- Google's Ngram Viewer is a basic distant reading tool for getting a macro-level picture of a particular topic (http://ngrams.google labs.com).
- The Perseus Project's distant reading component accesses and analyzes information using automated systems to generate knowledge across a vast collection of texts and artifacts. Researchers can deal with scatter at an abstract scale by algorithmically tracking the appearance of terms, phrases, and authors during a specified time period (http://www.perseus.tufts.edu/hopper/).

Alert services and RSS feeds provide a more detailed capture than distant reading tools. In fact, many resources for this book came from sifting through returns in daily Google Alerts (http://www.google.com/alerts). By entering a specific string of search terms, alert services allow researchers to control the range of search returns while receiving frequent updates. A Google Alert for "digital + humanities," for example, returns regular hits per day with minimal redundancy and a high usability. In addition, researchers need to be alert to new resources from expert groups. To name a few final examples, in 2011 the Association of Research Libraries advertised then published the *Digital Humanities SPEC Kit 326* (www.arl.org/storage/documents/publications/spec-326-web.pdf). Publications such as *Archaeology 2.0*, mentioned in chapter 2 on "Defining," provide state-of-the-art accounts in particular areas. And, scrolling through tables of contents of anthologies of essays on Digital Humanities is a good way of identifying both general and area-specific resources. To reiterate, library guides that are updated also merit checking periodically. Finally, new tools will continue to emerge. In 2012, for instance, Google launched a new search engine called "The Knowledge Graph," aimed at dealing with scatter by finding relationships between terms. Google is a popular rather than academic engine so should not be viewed as a one-stop resource (http://www. google.com/insidesearch/features/search/knowledge.html). For that matter, no sites and tools for finding knowledge and information should be considered one-stops. The sites annotated in this chapter, though, provide sound starting points for navigating the scatter and developing customized pathways for keeping up to date.

References for Resourcing Chapter

Klein, Julie Thompson, and William Newell. "Strategies for Using Interdisciplinary Resources." *Issues in Integrative Studies* 20 (2002): 139–60.

Moretti, Franco. "Conjectures on World Literature," *New Left Review* 1 (January/February 2000): 54–68.

Turchi, Peter. *Maps of the Imagination: The Writer as Cartographer* (San Antonio, TX: Trinity University Press, 2004).

Print References for Chapters 1–6

NOTE: Print and online sources are equally important in this book. URLs for online resources cited in chapters 1–6 appear at the end of the respective chapters.

Addelson, Kathryn Pyne, and Elizabeth Potter. "Making Knowledge." *(En)Gendering Knowledge: Feminists in Academe.* Ed. Joan E. Hartman and Ellen Messer-Davidow. Knoxville: U of Tennessee P, 1991. 259–77. Print.

Alexander, Bryan, and Rebecca Frost Davis. "Should Liberal Arts Campuses Do Digital Humanities? Process and Products in the Small College World." *Debates in the Digital Humanities*, ed. Matthew Gold. Minneapolis: U of Minnesota P, 2012. 368–89. Print.

Alvarado, Rafael C. "The Digital Humanities Situation." *Debates in the Digital Humanities.* Ed. Matthew Gold. Minneapolis: U of Minnesota P, 2012. 50–55. Print.

American Council of Learned Societies. *Our Cultural Commonwealth.* Report of the American Council of Learned Societies Commission on Cyberinfrastructure for the Humanities and Social Sciences Societies. 2006. Print and Web. http://www.acls.org/cyberinfrastructure/ourculturalcommonwealth.pdf

Andersen, Deborah Lines. "Introduction." *Digital Scholarship in the Tenure, Promotion, and Review Process.* Ed. Deborah Lines Andersen. Armonk, NY: M. E. Sharpe, 2003. 3–24. Print.

Armstrong, Cheryl, and Sheryl I. Fontaine. "The Power of Naming: Names That Create and Define the Discipline." *WPA: Writing Program Administration*, 13.1–2 (1989): 5–14. Print.

Arthurs, Alberta. "The Humanities in the 1990s." *Higher Learning in America, 1980–2000.* Ed. Arthur Levine. Baltimore: Johns Hopkins UP, 1993. 259–72. Print.

Bal, Mieke. *Travelling Concepts in Humanities: A Rough Guide.* Toronto: U of Toronto P, 2002. Print.

Balsamo, Anne. *Designing Culture: The Technological Imagination at Work.* Durham: Duke UP, 2011. Print.

Balsamo, Anne, and Carl Mitcham. "Interdisciplinarity in Ethics and the Ethics of Interdisciplinarity." *The Oxford Handbook of Interdisciplinarity*. Ed. Robert Frodeman, Julie Thompson Klein, and Carl Mitcham. Oxford and New York: Oxford UP, 2010. 206–19. Print.

Barthes, Roland. "From Work to Text." *Image, Music, Text*. Trans. Stephen Heath. New York: Hill and Wang; Fontana: Collins, 1977. l55–64. Print.

Bathrick, David. "Cultural Studies." *Introduction to Scholarship, in Modern Languages and Literatures*. Ed. Joseph Gibaldi. New York: Modern Language Association of America, 1992, 320–40. Print.

Becher, Tony. "The Counter-Culture of Specialization." *European Journal of Education*, 2.2 (1990): 333–46. Print.

Bender, Thomas, and Carl E. Schorske. "Introduction." *American Academic Culture in Transformation: Fifty Years, Four Disciplines*. Ed. Thomas Bender and Carl Schorske. Princeton: Princeton UP, 1997. 3–13. Print.

Bergmann, Matthias, Thomas Jahn, Tobias Knobloch, Wolfgang Krohn, Christian Pohl, and Englebert Schramm. *Methoden transdisziplinärer forschung: Ein uberblick mit anwendungsbeispielen*. Frankfurt/Main and New York: Campus Verlag; in English translation (2012); *Transdisciplinary Research Methods*. Chicago: University of Chicago Press [for Campus Verlag], 2010. Print.

Berry, David M., ed. *Understanding Digital Humanities*. Hampshire, UK: Palgrave, Macmillan, 2012. Print.

Bianco, Jamie "Skye." "This Digital Humanities Which is Not One." *Debates in the Digital Humanities*. Ed. Matthew Gold. Minneapolis: U of Minnesota P, 2012. 96–112. Print.

Bjork, Olin. "Digital Humanities and the First-Year Writing Course." *Digital Humanities Pedagogy: Practices, Principles and Policies*. Ed. Brett D. Hirsch. Open Book Publishers, 2012. 97–119. Print.

Bodenhamer, David J. "The Potential of Spatial Humanities." *The Spatial Humanities: GIS and the Future of Humanities Scholarship*. Ed. David J. Bodenhamer, John Corrigan, and Trevor M. Harris. Bloomington: Indiana UP, 2010. 14–30. Print.

Bodenhamer, David J. "Narrating Space and Time." *Deep Maps and Spatial Narratives*. Ed. David J. Bodenhamer, John Corrigan, and Trevor M. Harris. Bloomington: Indiana UP, forthcoming in 2015. Print.

Boix-Mansilla, Veronica. "Assessing Expert Interdisciplinary Work at the Frontier: An Empirical Exploration." *Research Evaluation*, 15.1 (2006): 17–29. Print.

Boix-Mansilla, Veronica, Irwin Feller, and Howard Gardner. "Quality Assessment in Interdisciplinary Research and Education." *Research Evaluation*, 15.1 (2006): 69–74. Print.

Boix-Mansilla, Veronica, Michele Lamont, and K. Sato. "Cognitive-Emotional Interactional Platforms: Markers and Conditions for Successful Interdisciplinary Collaborations." Unpublished ms.

Boix-Mansilla, Veronica, Michele Lamont, and K. Sato. "Successful Interdisciplinary Collaborations: Toward a Socio-Emotional-Cognitive Platform for Interdisciplinary Collaborations." Unpublished ms.

Bolter, Jay David. "Critical Theory and the Challenge of New Media." *Eloquent Images: Word and Image in the Age of New Media*. Ed. Mary E. Hocks and Michelle R. Kendrick. Cambridge: MIT Press, 2003. 19–36. Print.

Bolter, Jay David. "Theory and Practice in New Media." *Digital Media Revisited: Theoretical and Conceptual Innovations in Digital Domains*. Ed. Gunnar Liestol, Andrew Morrison, and Terje Rasmussen. Cambridge: MIT Press, 2003. 15–34. Print.

Bourdieu, Pierre. *The Field of Cultural Production: Essays on Art and Literature*. New York: Columbia UP, 1993. Print.

Boxer, Marilyn J. "For and About Women: The Theory and Practice of Women's Studies in the United States." *Signs*, 7.3 (1982): 661–95. Print.

Brantlinger, Patrick. *Crusoe's Footprints: Cultural Studies in Britain and America*. New York: Routledge, 1990. Print.

Brier, Stephen. "Where's the Pedagogy? The Role of Teaching and Learning in the Digital Humanities." *Debates in the Digital Humanities*. Ed. Matthew Gold. Minneapolis: U of Minnesota P, 2012. 390–401. Print.

Brown, John Seely, and Paul Duguid. "Universities in the Digital Age." *Change*, 24.4 (1996): 10–19. Print.

Burdette, Alan R. "EVIA Digital Archive Project." *Online Humanities Scholarship: The Shape of Things to Come*. Ed. Jerome McGann. Houston: Rice UP, 2010. 189–209. Print.

Burdette, Alan R. "A Response to the Responses of John Unsworth and John Rink on 'The EVIA Digital Archive Project: Challenges and Solutions.'" *Online Humanities Scholarship: The Shape of Things to Come*. Ed. Jerome McGann. Houston: Rice UP, 2010. 237–50. Print.

Burdick, Anne, Johanna Drucker, Peter Lunenfeld, Todd Presner, and Jeffrey Schnapp. *Digital_Humanities*. Cambridge: MIT Press, 2012. Print.

Burke, Kenneth. *Language as Symbolic Action: Essays on Life, Literature, and Method*. Berkeley: U of California P, 1966. Print.

Caldwell, Lynton K. "Environmental Studies: Discipline or Metadiscipline?" *Environmental Professional*, 5 (1983): 247–59. Print.

Carp, Richard. "Relying on the Kindness of Strangers: CEDD's Report on Hiring, Tenure, Promotion in IDS." *Association for Integrative Studies Newsletter*, 30.2 (2008): 1–6. Print.

Clark, B. R. *Places of Inquiry: Research and Advanced Education in Modern Universities*. Berkeley: U of California P, 1995. Print.

Clarke, John, and Russell Agne, eds. *Interdisciplinary High School Teaching*. Boston: Allyn and Bacon, 1996. Print.

Clayton, Keith. "The University of East Anglia." *Inter-Disciplinarity Revisited: Re-Assessing the Concept in Light of Institutional Experience*. Ed. L. Levin and I. Lind. OECD/CERI, Swedish National Board of Universities and Colleges, Linköping U. 1985. 189–96. Print.

Clement, Tanya. "Multiliteracies in the Undergraduate Digital Humanities Curriculum." *Digital Humanities Pedagogy: Practices, Principles and Policies.* Ed. Brett D. Hirsch. Open Book Publishers, 2012. 365–88. Print.

Collins, Harry, Robert Evans, and Michael E. Gorman. "Trading Zones and Interactional Expertise." *Trading Zones and Interactional Expertise: Creating New Kinds of Collaboration.* Ed. Michael E. Gorman. Cambridge: MIT Press, 2010. 7–23. Print.

Committee on Facilitating Interdisciplinary Research. *Facilitating Interdisciplinary Research.* Washington, D.C.: National Academies P, 2004. Print.

Cornwall, Grant H., and Eve W. Stoddard. "Toward an Interdisciplinary Epistemology: Faculty Culture and Institutional Change." *Reinventing Ourselves: Interdisciplinary Education, Collaborative Learning, and Experimentation in Higher Education.* Ed. Barbara Leigh Smith and John McCann. Bolton, MA: Anker, 2001. Print.

Council of Environmental Deans and Directors. *Interdisciplinary Hiring and Career Development: Guidance for Individuals and Institutions.* Washington, D.C.: National Council for Science and the Environment, 2011. Print.

Courant, Paul. "Perpetual Stewardship: Comments on Penelope Kaiserlian's Paper on the Rotunda Press." *Online Humanities Scholarship: The Shape of Things to Come.* Ed. Jerome McGann. Houston: Rice UP, 2010. 365–74. Print.

Cowan, Michael. "American Studies: An Overview." *Encyclopedia of American Studies.* Ed. George T. Kurian et al. New York: Grolier Education, Scholastic Incorporated, 2001. V. I: 105–17. Print.

Coyner, Sandra. "Women's Studies." *NWSA Journal* [National Women's Studies Association], 3.3 (1991): 349–54. Print.

Crane, Greg. "Give us Editors! Re-inventing the Edition and Rethinking the Humanities." *Online Humanities Scholarship: The Shape of Things to Come.* Ed. Jerome McGann. Houston: Rice UP, 2010. 137–69. Print.

Daniel, Philip T. K. "Theory Building in Black Studies." *The Black Scholar,* 12, 13 (1981): 29–36. Reprinted in *The African American Studies Reader.* Ed. Nathaniel Norment Jr. Durham, NC: Carolina Academic P, 2001. 372–79. Print.

Davidson, Cathy. "Humanities 2.0: Promise, Perils, Predictions." *PMLA,* 123.3 (2008): 707–17. Print.

Davidson, Cathy. "Humanities and Technology in the Information Age." *The Oxford Handbook of Interdisciplinarity.* Ed. Robert Frodeman, Julie Thompson Klein, and Carl Mitcham. Oxford and New York: Oxford UP, 2010. 206–19. Print.

Davidson, Cathy, and David Theo Goldberg. *The Future of Learning Institutions in a Digital Age.* Cambridge: MIT Press, 2009. Print and Web. http://mitpress.mit.edu/books/chapters/Future_of_Learning.pdf

de Certeau, Michel. *The Practice of Everyday Life.* Trans. Steven Randall. Berkeley: U of California P, 1984. Print.

Derrida, Jacques. "The Principle of Reason: The University in the Eyes of its Pupils." *Diacritics,* Fall (1983): response section 3–20. Print.

Dhareshwar, Vivek. "The Predicament of Theory." *Theory Between the Disciplines: Authority, Vision, Politics.* Ed. Martin Kreiswirth and Mark A. Cheetham. Ann Arbor: U of Michigan P, 1990. 231–50. Print.

Dougherty, Jack, and Kristen Nawrotzki, eds. *Writing History in the Digital Age.* Ann Arbor: U of Michigan P, 2013. 1–18. Print. Web version at http://writinghistory. trincoll.edu (a site maintained by the editors for an unspecified period of time).

Dougherty, Jack, Kristen Nawrotzki, Charlotte D. Rochez, and Timothy Burke. "Conclusions: What We Learned from *Writing History in the Digital Age.*" *Writing History in the Digital Age.* Ann Arbor: U of Michigan P, 2013. 1–18. Print. Web version at http://writinghistory.trincoll.edu

Drucker, Johanna. "Humanistic Theory and Digital Scholarship." Ed. Matthew Gold. Minneapolis: U of Minnesota P, 2012. 85–95. Print.

Drucker, Johanna. *SpecLab: Digital Aesthetics and Projects in Speculative Computing.* Chicago: U of Chicago P, 2009. Print.

Drucker, Johanna, and Bethany Nowviskie. "Speculative Computing: Aesthetic Provocations in Humanities Computing." *A Companion to Digital Humanities.* Ed. Susan Schreibman, Raymond Siemens, and John Unsworth. Malden, MA and Oxford, UK: Blackwell, 2004. 431–47. Print.

Earhart, Amy E. "Can Information Be Unfettered? Race and the New Digital Humanities Canon." *Debates in the Digital Humanities.* Ed. Matthew Gold. Minneapolis: U of Minnesota P, 2012. 309–18. Print.

Edwards, Charlie. "The Digital Humanities and Its Users." *Debates in the Digital Humanities.* Ed. Matthew Gold. Minneapolis: U of Minnesota P, 2012. 213–32. Print.

Eiteljorg, Harrison II. "Computing for Archaeologists." *A Companion to Digital Humanities.* Ed. Susan Schreibman, Raymond Siemens, and John Unsworth. Malden, MA and Oxford, UK: Blackwell, 2004. 20–30. Print.

Elam, Diane. "Ms. en Abyme: Deconstruction and Feminism." *Social Epistemology,* 4.3 (1990): 293–308. Print.

Elam, Diane. "Taking Account of Women's Studies." *Women's Studies on Its Own: A Next Wave Reader in Institutional Change.* Ed. R. Wiegman. Durham, NC: Duke UP, 2002. Print.

Eyman, Douglas. *Digital Rhetoric: Theory, Practice, and Method.* Ann Arbor: U of Michigan P, forthcoming. Print.

Feller, I. "Multiple Actors, Multiple Settings, Multiple Criteria: Issues in Assessing Interdisciplinary Research." *Research Evaluation,* 15.1 (2006): 5–15. Print.

Feller, I. "New Organizations, Old Cultures: Strategies and Implementation of Interdisciplinary Programs." *Research Evaluation,* 1.2 (2002): 109–110. Print.

Fiscella, Joan, and Stacey Kimmel. *Interdisciplinary Education: A Guide to Resources.* New York: The College Board, 1998. Print.

Fish, Stanley. "Being Interdisciplinary is So Very Hard To Do." *Profession 89.* New York: Modern Language Association, 1985. 15–22. Print.

Fisher, D. *Fundamental Development of the Social Sciences: Rockefeller Philanthropy and the United States Social Science Research Council.* Ann Arbor: U of Michigan P, 1993. Print.

Fitzpatrick, Kathleen. "Comment." *Hacking the Academy: New Approaches to Scholarship and Teaching from Digital Humanities.* Ed. Daniel Cohen and Thomas Scheinfeldt. Ann Arbor: U of Michigan P, 2013. Print.

Fitzpatrick, Kathleen. "The Humanities, Done Digitally." *Debates in the Digital Humanities.* Ed. Matthew Gold. Minneapolis: U of Minnesota P, 2012. 12–15. Print.

Flanders, Julia. "Collaboration and Dissent: Challenges of Collaborative Standards for Digital Humanities." *Collaborative Research in the Digital Humanities.* Ed. Marilyn Deegan and Willard McCarty. Farnham, UK: Ashgate, 2012. 67–80. Print.

Fountain, Kathleen Carlisle. "To Web or Not to Web? The Evaluation of World Wide Web Publishing in the Academy." *Digital Scholarship in the Tenure, Promotion, and Review Process.* Ed. Deborah Lines Andersen. Armonk, NY: M. E. Sharpe, 2003. 44–60. Print.

Fraistat, Neil. "The Function of Digital Humanities Centers at the Present Time." *Debates in the Digital Humanities.* Ed. Matthew Gold. Minneapolis: U of Minnesota P, 2012. 281–91. Print.

Frey, Gerhard. "Methodological Problems of Interdisciplinary Discussions." *RATIO,* 15.2 (1973): 161–82. Print.

Friedlander, Amy. "Foreword." *A Survey of Digital Humanities Centers in the United States.* Washington, D.C. Council on Library and Information Resources, 2008. vi. Print and Web. http://www.clir.org/pubs/reports/pub143/pub143.pdf

Friedman, Susan. "Academic Feminism and Interdisciplinarity." *Feminist Studies.* Spec. issue on *Doing Feminism in Interdisciplinary Contexts,* 27.2 (2001): 499–531. Print.

Galison, Peter. *Image & Logic: A Material Culture of Microphysics.* Chicago: U of Chicago P, 1997. Print.

Gallagher, Catherine. "The History of Literary Criticism." *American Academic Culture in Transformation: Fifty Years, Four Disciplines.* Ed. Thomas Bender and Carl Schorske. Princeton: Princeton UP, 1997. 151–71. Print.

Giroux, Henry, David Shumway, and James Sosnoski. "The Need for Cultural Studies: Resisting Intellectuals and Oppositional Public Spheres." *Dalhousie Review,* 64 (1984): 472–86. Print.

Gold, Matthew K., ed. *Debates in the Digital Humanities.* Minneapolis: U of Minnesota P, 2012. Print.

Gold, Matthew K. "The Digital Humanities Moment." *Debates in the Digital Humanities.* Ed. Matthew Gold. Minneapolis: U of Minnesota P, 2012. ix–xvi. Print.

Gold, Matthew K. "Looking for Whitman: A Multi-Campus Experiment in Digital Pedagogy." *Digital Humanities Pedagogy: Practices, Principles and Policies.* Ed. Brett D. Hirsch. Open Book Publishers, 2012. 151–76. Print.

Gold, Matthew K., and Jim Groom. "Looking for Whitman: A Grand, Aggravated

Experiment." *Debates in the Digital Humanities*. Ed. Matthew Gold. Minneapolis: U of Minnesota P, 2012. 406–8. Print.

Goodwin, Andrew, and Janet Woolf. "Conserving Cultural Studies." *From Sociology to Cultural Studies: New Perspectives*. Ed. Elizabeth Long. Malden, MA; Oxford, UK: Blackwell, 1997. 123–49. Print.

Gorman, Michael. "Introduction: Trading Zones, Interactional Expertise, and Collaboration." *Trading Zones and Interactional Expertise: Creating New Kinds of Collaboration*. Ed. Michael E. Gorman. Cambridge: MIT P, 2010. 1–4. Print.

Gray, Barbara. "Enhancing Transdisciplinary Research Through Collaborative Leadership." *American Journal of Preventive Medicine*, 35.2 (2008): S124–S132. Print.

Graybill, J. K., and V. Shandas. "Doctoral Student and Early Career Academic Perspectives on Interdisciplinarity." *The Oxford Handbook of Interdisciplinarity*. Ed. Robert Frodeman, Julie Thompson Klein, and Carl Mitcham. Oxford and New York: Oxford UP, 2010. 403–18. Print.

Greenhalgh, Michael. "Art History." *A Companion to Digital Humanities*. Ed. Susan Schreibman, Raymond Siemens, and John Unsworth. Malden, MA and Oxford, UK: Blackwell, 2004. 31–45. Print.

Gunn, Giles. "Interdisciplinary Studies." *Introduction to Scholarship in Modern Languages and Literatures*. Ed. J. Gibaldi. New York: Modern Language Association, 1992. 2nd ed. 239–61. Print.

Gurak, Laura, and Smiljana Antonijevic. "Digital Rhetoric and Public Discourse." *The SAGE Handbook of Rhetorical Studies*. Ed. Andrea Lunsford, Kirt H. Wilson, and Rosa A. Eberly. Thousand Oaks, CA: SAGE, 2009. 497–508. Print.

Hajic, Jan. "Linguistics Meets Exact Sciences." *A Companion to Digital Humanities*. Ed. Susan Schreibman, Raymond Siemens, and John Unsworth. Malden, MA and Oxford, UK: Blackwell, 2004. 79–87. Print.

Hall, Stuart. "Emergence of Cultural Studies and the Crisis of the Humanities." *October*, 53 (1990): 11–23. Print.

Hayles, N. Katherine. *How We Think: Digital Media and Contemporary Technogenesis*. Chicago: U Chicago P, 2012. Print.

Hayles, N. Katherine. *Chaos Bound: Orderly Disorder in Contemporary Literature and Science*. Ithaca: Cornell UP, 1990. Print.

Henry, Chuck. "Removable Type." *Online Humanities Scholarship: The Shape of Things to Come*. Ed. Jerome McGann. Houston: Rice UP, 2010. 385–400. Print.

Herbert, James. "Masterdisciplinarity and the Pictorial Turn." *The Art Bulletin*, 77.4 (1995): 537–40. Print.

Hirsch, Brett. "Introduction." *Digital Humanities Pedagogy: Practices, Principles and Politics*. Ed. Brett D. Hirsch. Cambridge, UK: Open Book Publishers, 2012. 3–30. Print.

Hockey, Susan. "The History of Humanities Computing." *A Companion to Digital Humanities*. Ed. Susan Schreibman, Raymond Siemens, and John Unsworth. Malden, MA and Oxford, UK: Blackwell, 2004. 3–19. Print.

Hockey, Susan. "Workshop on Teaching Computers and the Humanities Courses." *Literary and Linguistic Computing*, 1.4 (1986): 228–29. Print.

Hunyadi, Laszlo. "Collaboration in Virtual Space in Digital Humanities." *Collaborative Research in the Digital Humanities*, ed. Marilyn Deegan and Willard McCarty. Farnham, UK: Ashgate, 2012. 93–103. Print.

Ide, Nancy. "Preparation and Analysis of Linguistic Corpora." *A Companion to Digital Humanities*. Ed. Susan Schreibman, Raymond Siemens, and John Unsworth. Malden, MA and Oxford, UK: Blackwell, 2004. 273–88. Print.

Interdisciplinarity: Problems of Teaching and Research in Universities. Washington, D.C.: Organization for Economic Cooperation and Development, 1972. Print.

Jenkins, Henry. *Convergence Culture: Where Old and New Media Collide*. New York: NYU P, 2006. 4. Print.

Jones, Steven E. *The Emergence of the Digital Humanities*. New York: Routledge, 2014. Print.

Juola, Patrick. "Killer Applications in Digital Humanities." *Literary and Linguistic Computing*, 23.1 (2008): 73–83. Print.

Kaplan, Ann, and George Levine. "Introduction." *The Politics of Research*. Ed. Ann Kaplan and George Levine. New Brunswick: Rutgers UP, 1997. 1–18. Print.

Katz, Stanley. "Beyond the Disciplines." The Role of the New American College in the Past, Present, and Future of American Higher Education. Saint Mary's College of California. Moraga, California, June 17, 1996. Address.

Keller, Michael. "Response to *Rotunda*: A University Press Starts a Digital Imprint." *Online Humanities Scholarship: The Shape of Things to Come*. Ed. Jerome McGann. Houston: Rice UP, 2010. 375–83. Print.

Kerber, Linda. "Diversity and the Transformation of American Studies." *American Quarterly*, 41.3 (1989): 415–32. Print.

Kinder, Marsha, and Tara McPherson, eds. *Transmedia Frictions: The Digital, The Arts, and The Humanities*. Berkeley: U of California P, 2014. Print.

Kirschenbaum, Matthew. "Digital Humanities As/Is a Tactical Term." *Debates in the Digital Humanities*. Ed. Matthew Gold. Minneapolis: U of Minnesota P, 2012. 415–28. Print.

Kirschenbaum, Matthew. *Mechanisms: New Media and the Forensic Imagination*. Cambridge: MIT Press, 2008. Print.

Kirschenbaum, Matthew. "What is Digital Humanities and What's it Doing in English Departments?" *Debates in the Digital Humanities*. Ed. Matthew Gold. Minneapolis: U of Minnesota P, 2012. 3–11. Print.

Klein, Julie Thompson. *Crossing Boundaries: Knowledge, Disciplinarities, and Interdisciplinarities*. Charlottesville: U of Virginia P, 1996. Print.

Klein, Julie Thompson. *Creating Interdisciplinary Campus Cultures*. San Francisco: Jossey-Bass and Association of American Colleges and Universities, 2010. Print.

Klein, Julie Thompson. "Evaluation of Interdisciplinary and Transdisciplinary Research: A Literature Review." *American Journal of Preventive Medicine*, 35.2S (2008): S116–S123. Print.

Klein, Julie Thompson. *Humanities, Culture and Interdisciplinarity: The Changing American Academy.* Albany, NY: SUNY P, 2005. Print.

Klein, Julie Thompson. *Interdisciplinarity: History, Theory, and Practice.* Detroit: Wayne State UP, 1990. Print.

Klein, Julie Thompson. "Introduction: Interdisciplinarity Today: Why? What? And How?" *Interdisciplinary Education in K-12 and College: A Foundation for K-16 Dialogue.* Ed. Julie Thompson Klein. New York: The College Board, 2002.1–17. Print.

Klein, Julie Thompson. "A Taxonomy of Interdisciplinarity." *The Oxford Handbook of Interdisciplinarity.* Ed. Robert Frodeman, Julie Thompson Klein, and Carl Mitcham. Oxford and New York: Oxford UP, 2010. 15–30. Print.

Klein, Julie Thompson, and William Newell. "Advancing Interdisciplinary Studies." *Handbook on the Undergraduate Curriculum.* Ed. Jerry Gaff and James Ratcliffe. San Francisco: Jossey-Bass, 1996. 393–415. Print.

Kleinberg, Ethan. "Interdisciplinary Studies at a Crossroads." *Liberal Education,* 94.1 (2008): 6–11. Print.

Kling, Rob, and Lisa B. Spector. "Rewards for Scholarly Communication." *Digital Scholarship in the Tenure, Promotion, and Review Process.* Ed. Deborah Lines Andersen. Armonk, NY: M. E. Sharpe, 2003. 78–103. Print.

Krauss, Robert M., and Susan Fussell. "Mutual Knowledge and Communicative Reflectiveness." *Intellectual Teamwork: Social and Technological Foundations of Cooperative Work.* Ed. Jolene Galegher, Robert E. Kraut, and Carmen Egido. Hillsdale, NJ: Erlbaum, 1990. 111–45. Print.

Kuhn, Virginia, and Vicki Callahan. "Nomadic Archives: Remix and the Drift to Praxis." *Digital Humanities Pedagogy: Practices, Principles and Policies.* Ed. Brett D. Hirsch. Open Book Publishers, 2012. 291–308. Print.

Lange, Peter. "Quality Assessment in Interdisciplinary Research and Education." Washington, D.C.: American Association for the Advancement of Science. February 8, 2006. Comments.

Lave, Jean, and Etienne Wenger. *Situated Learning: Legitimate Peripheral Participation.* Cambridge: Cambridge UP, 1991. Print.

Ledford, Heidi. "With All Good Intentions." *Nature,* 452, April 10, 2008, 682–84. Print.

Lin, Yu-wei. "Transdisciplinarity and Digital Humanities: Lessons Learned from Developing Text-Mining Tools for Textual Analysis." *Understanding Digital Humanities.* Ed. David M. Berry. Hampshire, UK: Palgrave, Macmillan, 2012. 295–314. Print.

Lipsitz, George. *American Studies in a Moment of Danger.* Minneapolis: U of Minnesota P, 2001. Print.

Liu, Alan A. *Local Transcendence: Essays on Postmodern Historicism and the Database.* Chicago: U of Chicago P, 2008. Print.

Losh, Elizabeth. "Hacktivism and the Humanities: Programming Protest in the Era of the Digital University." *Debates in the Digital Humanities.* Ed. Matthew Gold. Minneapolis: U of Minnesota P, 2012. 161–86. Print.

Lyotard, Jean-Francois. *The Postmodern Condition: A Report on Knowledge.* Trans. G. Bennington and B. Massumi, with foreword by F. Jameson. 1988. Print.

Maddox, Lucy, ed. *Locating American Studies: The Evolution of a Discipline.* Baltimore: Johns Hopkins UP, 1999. Print.

Mahoney, Simon, and Elena Pierazzo. "Teaching Skills of Teaching Methodology?" *Digital Humanities Pedagogy: Practices, Principles and Policies.* Ed. Brett D. Hirsch. Open Book Publishers, 2012. 215–25. Print.

Manovich, Lev. "What is New Media?" *The New Media Theory Reader.* Ed. Robert Hassan and Julian Thomas. Maidenhead, UK: Open UP, 2006. 5–10. Print.

McCarty, Willard. "Collaborative Research in the Digital Humanities." *Collaborative Research in the Digital Humanities.* Ed. Marilyn Deegan and Willard McCarty. Farnham, UK: Ashgate, 2012. 2–10. Print.

McCarty, Willard. *Humanities Computing.* London and New York: Palgrave Macmillan, 2005. Print.

McCarty, Willard. "The Ph.D. in Digital Humanities." *Digital Humanities Pedagogy: Practices, Principles and Policies.* Ed. Brett D. Hirsch. Open Book Publishers, 2012. 33–46. Print.

McCorcle, Mitchell D. "Critical Issues in the Functioning of Interdisciplinary Groups." *Small Group Behavior,* 12.3 (1982): 291–301. Print.

McGann, Jerome. "Sustainability: The Elephant in the Room." *Online Humanities Scholarship: The Shape of Things to Come.* Ed. Jerome McGann. Houston: Rice UP, 2010. 3–24. Print.

McGann, Jerome, Andrew Stauffer, Dana Wheeles, and Michael Pickard. "Abstract of Roger Bagnall, 'Integrating Digital Papyrology.'" *Online Humanities Scholarship: The Shape of Things to Come.* Ed. Jerome McGann. Houston: Rice UP, 2010. 135. Print.

McKeon, Richard. "The Uses of Rhetoric in a Technological Age: Architectonic Productive Arts." *The Prospect of Rhetoric: Report of the National Development Project.* Ed. Lloyd. F. Bitzer and Edwin Black. Upper Saddle River, NJ: Prentice Hall, 1979. Print.

McPherson, Tara. "Introduction: Media Studies and the Digital Humanities." *Cinema Journal,* 48.2 (2009): 119–23. Print.

McPherson, Tara. "*Vectors*: An Interdisciplinary Digital Journal." *The Oxford Handbook of Interdisciplinarity.* Ed. Robert Frodeman, Julie Thompson Klein, and Carl Mitcham. Oxford and New York: Oxford UP, 2010. 210–11. Print.

McPherson, Tara. "Why are the Digital Humanities So White? Or Thinking the Histories of Race and Computation." *Debates in the Digital Humanities.* Ed. Matthew Gold. Minneapolis: U of Minnesota P, 2012. 139–60. Print.

Marcell, David. "Characteristically American: Another Perspective on American Studies." *Centennial Review,* 21.4 (1977): 388–400. Print.

Mechling, Jay, Robert Meredith, and David Wilson. "American Culture Studies: The Discipline and the Curriculum." *American Quarterly,* 25.4 (1973): 363–89. Print.

Menand, Louis. *The Marketplace of Ideas: Reform and Resistance in the American University.* New York: W. W. Norton, 2010. Print.

Menand, Louis. "Undisciplined." *The Wilson Quarterly,* 51 (2001): 51–59. Print.

Messer-Davidow, Ellen. *Disciplining Feminism: From Social Activism to Academic Discourse.* Durham, NC: Duke UP, 2002. Print.

Messer-Davidow, Ellen, David Shumway, and David Sylvan. "Preface." *Knowledges: Historical and Cultural Studies in Disciplinarity.* Ed. Ellen Messer-Davidow, David Shumway, and David Sylvan. Charlottesville: U of Virginia P, 1993. vii. Print.

Miller, Raymond. "Varieties of Interdisciplinary Approaches in the Social Sciences." *Issues in Integrative Studies,* 1 (1982): 1–37. Print.

Mirzoeff, Nicholas. *An Introduction to Visual Culture.* London and New York: Routledge, 1999. Print.

Mirzoeff, Nicholas. "What is Visual Culture?" *The Visual Culture Reader,* Ed. Nicholas Mirzoeff. London and New York: Routledge, 1998. 3–13. Print.

Moran, Joe. *Interdisciplinarity.* London and New York: Routledge, 2002. Print.

Muri, Allison. "The Grub Street Project." *Online Humanities Scholarship: The Shape of Things to Come.* Ed. Jerome McGann. Houston: Rice UP, 2010. 25–58. Print.

Nawrotzki, Kristen, and Jack Dougherty. "Introduction." *Writing History in the Digital Age.* Ed. Jack Dougherty and Kristen Nawrotzki. Ann Arbor: U of Michigan P, 2013. 1–18. Print.

Nelson, Janet L. "From Building Site to Building: The Prosopography of Anglo-Saxon England PASE Project." *Collaborative Research in the Digital Humanities.* Ed. Marilyn Deegan and Willard McCarty. Farnham, UK: Ashgate, 123–34. Print.

Newell, William H. "The Political Life Cycle of a Cluster College: The Western College Program at Miami University." *Politics of Interdisciplinary Studies: Essays on Transformations in American Undergraduate Programs.* Ed. Tanya Augsburg and Stuart Henry. Jefferson, NC: McFarland, 2009. 29–50. Print.

Nowviski, Bethany. "Skunks in the Library: A Path to Production for Scholarly R&D." *Journal of Library Administration,* 53 (2013): 53–66. Print.

Nuffield Foundation. *Interdisciplinarity.* London: Nuffield Foundation, 1975. Print.

O'Donnell, James J. "Engaging the Humanities: The Digital Humanities." *Daedalus.* 138.1 (2009): 99–104. Print.

O'Donnell, Angela N., and Sharon J. Derry. "Cognitive Processes in Interdisciplinary Groups: Problems and Possibilities." *Interdisciplinary Collaboration: An Emerging Cognitive Science.* Ed. Sharon Derry, Christopher D. Schunn, and Morton A. Gernsbacher. Mahwah, NJ: Earlbaum, 2005. Print. 51–82

Orvell, Miles, Johnnela Butler, and Jay Mechling. "Preface." *Encyclopedia of American Studies.* Ed. George T. Kurian et al. New York: Grolier Education, Scholastic Incorporated, 2001. V. I: vii–xii. Print.

Ostriker, J. P., and C. V. Kuh, eds. *Assessing Research-Doctorate Programs: A Methodology Study.* Washington, D.C.: National Academies P, 2003. Print.

Ostriker, J. P., P. W. Holland, C. Kuh, and J. A. Voytuk, eds. *A Guide to the Method-*

ology of the National Research Council Assessment of Doctorate Programs. Washington, D.C.: National Academies P, 2009. Print.

Palmer, Carole L. "Thematic Research Collections." *Online Humanities Scholarship: The Shape of Things to Come.* Ed. Jerome McGann. Houston: Rice UP, 2010. 348–65. Print.

Palmer, Carole L. "Information Research on Interdisciplinarity." *The Oxford Handbook of Interdisciplinarity.* Ed. Robert Frodeman, Julie Thompson Klein, and Carl Mitcham. Oxford and New York: Oxford UP, 2010. 174–88. Print.

Parker, Joe, Ranu Samantrai, and Mary Romero, eds. *Interdisciplinarity and Social Justice: Revisioning Academic Accountability.* Albany, NY: SUNY P, 2010. Print.

Parry, Dave. "The Digital Humanities as a Digital Humanism." *Debates in the Digital Humanities.* Ed. Matthew Gold. Minneapolis: U of Minnesota P, 2012. 429–37. Print.

Pfirman, Stephanie, and Paula J. S. Martin. "Facilitating Interdisciplinary Scholars." *The Oxford Handbook of Interdisciplinarity.* Ed. Robert Frodeman, Julie Thompson Klein, and Carl Mitcham. Oxford and New York: Oxford UP, 2010. 387–403. Print.

Presner, Todd. "Hypercities." *Online Humanities Scholarship: The Shape of Things to Come.* Ed. Jerome McGann. Houston: Rice UP, 2010. 251–72. Print.

Presner, Todd, David Shepard, and Yoh Kawano. *HyperCities: Thick Mapping in the Digital Humanities.* Cambridge: Harvard U P, 2014. Print.

Price, Kenneth. "Civil War Washington Project." *Online Humanities Scholarship: The Shape of Things to Come.* Ed. Jerome McGann. Houston: Rice UP, 2010. 287–310. Print.

Ramsay, Stephen, and Geoffrey Rockwell. "Developing Things: Notes toward an Epistemology of Building in the Digital Humanities." *Debates in the Digital Humanities.* Ed. Matthew Gold. Minneapolis: U of Minnesota P, 2012. 75–84. Print.

Readings, Bill. *The University in Ruins.* Cambridge: Harvard UP, 1996. Print.

Repko, A. "Transforming an Experimental Innovation into a Sustainable Mainstream Academic Program: The New Interdisciplinary Studies Program at the University of Texas at Arlington." *Disciplining Interdisciplinary Studies? The Politics of Interdisciplinary Transformation in Undergraduate American Higher Education.* Ed. Tanya Augsburg and Stuart Henry. Jefferson, NC: McFarland, 2009. 144–62. Print.

Rice, Jeff. *The Rhetoric of Cool.* Southern Illinois UP, 2007. Print.

Rich, D., and R. Warren. "The Intellectual Future of Urban Affairs: Theoretical, Normative, and Organizational Options." *Social Science Research,* 17.2 (1980): 53–66. Print.

Robinson, Peter. "Response to Roger Bagnall, 'Integrating Digital Papyrology.'" *Online Humanities Scholarship: The Shape of Things to Come.* Ed. Jerome McGann. Houston: Rice UP, 2010. 171–88. Print.

Rockwell, Geoffrey. "Crowdsourcing the Humanities: Social Research and Collaboration." *Collaborative Research in the Digital Humanities*. Ed. Marilyn Deegan and Willard McCarty. Farnham, UK: Ashgate, 2012. 135–54. Print.

Rockwell, Geoffrey, and Andrew Mactavish. "Multimedia." *A Companion to Digital Humanities*. Ed. Susan Schreibman, Raymond Siemens, and John Unsworth. Malden, MA and Oxford: Blackwell, 2004. 108–20. Print.

Rockwell, Geoffrey, and Stefan Sinclair. "Acculturation and the Digital Humanities Community." *Digital Humanities Pedagogy: Practices, Principles and Politics*. Ed. Brett D. Hirsch. Cambridge, UK: Open Book Publishers, 2012. 177–211. Print.

Rogoff, Irit. 1998. "Studying Visual Culture." *The Visual Culture Reader*. Ed. Nicholas Mirzoeff. New York: Routledge, 1998. 14–26. Print.

Ross, Claire. "CASE STUDY: QRator Project: Enhancing Co-creation of Content in Practice." *Digital Humanities in Practice*. Ed. Claire Warwick, Melissa Terras, and Julianne Nyhan. London: Facet in Association with UCL Center for Digital Humanities, 2012. 37–39. Print.

Russell, Isabel Galina. "CASE STUDY: Digital Humanities in Mexico." *Digital Humanities in Practice*. Ed. Claire Warwick, Melissa Terras, and Julianne Nyhan. London: Facet in Association with UCL Center for Digital Humanities, 2012. 202–4. Print.

Saklofske, Jon, Estelle Clements, and Richard Cunningham. "On the Digital Future of Humanities." *Digital Humanities Pedagogy: Practices, Principles and Policies*. Ed. Brett D. Hirsch. Open Book Publishers, 2012. 311–30. Print.

Sample, Mark L. "Unseen and Unremarked On: Don DeLillo and the Failure of the Digital Humanities." *Debates in the Digital Humanities*. Ed. Matthew Gold. Minneapolis: U of Minnesota P, 2012. 187–201. Print.

Scheinfeld, Tom. "Sunset for Ideology, Sunrise for Methodology?" *Debates in the Digital Humanities*. Ed. Matthew Gold. Minneapolis: U of Minnesota P, 2012. 124–26. Print.

Scholle, David. "Resisting Disciplines: Repositioning Media Studies in the University." *Communication Theory*, 5 (1995): 130–43. Print.

Schreibman, Susan, Ray Siemens, and John Unsworth, eds. *A Companion to Digital Humanities*. Malden, MA and Oxford: Blackwell, 2004. Print.

Schreibman, Susan, Raymond Siemens, and John Unsworth. "The Digital Humanities and Humanities Computing: An Introduction." *A Companion to Digital Humanities*. Ed. Susan Schreibman, Raymond Siemens, and John Unsworth. Malden, MA and Oxford: Blackwell, 2004. xxiii–xxvii. Print.

The Science of Team Science. *American Journal of Preventive Medicine*, 35.2, Supplement 1 (August 2008): A1–A8, S77–S252. Print.

Shapin, Steven. "Discipline and Bonding: The History and Sociology of Science as Seen through the Externalism-Internalism Debates." *History of Science*, 30.4 (1992): 333–69. Print.

Siemens, Lynne. "It's a Team If You Use 'Reply All': An Exploration of Research Teams in Digital Humanities Environments." *Literary and Linguistic Computing*, 24.2 (2009): 225–33. Print.

Siemens, Raymond G. "Underpinnings of the Social Edition." *Online Humanities Scholarship: The Shape of Things to Come.* Ed. Jerome McGann. Houston: Rice UP, 2010. 401–60. Print.

Siemens, Raymond, et al. "Human-Computer Interface/Interaction and the Book: A Consultation-derived Perspective on Foundational E-Book Research." *Collaborative Research in the Digital Humanities.* Ed. Marilyn Deegan and Willard McCarty. Farnham, UK: Ashgate, 2012. 162–89. Print.

Smelser, N. J. "Interdisciplinarity in Theory and Practice." *The Dialogical Turn: New Roles for Sociology in the Postdisciplinary Age.* Ed. C. Camic and H. Joas. Lanham, MD.: Rowman and Littlefield, 2004. Print.

Smith, Martha Nell. "Electronic Scholarly Editing." *A Companion to Digital Humanities.* Ed. Susan Schreibman, Raymond Siemens, and John Unsworth. Malden, MA and Oxford, UK: Blackwell, 2004. 306–22. Print.

Star, Susan L., and James R. Griesemer. "Institutional Ecology, 'Translations' and Boundary Objects: Amateurs and Professionals in Berkeley's Museum of Vertebrate Zoology, 1907–39." *Social Studies of Science,* 19.3 (1989): 387–420. Print.

Sternfeld, Joshua. "Pedagogical Principles of Digital Historiography." *Digital Humanities Pedagogy: Practices, Principles and Policies.* Ed. Brett D. Hirsch. Open Book Publishers, 2012. 255–90. Print.

Stokols, Daniel, et al. "Cross Disciplinary Team Science Initiatives: Research, Training, and Translation." *The Oxford Handbook of Interdisciplinarity.* Ed. Robert Frodeman, Julie Thompson Klein, and Carl Mitcham. Oxford and New York: Oxford UP, 2010. 471–93. Print.

Stone, Anthony R. "The Interdisciplinary Research Team." *Journal of Applied Behavioral Science,* 5.3 (1969): 351–65. Print.

Strain, Ellen, and Greg Van Hoosier-Carey. "Eloquent Interfaces." *Eloquent Images.* Ed. Mary Hocks and Michelle Kendrick. Cambridge: MIT Press, 2003. 257–81. Print.

Terras, Melissa. "Being the Other." *Collaborative Research in the Digital Humanities.* Ed. Marilyn Deegan and Willard McCarty. Farnham, UK: Ashgate, 2012. 213–30. Print.

Terras, Melissa. "Digitization and Digital Resources in the Humanities." *Digital Humanities in Practice.* Ed. Claire Warwick, Melissa Terras, and Julianne Nyhan. London: Facet in Association with UCL Center for Digital Humanities, 2012. 47–70. Print.

Terras, Melissa. "Disciplined: Using Educational Studies to Analyze Humanities Computing." *Literary and Linguistic Computing,* 21.2 (2006): 229–46. Print.

Terras, Melissa, Julianne Nyhan, and Edward Vanhoutte, eds. *Defining Digital Humanities: A Reader.* Farnham, UK: Ashgate, 2013. Print.

Thomas, William. "Computing and the Historical Imagination." *A Companion to Digital Humanities.* Ed. Susan Schreibman, Raymond Siemens, and John Unsworth. Malden, MA and Oxford, UK: Blackwell, 2004. 56–68. Print.

Toombs, W., and W. Tierney. *Meeting the Mandate: Reviewing the College and De-*

partment Curriculum. ASHE-ERIC Higher Education Report No. 6. Washington, D.C.: School of Educational and Human Development, George Washington University, 1991. Print.

Trowler, P. R., and P. T. Knight. "Exploring the Implementation Gap: Theory and Practices in Change Interventions." *Higher Education Policy and Institutional Change: Intentions and Outcomes in Turbulent Environments.* Ed. P. R. Trowler. Buckingham, U.K.: Society for Research into Higher Education/Open UP, 2002. 142–63. Print.

Turkle, Sherry. *Life on the Screen: Identity in the Age of the Internet.* New York: Simon & Schuster, 1995. Print.

Unsworth, John. "University 2.0." *The Tower and the Cloud: Higher Education in the Age of Cloud Computing.* Ed. R. N. Katz. Washington, D.C.: EDUCAUSE, 2008. Print.

Unsworth, John, and Charlotte Tupman. "Interview with John Unsworth, April 2011, carried out and transcribed by Charlotte Tupman." *Collaborative Research in the Digital Humanities.* Ed. Marilyn Deegan and Willard McCarty. Farnham, UK: Ashgate, 2012. 231–39. Print.

Vershbow, Ben. "NYPL Labs: Hacking the Library." *Journal of Library Administration,* 53 (2013): 79–96. Print.

Vickers, Jill. "Diversity, Globalization, and 'Growing Up Digital': Navigating Interdisciplinarity in the Twenty-First Century." *History of Intellectual Culture,* 3.1 (2003). Web publication. http://www.ucalgary.ca/hic/issues/vol3

Vickers, Jill. "'Unframed in Open, Unmapped Fields': Teaching and the Practice of Interdisciplinarity." *Arachne: An Interdisciplinary Journal of the Humanities,* 4.2 (1997): 11–42. Print.

Vosskamp, Wilhelm. "Crossing of Boundaries: Interdisciplinarity as an Opportunity for Universities in the l980's?" *Issues in Integrative Studies,* 12 (1994): 43–54. Print.

Vosskamp, Wilhelm. "From Scientific Specialization to the Dialogue Between the Disciplines." *Issues in Integrative Studies,* 4 (1986). l7–36. Print.

Warhol, Robyn R. "Nice Work If You Can Get It—and If You Can't? Building Women's Studies Without Tenure Lines." *Women's Studies on Its Own: A Next Wave Reader in Institutional Change.* Ed. Robyn Wiegman. Durham: Duke UP, 2002. 224–32. Print.

Waltzer, Luke. "Digital Humanities and the 'Ugly Stepchildren' of American Higher Education." *Debates in the Digital Humanities.* Ed. Matthew Gold. Minneapolis: U of Minnesota P, 2012. 335–49. Print.

Walzer, Arthur E., and David Beard. "Historiography and the Study of Rhetoric." *The SAGE Handbook of Rhetorical Studies.* Ed. Andrea Lunsford, Kirt H. Wilson, and Rosa A. Eberly. Thousand Oaks, CA: SAGE, 2009. 13–34. Print.

Warwick, Claire. "Institutional Models for Digital Humanities." *Digital Humanities in Practice.* Ed. Claire Warwick, Melissa Terras, and Julianne Nyhan. London: Facet in Association with UCL Center for Digital Humanities, 2012. 193–216. Print.

Warwick, Claire, Melissa Terras, and Julianne Nyhan. "Introduction." *Digital Hu-*

manities in Practice. Ed. Claire Warwick, Melissa Terras, and Julianne Nyhan. London: Facet in Association with UCL Center for Digital Humanities, 2012. 1–21. Print.

Wátzlawick, Paul, John H. Weakland, and Richard Fisch. *Change: Principles of Problem Formation and Problem Resolution.* New York: W. W. Norton, 1974. Print.

Weingart, Peter. "Interdisciplinarity: The Paradoxical Discourse." *Practicing Interdisciplinarity.* Ed. Peter Weingart and Nico Stehr. Toronto: U of Toronto P, 2000. 25–41. Print.

Williams, Raymond. *Keywords: A Vocabulary of Culture and Society. Revised Edition.* New York: Oxford UP, 1983. Print.

Williford, Christa, and Charles Henry. *One Culture: Computationally Intensive Research in the Humanities and Social Sciences. A Report on the Experiences of First Respondents to the Digging Into Data Challenge.* Washington, D.C.: Council on Library and Information Resources, 2012. Print.

Winter, Michael. "Specialization, Territoriality, and Jurisdiction in Librarianship." *Library Trends,* 45.2 (1996): 343–63. Print.

Wise, Gene. "Paradigm Dramas in American Studies." *American Quarterly,* 31.3 (1979): 293–337. Print.

Wise, Gene. "Some Elementary Axioms for an American Culture Studies." *Prospects: The Annual of American Cultural Studies* (1978). 517–47. Print.

Wosh, Peter J., Cathy Moran Hajo, and Esther Katz. "Teaching Digital Skills in an Archives and Public History Curriculum." *Digital Humanities Pedagogy: Practices, Principles and Policies.* Ed. Brett D. Hirsch. Open Book Publishers, 2012. 97–119. Print.

Zorich, Diane. *A Survey of Digital Humanities Centers in the United States.* Washington, D.C. Council on Library and Information Resources, 2008. Print and Web. http://www.clir.org/pubs/reports/pub143/pub143.pdf

Index